D0729933

www.wadsworth.com

www.wadsworth.com is the World Wide Web site for
Thomson Wadsworth and is your direct source to dozens
of online resources.

At *www.wadsworth.com* you can find out about supple-
ments, demonstration software, and student resources.
You can also send e-mail to many of our authors and
preview new publications and exciting new technologies.

www.wadsworth.com
Changing the way the world learns[®]

Research Methods

Planning, Conducting and Presenting Research

Ann Sloan Devlin, Ph.D.
Connecticut College

THOMSON
WADSWORTH

Australia • Brazil • Canada • Mexico • Singapore •
Spain • United Kingdom • United States

THOMSON

WADSWORTH

Publisher: *Vicki Knight*
Editorial Assistant: *Juliet Case*
Technology Project Manager: *Erik Fortier*
Marketing Manager: *Dory Schaeffer*
Marketing Assistant: *Nicole Morinon*
Executive Marketing Communications
 Manager: *Brian Chaffee*
Project Manager, Editorial Production:
 Karol Jurado
Creative Director: *Rob Hugel*
Senior Art Director: *Vernon Boes*
Senior Print Buyer: *Judy Inouye*
Senior Permissions Editor: *Joohee Lee*

Production Service: *Interactive
 Composition Corporation*
Text Designer: *Lisa Henry*
Copy Editor: *Margaret Berson*
Illustrator: *Interactive Composition
 Corporation*
Cover Designer: *Lisa Henry*
Cover Image: *Indivision/DEX Image*
Cover Printer: *Banta Book Group/
 Harrisonburg*
Compositor: *Interactive Composition
 Corporation*
Printer: *Banta Book Group/Harrisonburg*

© 2006 Thomson Wadsworth, a part of The
Thomson Corporation. Thomson, the Star
logo, and Wadsworth are trademarks used
herein under license.

ALL RIGHTS RESERVED. No part of this
work covered by the copyright hereon may
be reproduced or used in any form or by
any means—graphic, electronic, or mechan-
ical, including photocopying, recording,
taping, web distribution, information storage and retrieval systems, or in any other
manner—without the written permission of
the publisher.

Printed in the United States of America
1 2 3 4 5 6 7 09 08 07 06 05

For more information about our products,
contact us at:
Thomson Learning Academic Resource Center
1-800-423-0563

For permission to use material from this text or
product, submit a request online at
http://www.thomsonrights.com.
Any additional questions about permissions can
be submitted by e-mail to
thomsonrights@thomson.com.

Library of Congress Control
Number: 2005922786

ISBN 0-534-61714-X

Thomson Higher Education
10 Davis Drive
Belmont, CA 94002-3098
USA

Asia
Thomson Learning
5 Shenton Way #01-01
UIC Building
Singapore 068808

Australia/New Zealand
Thomson Learning
102 Dodds Street
Southbank, Victoria 3006
Australia

Canada
Nelson
1120 Birchmount Road
Toronto, Ontario M1K 5G4
Canada

Europe/Middle East/Africa
Thomson Learning
High Holborn House
50/51 Bedford Row
London WC1R 4LR
United Kingdom

Latin America
Thomson Learning
Seneca, 53
Colonia Polanco
11560 Mexico
D.F. Mexico

Spain/Portugal
Paraninfo
Calle Magallanes, 25
28015 Madrid, Spain

ANN SLOAN DEVLIN is the May Buckley Sadowski '19 Professor of Psychology at Connecticut College and the College Marshal. In her teaching career at Connecticut College, she has engaged generations of students in the process of conducting their own research. She received her undergraduate degree, M. A., and Ph.D. from the University of Michigan. Her first book, Mind and Maze: Spatial Cognition and Environmental Behavior (Praeger, 2001), focused on the relationship between spatial behavior, such as navigation, and its application to environmental psychology and urban planning. She is a Fellow of Division 34, Population and Environment, of the American Psychological Association, on the editorial review board of the journal *Environment and Behavior*, and a past Secretary of the Environmental Design Research Association.

This book is dedicated to my students.

BRIEF CONTENTS

CONTENTS

CHAPTER 2
Research Design and Statistical Considerations   41

CHAPTER 3
Sources of Measures   89

CHAPTER 4
Obtaining Your Subjects: Never Appear on Stage with Animals or Children   117

CHAPTER 7
The Light at the End of the Tunnel: Report Writing and Presentations   205

Students in the social sciences are often overwhelmed by a one-semester research project. All too often, students are bogged down by the very real aspects of the project. These practical aspects include obtaining a questionnaire that is referenced but not printed along with an article, getting through the IRB review process, recruiting subjects (and a sufficient number of them), and so on. This volume is written with the goal of addressing the practical aspects of a one-semester research project, from generating your idea to handing in your paper at the end of the semester.

Contents

Each of the seven chapters combines practical advice with justification from the literature, where applicable. In this way, students learn that even these practical aspects have a justification based on research. As just one example, Church's (1993) meta-analysis on the use of incentives in mail survey research shows that only inducements given initially (either monetary or non-monetary) improve response rates.

CHAPTER 1
Generating and Shaping Ideas: The Challenge of the One-Semester Project

One of the most difficult aspects of doing research, but particularly for the novice researcher doing a one-semester project for a research methods course, is generating a workable idea. This chapter gives students suggestions for creating a research timeline and for sources of ideas, including themselves, their families and friends, the media, and the literature (journals, abstracts from professional meetings, etc.). The chapter discusses the literature review as a source of ideas, the challenge of psychology as both derivative and innovative, and the use of the library/information services, with a special emphasis on electronic resources and the assistance librarians/information specialists can provide. The chapter ends with examples of transforming research ideas into testable hypotheses.

CHAPTER 2
Research Design and Statistical Considerations

In this chapter, the relationship between the stated hypotheses, possible research designs, and the appropriate statistical approaches is considered. In particular, the chapter emphasizes the importance of thinking through the project to the point of data analysis, before any subject participates. The chapter does not duplicate the statistical emphasis that is found in a longer research methods book. Rather, it concentrates on getting students to see the relationship between the way the research questions (and hypotheses) are framed, the kinds of data that need to be collected to answer the questions posed, and the appropriate approaches to data analysis. It is my hope that students will come away better understanding how to examine cause-and-effect relationships, the role of quasi-independent variables, correlational analyses, and questions posed in a yes/no manner (i.e., the role of nominal data).

The chapter poses a series of questions leading students to see the relationship between hypotheses, the way questions are asked, and data analysis. For example, are relationships explored, which will generally lead to correlational analyses? What conclusions can one draw from the data in such relationships? Such an approach is contrasted with an examination of group differences, approached by analysis of variance, and the potential issue of cause and effect. This chapter examines how slightly different statements of the research hypotheses can lead to different research designs. It takes some practice before students understand the implications of research design and whether you are asking questions in a way that leads to analysis for interval scale data (e.g., *t*-tests) or nominal data (e.g., chi-squares).

CHAPTER 3
Sources of Measures

Although in real time many of these tasks (developing a research design and selecting measures) are approached on parallel tracks, an artificial sequence of steps must be imposed in a book. The results of a search for research measures may sometimes lead you to modify your research design. But at some point early on you will have to determine your variables of interest and the degree to which it is possible to measure them. In this chapter, a useful conceptual representation is offered, which shows the overlap between the theoretical construct or idea that you want to measure (e.g., leadership) and the actual measures available to assess that construct. The goal is to obtain the most significant degree of overlap you can between the theoretical construct and the actual measure(s).

The chapter will concentrate on practical ways to secure measures including source books and previous articles, and how to obtain complete questionnaires and scoring instructions, which are critical to the success of a project. The chapter makes clear the pitfalls in developing your own measures, and the kinds of questions (typically demographic) it is reasonable to generate yourself. Students learn about measures that are copyrighted and issues of payment. Another major aspect of this chapter is explaining how to evaluate the reliability and validity of instruments, and why those issues are important in selecting a measure. Practical aspects like the length of the measure(s), the difficulty of the items, and the number of questionnaires (and implications for administration such as length of time it will take) are considered.

CHAPTER 4

Obtaining Your Subjects: Never Appear on Stage with Animals or Children

Obtaining a sufficient number of participants for your study is a challenge, and this chapter deals with recommendations for the kinds of approaches that have proven effective in getting people to participate. As Chapter 1 makes clear, college students are well advised to focus on topics that they know something about and to enlist the participation of those who can provide the answers (that is, other college students). The focus in this chapter is thus on recruiting other college students from subject pools or other means, but there is also a discussion of doing research in the field and with vulnerable populations. The challenges of field research and vulnerable populations are considered within the context of the one-semester project. The chapter also discusses ethical and practical issues associated with incentives and payment of subjects.

The chapter ends with "Dustin's Dozen," a series of 12 tips for conducting survey research in the field. These tips are the recommendations of an MA student who had great success recruiting subjects from train stations, laundromats, and other facilities in the community.

CHAPTER 5

Ethics and the IRB Review Process: I'm From the IRB and I'm Here to Help You

Chapter 5 provides a thorough understanding of the purpose and history of Institutional Review Boards and the series of steps that are typically required to prepare a proposal for IRB review. The various levels of IRB review are presented so that students can assess ahead of time the kind of review they will likely undergo. Sample informed consent and debriefing explanations are included. The issues surrounding deception in research are addressed, and there is some discussion about the resistance to IRB review among social and behavioral scientists. Students are also provided with website addresses for IRB training modules.

CHAPTER 6
Managing Your Data: A Penny Saved . . .

The chapter stresses the importance of careful record keeping and data labeling. Such basics as how to get a preliminary feel for your data (and why that is important), frequent backing up of computer files, dating your drafts, and other prudent steps are reviewed. For example, the chapter shows what you can learn from initial steps such as running frequencies and descriptive statistics. Not only can you get a sense of the convergence vs. spread of your data, but you can also tell whether you have entered the data correctly (i.e., seeing whether any values are out of range). There is also a discussion of how to approach content analysis and to transform qualitative data to a quantitative expression of that information.

CHAPTER 7
The Light at the End of the Tunnel: Report Writing and Presentations

In this chapter, students are given a list of the most frequently confronted issues in APA style, such as what goes in the abstract, reference citations in text and the reference list, use of direct quotations, citing secondary sources, and so on. There is practical advice about the importance of photocopying quotations for later verification, careful record keeping, legible handwriting, and language bias. There is also a review of common grammatical mistakes, including subject–pronoun agreement, use of relative pronouns, and the use of possessives.

The chapter provides advice about writing up results and elements of an effective discussion. An effective discussion begins with a summary of the results as they relate to the hypotheses, ties in the results of previous research (either supportive or not), states limitations of the current research, and poses directions for future studies.

The chapter also discusses venues in which students can present their work, including local (e.g., college Psi Chi conferences) and regional research conferences (e.g., New England Psychological Association), and even national and international conferences where students often present their work as posters (e.g., Environmental Design Research Association). Student research journals (e.g., *The Connecticut College Psychology Journal*), which also provide an opportunity for students to present their work, are discussed.

With the knowledge and tools students will have in hand by the end of this volume, they will be well-prepared to handle the challenges inherent in a one-semester research project. Moreover, they can return to this volume as a reference for use in future courses or projects that involve research.

ACKNOWLEDGMENTS

First, I want to thank the research methods students I have taught for motivating me to write this book. Their curiosity about research, and their frustration with many aspects of the process, served as an impetus to map out a "better way" to teach students about their first research project.

Next, I want to thank my colleagues in the social sciences at Connecticut College, particularly my department colleagues in psychology, for their help in providing information about measures and journals in their particular disciplines. A special note of thanks goes to Professor of Psychology Stuart Vyse, who was always willing to answer questions about statistics.

The librarians and information specialists at the Connecticut College Library deserve special thanks for their help with Chapter 1 and with ordering the many journal articles that I consulted for Chapter 5 on the IRB process.

I also want to thank the administration at Connecticut College for its generous sabbatical policy, which enabled me to take a semester off to work on this book project.

I was very fortunate to have reviewers who provided constructive and encouraging suggestions at each draft of the manuscript. I am most appreciative of the comments and suggestions they provided, which certainly help strengthen the book.

Thanks to:

Bill Gabrenya, *Florida Institute of Technology*

Jo Ann Farver, *University of Southern California*

Virginia Norris, *South Dakota State University*

Allen Salo, *University of Maine at Presque Isle*

Michael Clump, *Marymount University*

Pamela Stuntz, *Texas Christian University*

Susan Baillet, *University of Portland*

David Alfano, *Community College of Rhode Island*

Tanya Whitehead, *University of Missouri–Kansas City*

One could hardly ask for a better editor than Vicki Knight of Wadsworth/Thomson Learning. Vicki encouraged me to add a number of chapter features, such as the Reflect and Review sections, to make the book as engaging as possible to students.

Finally, I want to thank my husband, David, and my daughter, Sloan, for their support and encouragement. Sloan, who was a college student during the time this book was written, deserves special recognition for reminding me to "get to the point, Mom."

Generating and Shaping Ideas

The Challenge of the One-Semester Project

Introduction and Chapter Overview

Generating a workable idea is one of the most difficult, if not the most difficult, part of doing a research project, but particularly one to be conceived and completed during a single semester. This chapter will give you suggestions for creating a research timeline and for sources of ideas, including yourself, your family and friends, the media, and the literature (journals, books, abstracts from professional meetings, etc.). The chapter discusses the literature review of published articles as a source of ideas, the challenge of social science as both derivative and innovative, and the use of library resources. Special emphasis is given to electronic resources and the assistance librarians and information service personnel can provide. The chapter concludes with examples of transforming research ideas into testable hypotheses.

Research: The Tension Between the Old and the New

One of the real tensions in the discipline of psychology (or sociology, or anthropology, or human development, or any of the other behavioral sciences) is the push and pull of what I call the derivative vs. the innovative. On the one hand, you must understand what work has preceded you in a given area; you must build on that foundation to some degree. On the other hand, you are trying to ask worthwhile and perhaps innovative questions and to move knowledge forward. It is a high-wire act.

Students often seem to feel that they may have nothing new to offer, or that the questions that interest them have already been asked and addressed. This is hardly the case. In the book *Metamorphosis*, Schachtel (1959) discusses one of the drawbacks to developing into an adult—that it brings with it a conventionalization of thought. If you watch the way in which children play on playgrounds or with what seem to be rigid and static objects, there seems to be no limit to the creative ways in which they use these components. In the movie *Big* (Brooks, Greenhut, & Marshall, 1999), the actor Tom Hanks is transformed from 12-year-old Josh Baskin, a middle-schooler (played by another actor), into an adult body by wishing that he were "big," a wish granted by Zoltar, the fortune-telling machine. Josh (Tom Hanks) lands a job at Macmillan Toys in the data entry department and quickly becomes VP for Product Development. He succeeds in this adult world precisely because he retains the wonderful imagination and outlook of a child, an outlook lost by the majority of people surrounding him. The point here is that students *do* have wonderful and creative ways of looking at ideas. And *before* immersing yourself in the literature of a given topic (and in a sense becoming constrained by what you see has already been done), it is useful to write down your own questions and reflections. Once you begin looking at the literature, it is easy to become trapped or conventionalized so that you question the worth of your own ideas or approaches.

Topics Selected by Students

Cognitive Styles and Academic Major: Influence on Student-Professor Relationships

Motivational Differences of Division III College Athletes: Athletic Identity and Personal Satisfaction

The Effect of Parenting Style on College Success

Am I Hot or Not? How Peer Pressure Affects Ratings of Attractiveness

The Media's Effect on Women's Body Esteem and Body Dissatisfaction: Effect of Brief Media Exposure

What you have just read are examples of some of the projects done in a class of students taking a course in research methods—essentially their first research project. What themes do you see in these projects? Students often pick topics (and often are encouraged to pick topics) related to some aspect of their own experiences—achievement, sports, relationships with peers, relationships with parents and/or siblings, and health (see Figure 1.1). On occasion they also consider subjects related to some medical or emotional problem in the family, for example, a sibling with mental illness such as schizophrenia, or physical and social challenges, such as cerebral palsy or autism. Although it is conceivable that a student could conduct meaningful research on such family challenges, it is almost impossible to actually accomplish this in a one-semester project. Such projects are important for a variety of reasons, but they are better managed as the student progresses in his/her education. Projects that involve sensitive populations, such as individuals with autism, require a series of permissions from "gatekeepers," a process that involves a full meeting of your college or university's Human Subjects Institutional Review Board (a committee that evaluates the risks and benefits and ethical issues involved in research done with humans) (IRB; see Chapter 5). For that reason, among a host of others, such involved and complex projects are better suited to a senior honors thesis or two-semester individual study or independent research project.

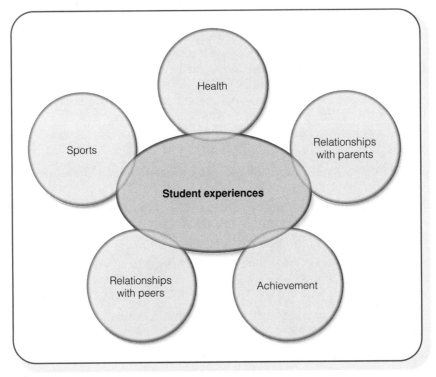

FIGURE 1.1 Common Student Research Themes

Time Pressure and Timelines

Students doing a one-semester research project with a completion deadline of the last day of class or the end of the semester (see the sample timeline on the following page) are under considerable pressure to manage their time effectively. One way to start the process of effective use of time is to create a timeline of due dates for components of the project: generating an idea, searching the literature for past research and related topics, devising an approach (research design), gathering and developing measures, obtaining approval from the IRB, soliciting participants, collecting the data, entering and analyzing the data, and interpreting the data. Then the actual report must be written including Introduction, Method (participants, apparatus/materials, procedure), Results, and Discussion. As you will see in the sample timeline, it is a wise idea to do some of your writing along the way, rather than waiting until the project's completion.

If you have a 12- or 13-week semester, divide it into weekly segments, and then work backwards from the deadline. How long will it take you to write? Some instructors will look at a draft and give you feedback. If you plan to have an instructor review your draft, factor that activity into your timeline. The sample timeline that follows is one possible model of a timeline based on the tasks you will undertake (for ease of understanding the steps in the research process, it is presented in order from beginning steps to completion, although it was generated in reverse order).

Sample Timeline

Week 1	Class begins; announcement of research project; begin generating ideas
Week 2	Continue to generate ideas and begin to consult the literature
Week 3	Refine and settle on an idea; order articles and books; decide on research approach (i.e., correlational vs. experimental)
Week 4	Obtain measures; generate IRB proposal; begin draft of Introduction
Week 5	Submit IRB proposal; continue writing Introduction; write References section
Week 6	Receive approval of IRB proposal; revise and resubmit to IRB if necessary
Week 7	Gather data
Week 8	Finish gathering data; write Method section
Week 9	Score, enter, and analyze data
Week 10	Write Results section and begin Discussion section
Week 11	Finish Discussion section and integrate paper into a draft
Week 12	Submit draft (if professor agrees)
Week 13	Receive draft comments, revise, and resubmit final paper

As you can see, there are many opportunities for this process to break down, especially with regard to what you can't control: other people's behavior. Thus, getting approval from the IRB or receiving comments on your draft may not happen in a week. Therefore, it is important that you manage the time you have for what *you* can control: generating ideas, consulting the literature, and writing sections of the manuscript.

Professors can actually help you prepare for a research methods course by alerting you in advance. For example, many schools have a two-semester sequence of statistics followed by research methods.

During the statistics class, the teacher can alert you to the project requirement in the methods course. You could be encouraged to keep a log or journal of ideas for projects. As mentioned earlier, it is important to write down some of your own ideas before immersing yourself in the literature. Even if the course is a combined statistics and research methods offering, professors can mention the research component in the introductory psychology courses. Forewarned is forearmed.

Sources of Ideas
Your Personal Sphere and Your College Environment

Whenever you wonder about why people do something (e.g., why women are more likely than men to raise their hands when volunteering to answer a question in class) or how decisions are made (e.g., the basis of roommate assignments in first-year student housing), that question has the potential to become a research project. Your curiosity about what goes on around you—around you personally, your family, your friends, your community, your culture—all provide fruitful ground for research. What do you and your friends talk about? Relationships? Campus culture? Television and other media? You and your family? Are parental authority and disciplinary style frequent points of "discussion"? Perhaps conversations about household chores, curfew hours, or responsibilities vis-à-vis cars and safe driving habits occupy significant amounts of time. What topics seem to provoke the most response in class discussions? Some students have work-study jobs and assist staff members in campus offices, from dining services, student life, and the library to physical plant and facilities and grounds. Other students have jobs that involve modeling for art classes; still others serve as lifeguards. Each of these venues provides opportunities for research.

Good ideas for research often come from people who are trying to solve a practical problem, such as those who work in your college or university's offices of physical plant or facilities, buildings and grounds, student life, or housing. Not infrequently, campus offices are understaffed and have plenty of research they want to do. For example, offices of student life are often interested in the care and upkeep of the residence halls. Many other aspects such as vandalism, litter, crowding, basement rooms, and so on may be developed into research projects that are not only workable but also meaningful and practical. Interviewing people who work in these offices may lead to a research project that has solving a practical problem as its focus.

Tackling such a project does not mean that it has no foundation in the literature, but it is possible to solve problems at the same time you are testing a theory. As an example, consider the relationships among vandalism, class year, residence hall programming, and residence hall size, and perhaps tie these indicators to the development of sense of community in residence halls. Is there more vandalism in the fall than in the spring semester? Can this be related to first-year students' adjustment to a set of rules? Is there more vandalism in residence halls with greater proportions of first year students than of students from the second-, third-, and fourth-year classes? These vandalism data may be obtained from the physical plant office—the cost of acts deemed vandalism rounded to the nearest dollar. You might also be able to obtain a breakdown of gender and class year per residence hall from your office of student life. What these examples indicate is that ideas for research surround us and are embedded in our lives. Thus, a research methods project might easily serve two purposes: your class assignment and the answer to a question a campus office needs answered.

Print Media

The print media provide an excellent source of ideas, from *The New York Times* to *The National Enquirer*. You can imagine investigating the beliefs of students regarding headlines in *The National Enquirer* or doing a **content analysis** of the depiction of serial killers by gender in *The New York Times* and other well-regarded papers (a project actually done by a student). A content analysis is a coding scheme you create based on themes that emerge from qualitative data such as written narratives or newspaper articles. *The Wall Street Journal* (*WSJ*) is also an excellent source of ideas, particularly if you are interested in work and family issues, technology in the workplace, or career strategies. The *WSJ* has weekly columns devoted to many of these topics.

Wall Street Journal. The *WSJ* has a number of weekly or biweekly columns that provide some terrific research ideas. Monday through Friday on the front page there is always a section entitled "What's News" where you can read about news in Business and Finance and World-wide. Then each day of the week has a number of special offerings. For example, on Mondays there is typically a column that deals with technology and something called "Portals," which offers articles that give a glimpse into some current issue, such as the technological savvy of Howard Dean's staff when he was running for the nomination of his party (8/13/03). Tuesdays there is something called "In the Lead," which deals with issues involving executives and people who are trendsetters. Wednesday there is "Cubicle Culture," which deals with aspects of work life such as "Why U.S. workers are losing the tug of war over toilet paper" (Sandberg, 2003), which may have parallels in residence hall life. You can obtain past columns about careers by using the web address www.CareerJournal.com. Thursday offers a column by Walter Mossberg entitled "Personal Technology," and Friday offers "Science Journal" and a section entitled "Weekend Journal" that offers ideas for travel, sports, and leisure activities, among others. I particularly enjoyed one called "Lobster chronicles" (Sokolov, 2003) about strategies for preparing and eating large lobsters, and whether they were "tougher" meat than smaller crustaceans. Consider a potential research project dealing with people's beliefs about food. Particularly with the current emphasis on counting carbohydrates, and other nutritional and dieting concerns, you could examine the difference in perspectives or attitudes about eating patterns and weight between student athletes and nonathletes. You could even focus the research more specifically by looking at athletes for whom maintaining a given weight is important (e.g., wrestling, gymnastics, lightweight crew) and those for whom a specific weight is less important (e.g., hockey, soccer). The *WSJ* has articles that deal with gadgets, catalogue orders, and anything that you can imagine dealing with in the world of work; it provides a cornucopia of ideas for research.

Chronicle of Higher Education.   For current ideas in education that may lead to research topics, *The Chronicle of Higher Education* provides a good starting point. Articles in *The Chronicle* may focus on curricular issues in higher education (think about student evaluation of instruction or distribution of core requirements), personnel issues (like the employment of part-time faculty and student satisfaction), or student culture (the relationship between vandalism, gender, and the Greek system). This weekly publication has sections dealing with The Faculty, Research, Government and Policies, Money and Management, Information Technology, Students, Athletes, and International. There are also small sections entitled "Verbatim," "Who knew?", and "Hot type" (which deals with issues in publishing). The "Who knew?" section often has useful tidbits that could lead to research projects. For example, in the September 19, 2003 issue, there was a short piece entitled "Drink to that" (p. A20), which reported that people who have an occasional drink are likely to earn more money than those who refrain altogether. David Bell, the researcher whose work the column highlights, speculates that pay raises may be linked to drinking socially with one's co-workers. Another piece indicated that people who nod their heads are more confident about the information being presented, whether positive or negative, than those who shake their heads from side to side.

There are also always a range of more "serious" articles dealing with a variety of topics, from the damaging role of athletics in colleges in the Ivy League and New England Small College Athletic Association to increasing student interest in Celtic studies, but the lack of faculty to teach such courses (see the September 19, 2003 issue). At the end of the summer, there is always an Almanac issue for the upcoming academic year that provides a great deal of data about student, faculty, and staff characteristics. Examples include students' SAT and ACT scores by race, sex, and ethnic group breakdowns, and faculty and staff salaries and attitudes toward their work.

Television

Commercials and trends in programming can be a good source of student research projects. For example, with the help of facilities like your institution's digital curriculum or visual resources center, students can do projects where different kinds of commercials are spliced into television programs to measure the retention of different products or other aspects of the commercial. Student interest in careers such as FBI behavioral profiler or medical examiner can be viewed in terms of television viewing habits or a host of other possibilities.

Previous Courses

Although it is tempting to sell your books at the end of each semester, the return on investment is not very good (our bookstore textbook manager states that the best-case scenario is typically 30%, and students often receive a much lower return on their investment). Many of those books, especially those in your major, will serve you well in the future, whether as a source of research ideas or as preparation for the GREs if you apply to graduate school. If you must sell those books, at least consider the idea of photocopying the indexes because such lists provide a really rich source of topics to consider for research.

By the time students register to take a course in research methods, they have typically taken one or two courses in an introductory sequence, and possibly one or two content courses in the major. If students are majoring in psychology, such content courses might be Personality, Abnormal, or Social Psychology. In Human Development, these courses might be Individual Differences in Development or Social and Personality Development. In Sociology, possibilities are Sociological Approaches to Social Problems, or Ethnic and Race Relations. You might use your notes from these courses as a source of ideas. For example, a theory that intrigued you, a finding with which you disagreed, or findings that are ambiguous might all be sources for future research projects.

Other Departmental Resources

Other possibilities for research ideas include research groups that professors often sponsor or past honors theses of students in your department. The honors theses (and most published research) typically include a section dealing with limitations of the study or directions for future research. Leafing through the past honors theses done by students in your department gives you a feeling for the scope of such projects (honors theses typically require two semesters) in relation to a one-semester project. These theses are also a very good source of measures and scales (see Chapter 3).

Some colleges and universities have research groups typically formed around a professor's area of interest. These groups meet periodically (once a week or less frequently) and talk about the research ideas of professors, graduate students, honors thesis students, or individual study students. Becoming involved in these groups is good practice for a variety of reasons—you may hear the projects proposed by other students (and professors) and hear the critiques of these projects that are given in the research group. Being a member of such a group is good training for future projects and for graduate school. One of the most important aspects of a successful application to graduate school in psychology or a related discipline is research experience, especially involving a project that is self-motivated (honors thesis or individual study). Becoming a member of one of the groups is an excellent way to start on this journey.

Even if your future goals do not include graduate study, research projects provide training in a variety of skills that focus on problem solving: what questions to ask, where to look for possible ways to examine these questions and measure the variables under examination, how to enlist the help of experts, and so on. These research groups also provide the opportunity to get to know upper-level students in the discipline and professors (and for them to get to know you). Further, potential employers are always interested in the characteristics of applicants that set them apart; doing research beyond what is required in courses may indicate a high level of motivation.

It is also refreshing for students to see that their professors struggle with similar kinds of challenges—shaping an idea, considering what aspects of the project may undermine its validity, and so on. Hearing other students ask professors the "what about" questions (have you thought about x? what happens if y occurs?) can build confidence!

Department publications. Some departments publish their students' work in college journals such as the series published by our local chapter of Psi Chi, the National Honors Society in Psychology. Many of the papers published in the journal are, in fact, projects completed in the research methods course. Consider the following sample of articles in the 2001–2003 issue of the journal *(Connecticut College Psychology Journal,* Vol. 15) that our department publishes:

> Cross-cultural differences in the evaluation and perception of body image in 18–24-year-old men and women *
>
> The effects of academic and social experiences on college satisfaction *
>
> The effects of the neuroactive steroid pregnanolone as a putative modulator of anxiety when administered to rats on an Elevated Plus Maze (EPM)
>
> The effects of lyrical and non-lyrical music on reading comprehension +
>
> Accuracy of memory recall for eyewitness events +
>
> Personality traits of introversion-extraversion as an indicator of performance on a task measuring visual creativity *

The ones marked with an asterisk (*) were research methods projects, and the ones marked with a + were conducted in an undergraduate course in cognition. As you can see, undergraduate research projects have the potential to be meaningful pieces of work.

Regional Association Meetings

Another excellent source of ideas, particularly because so many of the poster presentations are from students, or from the collaborative work of students and professors, are abstracts of the regional (or national) meetings of psychological, sociological, or anthropological associations. As an example, here are some of the abstracts from the 2000 annual meeting of the Eastern Psychological Association (EPA) in Baltimore. The lead authors Najjar and Wolf were both undergraduate students at the time of the conference:

> Najjar, L., & Devlin, A. S. (2000). Intercultural marriage: Satisfaction levels and gender roles.
>
> Wolf, J. F., & Singer, J. A. (2000). Substance abuse and ADHD in homeless men.

Many students present their work during poster sessions, where a condensed version of the research paper is posted on a bulletin board. The student researchers stand by their posters, answering questions from conference attendees who walk around to view the posters. A fuller discussion of a poster session as a way to present your work is discussed in Chapter 7. There are poster sessions spread throughout the three-day EPA conference in the following categories:

Community and Clinical Assessment

Personality: Experimental, Regression, and Methodology

Experimental Social

Health, Stress, and the Addictions

Gender, Race, and Applied Behaviors

Applied Social Psychology

Cognition and Cognitive Psychology

Physiological, Developmental Psychobiology, and Animal Learning and Behavior

Child and Developmental Psychology

The abstract of any given article will give you just enough sense of the project to know whether it interests you for further investigation. Here is a sample of the titles of some of the abstracts under the heading Applied Social Psychology:

"The relationship between tomboys, their siblings, and androgyny in adulthood" (van Volkom, 2000, p. 60).

"Is professional wrestling becoming more violent?" (Kather, Chestnut, Ellyson, & Yarab, 2000, p. 61).

"Campus stereotypes of student smokers" (Srebro, Hodges, Authier, & Chambliss, 2000, p. 61).

"What's in a name? A comparison of attitudes toward food names and their nutrient descriptions" (DePauli, Kelker, Slotterback, & Oakes, 2000, p. 61).

The titles of the articles in the preceding list from the 2000 EPA meeting certainly suggest areas of student interest and seem like plausible research methods projects. As you can see, almost anything you might be interested in, from professional wrestling to food names, provides "fodder" for research (see Figure 1.2).

● ●

REFLECT AND REVIEW

How does social science advance as a discipline without repeating itself? Why are you likely to develop a good research idea when you use your personal experience?

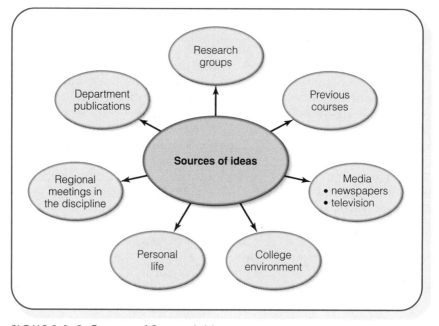

FIGURE 1.2 Sources of Research Ideas

● ●

APPLY YOUR KNOWLEDGE

Write down two or three potential research ideas that come out of your personal experience and two to three that come from recent television viewing or newspaper perusal.

Ideas in the Library

During freshman orientation, or soon thereafter, most students have an orientation to their institution's library or Information Services department. At many institutions, the head of the library is a vice president for information services or something similar, and technology is a critical aspect of the background and preparatory components of doing research (generating ideas, locating, and obtaining articles).

Before beginning your research project, it is a good idea to schedule a refresher seminar with one of your librarians/information specialists (according to the librarian I consulted, she is still a "research and instructional librarian"). Some institutions have librarians or information specialists who are assigned to a particular area of the curriculum, like Social Sciences or Humanities. Check with your library to see if this is the case, and then consult the appropriate staff member in your area.

Faculty consult the library staff as well, as not only do new sources become available for the many articles that students and faculty request, but also the ways in which the information is made available to users frequently change. Journal articles may be photocopied from the library's holdings of existing journals (hard copies), and they may be immediately available to download through electronic journal holdings. If articles are not immediately available through these routes, students and faculty may request articles (using a service like Interlibrary Loan) from another library. Students and faculty then receive either a photocopy in their campus mail or an electronic version to download through their campus e-mail.

When you begin to get an idea of the area of research that might interest you, finding a review article in *Psychological Bulletin*, the *Annual Review of Psychology*, or handbooks of psychology (e.g., *The Handbook of Environmental Psychology*) may give you an idea of the major issues the field is currently addressing. Your reference librarian can also help you find handbooks and review articles in other areas of social science, such as sociology, human development, and anthropology.

The Organization of the Library

Although the size of the library will vary dramatically depending on the institution, some aspects of libraries are essentially the same across institutions. Libraries in the United States use the Library of Congress Classification System for the call numbers of books, and it is worth becoming familiar with the call numbers that correspond to your area of interest. If you use a search engine such as Google™ and type in "Library of Congress Classification," the result will give you the Library of Congress classification outline. As examples, B is linked to Philosophy, Psychology, and Religion; G is linked to Geography, Anthropology, and Recreation; H is Social Sciences; L is Education; and R is Medicine. If you click on "B" you will get a subheading that indicates that the heading BF is the category for books in Psychology. As another example, if you click on "H" you will see a number of subheadings, including HM for sociology (General); HQ for Family, Marriage, Women; and HT for Communities, Classes, Races. Some students (and faculty) enjoy just "browsing the aisles" of their discipline's major call number (like looking at the books beginning with BF).

What may be true of smaller libraries is that their strengths tend to reflect the strength of the faculty at that institution, because faculty at a given institution will request books in their field of expertise. This area might otherwise be underrepresented at a small college. This use of specialized resources can work to the student's advantage in that you may end up doing research with a faculty member on campus, in his or her area of expertise, and you will have a solid base of resources from which to launch your own research projects. It is also likely that librarians are more accessible to students at smaller institutions with smaller libraries. These colleges are likely to have teaching rather than scholarship as their primary mission, and assisting students in the library goes hand in hand with this teaching mission. It is always a good idea to talk to a librarian about your research ideas before actually beginning your search for information, and certainly if you feel you are stuck or the keywords you are using yield fruitless searches.

Another way in which small colleges expand their resources is through participating in something like a consortium, where neighboring schools band together to share resources, incorporating the library holdings of each institution into the library database for each institution. Books requested through such a consortium typically arrive the next day.

Reference Materials

In addition to the circulating collection of books (books that may be borrowed), all libraries have an area dedicated to reference materials. In addition to the many print reference sources, most libraries offer a range of electronic databases, both general and discipline-specific.

Reference material: Style manuals and thesauruses. Perusing the Reference section is particularly useful before beginning a research project. Rather than immediately conducting a database search, it may be useful to look at the various reference encyclopedias and handbooks in a given discipline. The Reference section also typically includes style handbooks such as the *Publication Manual of the American Psychological Association* (5th ed.) (2001); the *MLA Handbook for Writers of Research Papers* (6th ed.) (Gilbaldi, 2003); *The Chicago Manual of Style* (15th ed.) (2003), used by the American Anthropological Association; and the *ASA Style Guide* (2nd ed.) (1997), used by the American Sociological Association.

The reference section also includes an array of thesauruses, such as the *Thesaurus of Psychological Index Terms* (8th ed.) (Walker, 1997), which can be an enormous help when you begin to do database searches for articles. Electronic databases such as **PsycINFO** also include a parallel thesaurus function. PsycINFO is a database of citations and summaries offered by the American Psychological Association. The database covers journals, books, technical reports, and dissertations in psychology and psychology-related disciplines such as psychiatry, medicine, nursing, education, sociology, anthropology, and linguistics. In 2003, the number of records offered in PsycINFO was more than 1.9 million ("Publications and Databases," 2004, p. 302). In PsycINFO, when you enter a keyword and click on the Map Subject Heading option, related terms appear and give you an indication of how many articles there are for each term.

Thesaurus of psychological index terms.   A thesaurus of index terms can be extremely useful to students in selecting the most effective keyword to search the literature on a topic. The thesaurus is usually arranged in such a way that if you look up a particular term, you will see a list of terms that are both broader and narrower. Often students initially enter keyword terms that either lead to "zero" hits or 1,000 hits; that is, the search leads to no relevant articles or so many that it is overwhelming to sort through them. If you look up the keyword "terrorism" in the PsycINFO database, you will get over 1,000 hits. If you click on the "Map Subject Heading" option in PsycINFO or consult a thesaurus of indexing terms (e.g., Walker, 1997) under "terrorism," you will see a definition (Scope note), and a broader term (B) antisocial behavior, and a list of related terms that are increasingly specific: Crime, Hostages, Political Revolution, and Radical Movements. If you enter "Radical Movements" into PsycINFO, you get 90 hits, a more manageable place to start (if this is the direction you are heading). At the very least, an indexing thesaurus or its online equivalent will give you some other keywords to test out.

Library holdings.   Another useful strategy before launching into a full-fledged database search is to look at your library's own holdings through its electronic catalogue. You can use the keywords you have identified through looking at the relevant thesaurus in your discipline. Try the Library of Congress subject headings for that topic. As an example, if I look up the term "personal space" in my institution's library catalogue, I see a listing of 166 entries that cover a wide range of topics, from art to medicine, that are in some way related to the topic of personal space. Students from small institutions often complain that their libraries are inadequate in terms of their physical holdings; however, most libraries have solid coverage in major areas and, in this electronic age, other materials are generally available within a week's time.

Reference section: Encyclopedias and handbooks.   The reference section of your library contains many handbooks and encyclopedias that can be invaluable sources of information. You can both obtain and refine ideas there.

Psychology.   In the Psychology section under the Library of Congress heading BF, you will find an array of reference materials related to psychology. The reference section contains various encyclopedias of psychology and handbooks covering a vast number of specialty areas, from a dictionary of Freud to encyclopedias of the paranormal and a dictionary of superstitions (which could be the starting point for a very interesting research project). There are also dictionaries or handbooks on more fundamental topics such as death and bereavement, emotions, stress, intelligence, health, adult development, aging and cognition, and sleep and dreams.

Although each library's holdings will obviously differ, the following list is a sample of the reference volumes you might typically find under the heading BF:

Companion Encyclopedia of Psychology, volumes 1 & 2 (Colman, 1994)

Encyclopedia of Psychology, volumes 1–8 (Kazdin, 2000)

Encyclopedia of Human Behavior, volumes 1–4 (Ramachandran, 1994)

Dictionary of Psychology (Bruno, 1986)

Dictionary of Psychology (Corsini, 1999)

The Freud Encyclopedia (Erwin, 2002)

Handbook of Child Psychology, 4 volumes (5th ed.) (Damon, 1998)

In addition to these relatively traditional areas of psychology, you might also find some newer areas represented:

Handbook of Multicultural Assessment: Clinical, Psychological, and Educational Applications (Suzuki, Meller, & Ponterotto, 1996)

Handbook of Environmental Psychology (Bechtel & Churchman, 2002)

Encyclopedia of Cognitive Science, 4 volumes (Nadel, 2003)

And of course there are always the areas that might be considered slightly off the beaten path:

Alternative Realities: The Paranormal, the Mystic, and the Transcendent in Human Experience (George, 1995)

The Encyclopedia of the Paranormal (Stein, 1996)

A Dictionary of Superstitions (Opie & Tatem, 1989)

The Reference section is also a good place to find sourcebooks of research measures and test critiques, a topic we will cover in more detail in Chapter 3:

Encyclopedia of Psychological Assessment (Fernandez-Ballesteros, 2003)

Measures for Clinical Practice (Corcoran & Fischer, 2000)

Test Critiques Compendium (Keyser & Sweetland, 1987)

Unpublished Experimental Mental Measures, 8 volumes (Goldman & Mitchell, 1996)

Under "H" in the Library of Congress headings, you are likely to find more general coverage of the social sciences such as:

Dictionary of the Social Sciences (Calhoun, 2002)

International Encyclopedia of Social and Behavioral Sciences (Smelser & Baltes, 2001)

And coverage of topics traditionally found in sociology:

Thesaurus of Sociological Indexing Terms (Booth, 1986)

Encyclopedia of Violence, Peace, and Conflict, 3 volumes (Kurtz, 1999)

Encyclopedia of Sociology, 4 volumes (Borgatta & Borgatta, 1992)

Encyclopedia of Family Life, 5 volumes (Bankston, 1999)

And important sources of attitudes such as:

Gallup Poll Public Opinion 2002 (Gallup, 2003) published annually

Other topics indexed under this heading include sexuality, women's issues, and criminal behavior such as:

The International Encyclopedia of Sexuality, 4 volumes (Francoeur, 1999)

Handbook of Sexuality-Related Measures (Davis, Yarber, Bauserman, Schreer, & Davis, 1998)

Women's Issues, 3 volumes (Dawson, 1997)

Encyclopedia of Drugs, Alcohol, and Addictive Behavior (Carson-DeWitt, 2001)

Encyclopedia of Criminology and Deviant Behavior, 4 volumes (Bryant, 2001)

Under the Library of Congress heading L, you will find topics in education. In addition to the college guides and evaluations, there are useful sources of information about research in education:

Encyclopedia of Educational Research, 4 volumes (Alkin, 1992)

Encyclopedia of Education, 8 volumes (Guthrie, 2003)

Handbook for Research for Educational Communications and Technology (Jonassen, 1996)

School Violence: A Reference Handbook (Kopka, 1997)

Dictionary of Multicultural Education (Grant & Ladson-Billings, 1997)

And there are many volumes related to the work of the Educational Testing Service, for example:

ETS Test Collection. Catalog: Vol. 5: Attitude tests (ETS, 1991)

Under the Library of Congress heading R, you will find material related to medicine. Examples include:

The Gale Encyclopedia of Alternative Medicine, 4 volumes (Krapp & Longe, 2001)

International Encyclopedia of Psychiatry, Psychology, Psychoanalysis, and Neurology, 12 volumes (Wolman, 1983)

Handbook of Abnormal Psychology (Eysenck, 1973)

Handbook of Psychiatric Measures (American Psychiatric Association, 2000)

Handbook of Behavioral Assessment (Ciminero, Calhoun, & Adams, 1986)

Handbook of Treatment for Eating Disorders (Garner & Garfinkel, 1997)

The Encyclopedia of Phobias, Fears, and Anxieties (Doctor & Kahn, 2000)

Encyclopedic Dictionary of Sports Medicine (Tver & Hunt, 1986)

Yearbook of Sports Medicine (Year Book Medical Publishers, 2002)

Handbook of Child and Adolescent Psychiatry (Adams & Bleiberg, 1998)

Handbook of Health Psychology (Baum, Reverson, & Singer, 2001)

REFLECT AND REVIEW

In what ways can librarians help with your research project?

APPLY YOUR KNOWLEDGE

Go to your own library, identify the Library of Congress call numbers for your area of interest, and see what reference books in that area are available to you.

Library Browsing

Journals. Spending time in the library looking at the current issues of journals in your field can generate ideas for your own project. In psychology, you might consider such journals as *Psychological Reports, Perceptual and Motor Skills*, the *Journal of Social Psychology*, the *Journal of Applied Social Psychology*, and somewhat more specialized journals such as the *Journal of College Student Development*, and the *Journal of College and University Student Housing*. Even if your library does not subscribe to these more specialized journals, it is often possible to look at their contents (article titles) online.

Journals frequently used by students in Sociology include *Ethnic and Racial Studies, Social Problems, Urban Studies, American Journal of Sociology, American Sociological Review, Journal of Marriage and the Family*, and *Media, Culture and Society*. In Anthropology, students may use such periodicals as *American Anthropologist* and *American Ethnologist* for cultural anthropology and *American Antiquity* for archaeology.

Ethnographies or published collections of articles are also valuable resources. In Human Development, my colleagues suggest *Child Development, Developmental Psychology, Exceptional Children, Pediatrics, Family Science Review, Journal of Marriage and the Family, Young Children, Children's Environmental Quarterly, Harvard Educational Review, The Journal of Black Psychology, Cultural Diversity and Mental Health*, and *Teaching Tolerance*.

In Education, frequently used journals are *Educational Researcher, American Educational Research Journal, Educational Studies*, and *Journal of Teacher Education*. Browsing through the tables of contents of recent journals in your particular discipline can give you a good sense of the kind of research that is being conducted.

Perceptual and Motor Skills vs. Journal of Personality and Social Psychology. It might be helpful to contrast the scope and depth of the articles in such journals as *Perceptual and Motor Skills* (*P&MS*) with those in such periodicals as the *Journal of Personality and Social Psychology* (*JPSP*) or the *Journal of Applied Psychology*. It could be argued that these journals define different ends of the spectrum with regard to the sophistication of work required for publication. *JPSP* and the *Journal of Applied Psychology* are among the premier journals in psychology in terms of the quality of the articles, and their rejection rate is exceedingly high, which might be interpreted as an indicator of quality. *JPSP* and the *Journal of Applied Psychology* often contain articles with multiple experiments, large numbers of participants, complex designs, and external funding. In the case of the *Journal of Applied Psychology*, a good many of the articles involve investigations in corporations rather than in college environments. In contrast, journals such as *Psychological Reports* and *Perceptual and Motor Skills* contain articles of much more modest proportions, in terms of the scope of the research. A good many of the articles could, in fact, be accomplished in a single semester. The articles in *P&MS* tend to be quite short (generally fewer than five pages), usually are about single experiments and somewhat limited sample sizes, are unlikely to involve external funding, and frequently have student authors. Some examples from the February, 2003 issue of *P&MS* illustrate these generalizations:

> "Tooth color: Effects on judgments of attractiveness and age" (pages 43–48) by Alexis Grosofsky, Sarah Adkins, Robert Bustholm, Leif Meyer, Lisa Krueger, Joshua Meyer, and Peter Torma of Beloit College. All but the first author are students.

> "Body image and eating attitudes among adolescent Chinese girls in Hong Kong" (pages 57–66) by Maria S. C. Fung and Mantak Yuen from The University of Hong Kong. This project was the MA thesis of the first author, who was supervised by the second author.

In contrast, from the February, 2003 issue of *JPSP,* take an example that involved grant support:

"Personality and the predisposition to engage in risky or problem behaviors during adolescence" by M. Lynne Cooper, Phillip K. Wood, Holly K. Orcutt, and Austin Albino of the University of Missouri-Columbia and Northern Illinois University (pages 390–410), a project that involved almost 2,000 participants. At the time this article was published, authors Cooper, Wood, and Orcutt were faculty members, and Albino was a graduate student, although when the project began in 1996, Orcutt was a graduate student and Albino, then an undergraduate, was not involved in the project (L. Cooper, personal communication, September 29, 2003). I mention the details of this authorship to illustrate that research, particularly large-scale research, often involves a considerable commitment of time and energy, and even, on occasion, a changing cast of characters!

What these contrasts between *P&MS* and *JPSP* illustrate is that there is a continuum of research sophistication and scope. When students are beginning their research careers with a one-semester project, a good phrase to remember may be "smaller is better."

REFLECT AND REVIEW

What do the number of authors, length of an article, and number of experiments included suggest about an article?

APPLY YOUR KNOWLEDGE

Check out the current issues of two to three journals in your disciplinary area (anthropology, education, psychology, sociology, etc.). Look at the differences in article length, section headings in the article, number of authors, indication of grant support, and so on. In your discipline, what might be the equivalents to *P&MS* and *JPSP*?

Electronic Resources

The Library Home Page

Although there is a lot to be said for the kind of browsing that involves taking books and journals off shelves (which typically is easier to do in the libraries of small, rather than large institutions, where access may be restricted), we increasingly do a lot of our browsing "online" using electronic resources (E-resources). It is therefore important to know what online resources are available to obtain literature about your project. Your library home page will probably contain a Catalogue (to find books), Electronic Resources such as Databases and Indexes (to find journals), access to Online Journals (full text), and Internet Resources such as course web pages, online dictionaries, and encyclopedias. The library home page may also contain subject and research guides, web reference sources, and search engines.

The library's electronic home page typically provides a wealth of information, particularly with regard to E-resources. Looking at this home page should give you information about how to access your library's catalogue and database indexes. First, we should distinguish between databases and indexes, on the one hand, and collections of online journals, on the other. Databases and indexes are typically used to locate an article of interest. Then, the question is whether the article you want is immediately available (downloadable) from an online journal. Databases such as PsycINFO allow the user to enter a keyword and then click on author name, article title, journal in which the article appears, or a combination of these in order to locate relevant articles. Then, the question becomes how to obtain that article (typically through your library's holdings of bound journals or its electronic journal holdings or access to such holdings in other libraries).

Databases and Indexes in the Social Sciences

Some of the most common databases and indexes in the social sciences are: PsycINFO, Psychology and Behavioral Sciences Collection, and Current Contents Connect (ISI). Often, under the heading

Databases and Indexes, there is the option of accessing the list alphabetically or by subject. For example, in many library systems, if you click on "listed by subject" under Databases and Indexes (to find journal articles), a list of subject areas appears alphabetically (from anthropology to zoology). You can click on the subject area of interest (e.g., education, psychology, sociology) and a list of the databases in that subject area appears. For example, if you click on Sociology in the Connecticut College library system, you will see a list of the following databases: Current Contents Connect (ISI), PAIS (Public Affairs Information Service [Via First Search]), Social Science Abstracts (via Wilson Web), and Web of Science (ISI). The other option is a list of databases and indexes alphabetically, from A and ABI/Inform to W and World-Cat. But if you don't know the names of the databases typically used in your field, the subject listing is a much better starting point.

Just as a comparison of resources, if you had gone to the Harvard University Libraries home page and clicked on their electronic resources option "Quick Jump to Selected Major Resources" in the summer of 2003, you would have seen that they offered the following (major) databases:

Academic Search Premier (EBSCO host)

Biography and Genealogy Master Index

Dissertation Abstracts/Digital Dissertations (UMI)

EconLit (OVID) (1969–)

ERIC (OVID) (1966–)

Historical Abstracts

JSTOR (Journal Storage)

LexisNexis® Academic

MEDLINE (OVID) (1966–)

MLA Bibliography (OVID) (Modern Language Association (1965–)

Oxford English Dictionary, 3rd Edition

PsycINFO (OVID) (1872–)

Science Citation Index Expanded (ISI Web of Science) (1945–)

WorldCat (First Search)

The list of selected major E-resources at Harvard is not substantially larger than the number of options at many small colleges, which should be reassuring.

To examine Harvard's resources in psychology, I went to their library's home page and looked under E-Resources by Subject, selected Psychology, and clicked on indexes to articles, which in the summer of 2003 produced the following list of indexes to journal articles (in Psychology) at Harvard: ERIC (OVID), Linguistics and Language Behavior Abstracts, PILOTS Database, PsycINFO (OVID) 1872–, and the Russian Academy of Sciences Bibliographies (Eureka on the Web) (1992–). With the exception of the PILOTS Database, which covers articles on traumatic stress, and the Russian Academy of Sciences Bibliographies, this list does not seem substantially more sophisticated than the offerings at my college. Our list includes Current Contents Connect (ISI), Medline, PsycArticles, Psychology and Behavioral Sciences Collection, PsycINFO, Science Direct, and Web of Science (ISI).

As one final exercise with Harvard, I examined their list of "New E-Resources" (under their heading of E-resources). On the day I checked (9/18/03), they listed 6 new non-E-journals and 95 new E-journals, resources that had been added over the previous three months. This domination of E-journals reflects the direction that journal publication is taking. Increasingly, journals that were once available in paper form are turning exclusively to an electronic means of publication. Libraries then pay for institutional subscriptions to these materials.

In the social sciences, broad and commonly used databases and indexes are ERIC (Education Resources Information Center), which is funded by the U.S. Department of Education and covers education and related issues, and InfoTrac® (which is the same database as Expanded Academic Index), covering news and periodical articles from 1980 onward in such areas as business, computers, current events, economics, health care, and sports, among others. There is also LexisNexis, which is almost always full text and covers almost 6,000 sources in news, business, legal, medical, and reference publications. Students may often find it useful to incorporate information that has appeared in newspapers or other current periodicals to supplement their academic work. In writing an article for publication, one of my students used InfoTrac and LexisNexis to check newspapers and magazines regarding vandalism on college campuses, and in particular the role of alcohol use and vandalism (Brown & Devlin, 2003). Using statistics from newspapers and magazines to include in the article provided the reader with some sense beyond academic journals regarding the increase in college student drinking nationwide and the role of fraternities and sororities in drinking behavior. Arguably this information added a different perspective to the article. Thus there may be reasons to look beyond traditional academic sources both in generating ideas and in developing them. Often, the inclusion of statistics from newspapers or other sources catches readers' interest. However, the researcher who uses information from popular magazines or newspapers should always question who the author is and the accuracy of the information. If you use popular magazines and newspapers, a good idea is to check the accuracy of the information by consulting primary sources.

Locating Journals Electronically

Once you have identified the journal that contains the article you seek, you need to obtain that article. Some libraries have a Journal Locator function for their electronic journal holdings on their home page (typically when you check a library's catalogue listings, there is an option to enter a journal name to see if the library subscribes to that journal). Imagine that you wanted a journal article from a 2002 issue of the *Journal of Environmental Psychology* (*JEP*). If you look under "J" in the electronic journal locator and scroll down to the *Journal of Environmental Psychology*, our library system indicates that articles for *JEP* are available from 1993 to the present through AP Ideal, which is presented as a hyperlink. You simply click on that link, locate the issue and article of interest, and download it and print it.

Take a second example from our system. If you are looking for an article in the *Journal of Social Psychology*, you may find that articles can be obtained through a number of electronic sources dating back from 1975 to the present (Psychology and Behavioral Sciences Collection), from 1998 to the present (LexisNexis Academic), from 1990 to the present (Expanded Academic Index ASAP and InfoTrac OneFile), and from 1995 to the present (Social Sciences Full Text). If you need an article earlier than 1975 in this case, you have to locate the bound volumes in your library (or another lending library). Bound volumes are hardcover, and each volume for a given journal contains all of the issues for a particular time period, usually a calendar year. Bound volumes are typically kept in the library stacks or sometimes even off-site for old volumes that are rarely used.

Some articles are linked directly to the database citation via a linking tool such as SFX, one of the most popular. When this happens, you don't even have to look up the journal title in the electronic journal locator; just click on the SFX link and your article will appear if your library has electronic access to your desired title. Otherwise, the SFX linking tool will provide options for obtaining the article (e.g., Interlibrary Loan). Librarians carefully select the combination of databases they provide to give library patrons the greatest coverage. For example, the library will decide which journals it wants to include in its First Search database to provide the broadest complement with other databases to which it subscribes.

● ●

REFLECT AND REVIEW

If you were starting your research, which source would you consult first, a database like PsycINFO, or an electronic journal locator?

● ●

APPLY YOUR KNOWLEDGE

Starting with your library's home page, find how many different ways you can access the *Journal of Social Psychology* through your library's electronic offerings.

Other Electronic Sources in the Library Worth Knowing

In addition to the journal locator resources we have already discussed, libraries typically have other ways to locate materials.

JSTOR (Journal Storage) is a collection of online academic journals containing older issues (with a moving wall of five years). You would *not* consult this collection if you wanted to electronically access a current journal article. **Project Muse** is an electronic source for current journals (over 220 scholarly journals).

Microfiche and microfilm are still available in most libraries, but their major function is to provide sources for newspapers and periodicals for the years not covered in the electronic sources (typically before 1980). Some students try to access newspaper articles by going directly to the newspaper's web address (e.g., www.nytimes.com) and then think they have to pay for full text articles. However, *The New York Times* is available through a library's LexisNexis server.

In my judgment, it makes the most sense to start with a solid database in your field, such as PsycINFO or Social Science Abstracts, locate articles of interest, and *then* consult the electronic journal holdings to see if a given article is available to download immediately from one of the electronic journal sources. If not, you can and should request the article through your library's version of interlibrary loan. Although it may be easier to limit yourself to electronic journal sources, the shortest path does not necessarily guarantee that you will secure the most important articles.

Interlibrary Loan Systems

You need to be familiar with the manner in which your library obtains materials (typically books and journal articles) that it does not own. These materials can be obtained through some kind of interlibrary loan system. Many libraries now use an interlibrary loan web interface called Illiad to make it easier to request books and journal articles.

Another useful resource related to obtaining materials from other libraries is WorldCat (World Catalogue). WorldCat is a worldwide database of books, monographs, videos, and sound recordings. In looking up a given book in WorldCat, you can see who in your region owns it, and beyond your region, if need be (which may give you a sense of how long it will take your library to obtain it).

Online Dictionaries and Encyclopedias

Colleges may also offer online dictionaries and encyclopedias, which are useful for general overviews of topic areas (the encyclopedias) or for looking up the derivation of words in the case of a source like the *Oxford English Dictionary*. Common sources for a library to offer online are the *Encyclopedia Britannica,* the *Grove Dictionary of Art,* and the *Oxford English Dictionary.*

Subject and Research Guides

Colleges and universities may also develop their own list of subject and research guides, which offer specific kinds of help to students including the proper form of citations, what constitutes plagiarism, and such listings as potential sources of internships. Each institution will obviously offer its own unique list. On our library site, there are citation guides for print and electronic resources, including links to MLA and APA; International Internships; Plagiarism Resources For Students, including material specific to our own institution and its honor code as well as links to other useful sites at the University of Michigan, the University of Oregon, and Purdue. There are Tests and Measurements Resources (from our own library holdings) and their call numbers.

Our site also provides search engines and their addresses, including AltaVista™, Google, HotBot, SurfWax, and WebCrawler®, among others. Each institution will have its own E-resources. What is important to recognize is that they exist and that these resources may be valuable to your research endeavor.

In addition to the traditional databases and indexes, search engines provide a way to explore research topics and keywords, but it is worth noting that there is no **peer review** *requirement* for the material you find on the web, and you may want to consider the validity of the sources of information that you find on the web. Most journal articles that are published, across disciplines, undergo what is called a peer review. In a peer review, a manuscript submitted for publication (usually with its identifying information removed, such as the author's name and affiliation) is evaluated or critiqued by other academics familiar with the topic of the research. Such peer review generally prevents articles from being published that are flawed from a methodological standpoint or that contribute no new knowledge to our understanding of a topic. No such review exists for materials on the web.

Therefore, when you consider using material you have found on the web, track down information about the author. Is he or she currently affiliated with an academic or research institution? Has the person published research in the area of your search? You can determine this by doing a search using a database like PsycINFO, entering the author's last name.

● ●

REFLECT AND REVIEW

Explain how you would obtain a book that your library does not own.

● ●

APPLY YOUR KNOWLEDGE

Go to your library's home page and see what specific subject and research guides your library offers.

GIS: Geographical Information Systems

Another research database tool that is becoming more widely available is **GIS:** Geographical Information Systems. GIS databases are archival sources of information from which it is possible to extract information about cities and towns, from the location and distribution of streets to the distribution of water, railroad lines, power plants, and so on. **Archival data** are pre-existing data such as statistics found in newspapers, the U.S. Census, and so forth. It is possible to merge data from other sources, such as the 2000 U.S. Census, with mapping data to create maps that contain **demographics**, information such as who lives where in a region, by race, sex, income, education, or any of the other census indicators.

Although the translation of this kind of information into research ideas is not immediately apparent for many people, there are certainly many possibilities for using GIS information in disciplines such as sociology. At a recent workshop on "Using GIS Across the Curriculum in the Liberal Arts," on October 4, 2003 at Connecticut College, a number of presenters described the course work projects using GIS that students have completed. John Grady, Professor of Sociology at Wheaton College, reviewed a project entitled "Attleboro: Poverty or Paradise," completed by two students in one of his courses. These students tested their hypothesis that mobile home parks are populated by poor and minority individuals. Using census data, aerial photographs of Attleboro to identify mobile home park clusters, and some "drive-by" observation, the two young men determined that their hypothesis was incorrect. In fact, at least in Attleboro, 75% of the occupants of mobile home parks are older than 55 years of age and the vast majority of them are White. According to the students, these occupants also own some "pretty nice" cars, and the students concluded that people may make an active choice to live in mobile homes or "manufactured housing parks," and may use their discretionary income for major purchases such as luxury vehicles.

Professor Grady commented that the humanities, social sciences, and sciences were taking a "visual turn," and he called himself a visual sociologist. He was guest editor for a special issue of *Sociological Imagination: The Quarterly Journal of the Wisconsin Sociological Association,* in which the special topic was "Challenging sociology visually," and wrote an article entitled "Becoming a visual sociologist" for that issue (Grady, 2001). For those of you who are interested in the applications of visual data in sociology, Grady's article is a good place to start. Another good reference book in this area is *Past Time, Past Place: GIS for History,* edited by Anne Knowles (2002). Figure 1.3 provides a summary of the library sources you may find useful.

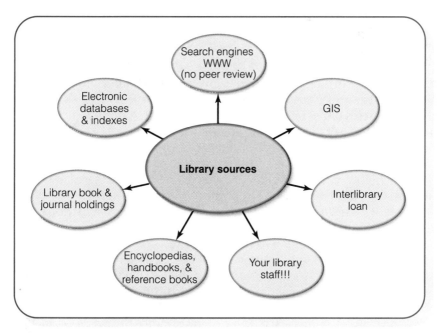

FIGURE 1.3 Library Sources

Next Steps: What to Do with Your Articles and Books

Don't be satisfied or complacent with reading an abstract! Although it is tempting to develop a research idea simply from reading abstracts, you will limit the quality of your research project if you do so. In a 120-word abstract, there is simply not enough information to make decisions related to the details of the project you want to undertake. On the other hand, you can go overboard with ordering articles without really considering their relevance to your project. I suggest to my students that their final research paper include citations from 15–20 articles. Perhaps because these journal articles are so easy to obtain, students print out large numbers of them to the point that some libraries are enforcing limits on "free" printing. For example, many institutions now permit "free" photocopying of a certain number of pages per semester (e.g., 300 pages per semester), after which a per-page fee is enforced.

Most of the articles you read will be divided into sections covering background literature (the literature review), what was accomplished with participants (the Method section in empirical work), some presentation of the findings (the Results section), and a discussion or interpretation of the findings (the Discussion section).

The Literature Review

When you read the literature in a given area, what should you note? Note how hypotheses are stated. Note what variables are involved. Your Results and Discussion section will be much easier to write up if the hypotheses are explicit. Even studies that seem to be exploring an area without particular hypotheses, such as looking at the relationship between student housing type and sense of community, can be turned into an explicit statement of hypothesis such as the following: Students living in suite arrangements will report a higher sense of community than students living in corridor arrangements.

Note whether the area is applied (practical applications) or basic research (about fundamental processes or concepts). Areas of social science differ in the degree to which they rest solidly on a theoretical foundation vs. the degree to which practical problems guide research. You will want to be sensitive to the applied vs. basic emphasis of a given area and ask yourself if you are more interested in pursuing one end of the continuum or the other. You can then focus more clearly on the kinds of questions each type of research asks. In the research described in the next paragraph on environmental preference, the emphasis was on basic research in the sense that the authors were trying to refine their model of the variables that predict judgments of environmental preference (i.e., how much we prefer a given scene in the environment). If you did a study asking people which kinds of environmental scenes they preferred with the goal of designing a new city park, the research would have a more applied emphasis.

Other questions you should ask yourself are: Who are the major theorists or key players? What theories are mentioned repeatedly? Is this an area of research with conflicting theories? For example, in the research on environmental preference, beginning work by Kaplan, Kaplan, and Wendt (1972) used pictures that varied in the degree of nature vs. built-environment emphasis. By taking into account the role of the environment, the research was designed to improve on earlier estimations of the relationship between preference and complexity by Berlyne (1963) and Wohlwill (1968, 1970). The research of Kaplan et al. demonstrated that the domain of the picture (whether it contained elements primarily of nature or an urban environment) had an impact on the preference judgment, which was not solely a matter of the degree of complexity, as hypothesized by earlier researchers. The Kaplan et al. research thus introduced a new wrinkle into the prediction of preference judgments. Their research showed that the theoretical variable of complexity was insufficient as a predictor of preference.

In reading the articles, you will want to pay attention to which hypotheses have been supported, which hypotheses have not, and which findings conflict with previous research. You will also want to note what questions seem to have been ignored or what areas have lain dormant. For example, a search of the literature will reveal that a number of studies on student housing were done in the 1970s, but that there have been few studies since then. Were all of the substantive questions really answered? With regard to our student housing example, perhaps questions related to gender, age, ethnicity, rural vs. urban upbringing, single sex vs. co-ed bathroom arrangements, and so on have not been addressed. Student housing today, in contrast to the 1970s, often includes more "liberal" arrangements with men and women living on the same floors and in some instances even using the same bathrooms. The impact of these kinds of arrangements on student satisfaction, studying habits, and so on might make a good study.

Conflicts and Gaps

In reading the literature in a given area, you will also want to note which approaches have been used and whether a particular approach seems to be a **paradigm**; that is, whether there is a single dominant approach that has been embraced in exploring a particular question.

Is research in a given area done by observation, through interviews and self-report, or have experimental manipulations been used? Perhaps you might try an experimental approach in an area that has not used one. For example, most studies of student housing use self-report surveys. If your college or university has remodeled housing over the summer and has assigned students more or less randomly to the old and new versions of this housing, it might be possible to assess the impact of this new form of housing using an experimental approach.

In the 1970s, the Herman Miller Research Corporation (Propst & Propst, 1973) conducted a study at the University of Massachusetts, Amherst, that involved providing a furniture store where students could select dormitory furniture for their rooms. In contrast to the amount of vandalism and damage to furniture that had occurred under the old system, student choice regarding their own furniture was related to a decrease in the average damage rate per student by as much as 55%. This research was conducted 30 years ago. Perhaps there are new questions about student housing you can ask. There may be archival means to examine satisfaction with housing reflected in the number of requests for room changes or the amount of vandalism that has occurred over a particular period of time.

Seminal Studies and Becoming an Expert

In your reading, another approach is to take note of what might be called the **seminal studies,** or keystone studies, in the field. What are the roots of the topic? What is its history? What are the core or seminal studies? Seminal studies are the foundational studies in an area that seem to be cited in most of the articles on a given topic. You can usually determine these seminal studies by looking at which references appear repeatedly across articles. For example, in the study of cognitive mapping and environmental cognition, the work of Kevin Lynch in his 1960 book *The Image of the City* almost always appears. Through examining the perceptions of residents of Boston, Jersey City, and Los Angeles, Lynch helped us understand how a city might vary in its legibility (the degree to which we understand its layout). It should come as no surprise that there are parts of Boston that baffle even its residents, who often perceive Boston Commons as a four-sided shape. In fact, it has five sides!

In becoming an "expert" in your field, so that you are knowledgeable about questions asked and findings, you may tree backward through references and tree forward (Martin, 1985, p. 39) using a database like the Social Sciences Citation Index. When you tree backward, you essentially look at the references in a given article, select those that seem promising to you (usually on the basis of the title), and then track down *those* articles, reading them and then using their references. This method obviously produces an exponential number of references, but eventually you will come to the point where each new article produces few articles that are new to you.

When you tree forward, using the Social Sciences Citation Index, you take a given article, and see in whose research it has later been cited. This later article presumably is on a topic of interest to you.

The Method Section

Pay particular attention to the Method section of the articles you read. The method section is typically divided into subsections involving participants, apparatus/materials, and procedure.

Participants. Who were the participants? Students? Community volunteers? A particular population like residents of a nursing home or a prison? How many participants were there? At small institutions, obtaining a sufficient number of people to serve as research participants may be a challenge (see Chapter 4). Also, be alert to whether a particular topic seems to involve a restricted and difficult-to-obtain population (e.g., prisoners).

How were the participants obtained? Randomly? With a mailing? A **convenience sample** (e.g., people who stop at your research table in the library or student union)? A **snowball sample** (i.e., asking people to participate who in turn recommend other people to participate)?

Apparatus/Materials. Keep close track of the scales and measures that you see repeatedly used in a given area. As an example, researchers evaluating student reactions to residence hall life often use the University Residence Environment Scales (Moos, 1988), a copyrighted measure that is available from Mind Garden® (www.mindgarden.com). For $120 (plus $30 for the sample set with the test manual), you can reproduce up to 150 questionnaires for a year's use (information retrieved 7/20/04). When budget constraints are a consideration, as is usually the case with student research, you may need to steer clear of measures for which a fee is charged. The issues surrounding obtaining measures will be discussed in Chapter 3.

Procedure. What did the participants do? How easy was it to accomplish? Did the researchers use questionnaires? Individual interviews? Experimental manipulation? How costly did the research seem to be (was there postage, payment to subjects, equipment, copyrighted questionnaires to purchase)? The cost of research may not be immediately evident from the write-up, but it is important to try to get a sense of whether the research is feasible from the standpoint of cost. You also need to determine whether any equipment is needed and whether your institution owns it or you can borrow it from another institution. One of my students learned about expensive projects the hard way in her thesis entitled "Color psychology, laterality, and spatial performance" (Brigham, 2002). She used the Torrance Tests of Creative Thinking (Torrance, 1977) but found that the tests were extremely time-consuming to score. She then considered having the tests scored professionally, but found that this was too costly. In the end she scaled back her research due to the time it took her to learn to score the tests.

Limitations and Future Directions

Many studies end with a section on the limitations of the study reported and directions for future research—to extend, expand, or improve upon the reported research. This section of research papers is extremely helpful for generating a specific research question once you have your general area of interest identified.

Critique, Critique, Critique

Simply because an article has been published does not mean it is flawless. And don't be afraid to poke as many holes in the research as you can, which will provide avenues for you to build upon. In one of the classes I teach, we spend a considerable amount of time reading articles in a variety of areas (social, personality, physiological, clinical, environmental, developmental) written by a range of authors (those eminent in the field, some of our own faculty, and some of our students whose work has been published). Students thus get a sense of the range of sophistication of the research and of the range of work that has been and can be published. When you look carefully at a given article, you might not be impressed with the **internal consistency** of the measure. The internal consistency is the degree to which each item of the measure is tapping the construct of interest. You might think that the sampling was flawed; for example, collecting data on Saturdays at the library might attract only a particular kind of student. Or you may see a way in which to extend the study, by adding a different population or an additional (or substitute) variable.

REFLECT AND REVIEW

Why is it so important to identify shortcomings in existing research?

APPLY YOUR KNOWLEDGE

Go to the library online, find an article of interest in your area, read it, and write down five ways you could improve upon it.

Organizing Your Articles and Books

Accumulating a large number of articles is relatively painless, and it is easy to lose track of how much material you have. Office supply stores make collapsible files, tinted files, and a myriad of other kinds of file organizers to help you compartmentalize and organize your material.

Do you use a highlighter to highlight passages on the originals you obtain through the library and work from that original? Or do you condense what you have by limiting yourself to an index card's worth of information for each article—its title, author(s), source, and essentials of the method, results, and discussion? You may find it useful to write executive summaries of the articles; that is, to condense the information and render it easier to use for your research. Some students work from full text and create condensed versions, using both approaches.

To create condensed versions of an article, you can use color-coded cards for articles to highlight different themes (e.g., aggression) from multiple articles. Another approach is to color-code sections *across* articles, so that different colors are used for (1) introductory or theoretical material, (2) method (about a particular scale), and (3) results. Some students even use three-hole binders, punch holes in their articles, and use color-coded tabs to identify different aspects of importance. Another approach is to create computer files for these different sections.

Especially for Interlibrary Loan (ILL) books, resources that are loaned to you from another library for a limited period of time and that must be returned to a lending library within two to three weeks, it is very important to accurately record the information you need. If you are using quotations in your paper, make sure that you photocopy the page(s) that contain the quotation(s) so that in your final version you can check the accuracy of your quotations. Don't rely on the legibility of your handwriting for accuracy.

Reasonable Questions and the Problem of Mediating Variables: Narrowing the Gap

On occasion students (and even professionals) ask important questions that seem to have a high probability of producing significant findings. Typically, the questions are broad, the constructs somewhat amorphous, and the path between the questions and any observed behavior or outcome may be littered with **mediating variables.** Mediating variables are those that impact or affect the relationship between the variables of interest. As an example, consider the somewhat surprising finding that there is a fairly small relationship between employee satisfaction and job performance (Iaffaldano & Muchinsky, 1985). Most students (most people, for that matter) assume that people who are more satisfied with their jobs will be more productive. Looking more closely, there are a lot of reasons why people may be productive in their jobs. Yes, satisfaction is one of those variables, but people may need to be productive to keep a job (and its benefits), because it gives them a certain amount of status, because no better job is available at the moment (a poor economy or a decline in that area of business), or a host of other reasons.

As you can see, lots of other pressures, concerns, or mediating variables influence the relationship between job productivity and worker satisfaction. When students start off with an idea like looking at the relationship between parental disciplinary style and student achievement, you might expect the same kind of difficulties; there are a number of explanations for any relationship. Particularly when you have a participant pool at a selective college or university, students who have experienced vastly different parenting styles are likely to have achieved at similarly high levels. Then, when students do a project examining the relationship between parenting styles and achievement, they are often disappointed by the results, which are unlikely to show a relationship between a particular parenting style and achievement.

Consider another example that a student proposed. She was interested in the relationship between the kind of high school (e.g., public, private, home school) a student attended and adjustment to college. The problem with trying to relate these two variables, again, is that there is so much "space" between them; that is, there are too many mediating variables. The student researcher may think that students who attended prep school would have an easier adjustment to college because they've already been away from home. The problem is that there are many alternative explanations and may be other reasons for the easier adjustment the researcher predicts. Think about people's lives. Students are involved in activities, have roommates, have things happening at home such as divorce or illness, and so on. Think about people's lives and the events that may mediate the relationship between type of high school and college adjustment. That gap is simply too wide. What the student needs to do is to narrow that gap—to ask questions that will give that

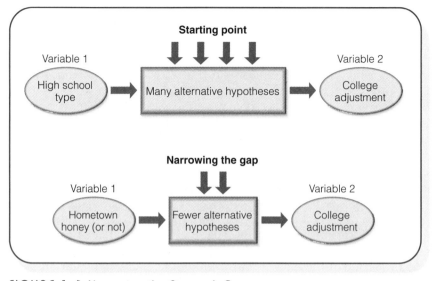

FIGURE 1.4 Narrowing the Research Gap

relationship of high school type and college adjustment somewhat more specificity. Perhaps the idea could be modified by looking at those who took a year off before college and their adjustment, or at those who maintain high school (dating) relationships (the "hometown honey syndrome") and college adjustment. So, when the variables are too far apart, you need to close the gap by looking at specific aspects of the variable(s) in question. Your job is to narrow the gap to rule out as many pre-existing alternative explanations as possible. Figure 1.4 illustrates the concept of closing the gap between variables.

You can help rule out many alternative hypotheses by including background or demographic variables (e.g., age, sex, number of siblings, parents' marital status) that you think might contribute to an alternative hypothesis. Demographic variables are background variables about the participants. For example, it is possible that parents' marital status may be a variable that mediates the relationship between high school type and college adjustment. In some families, a divorce may mean that teenage offspring are sent to private schools. Adding a question about parents' marital status (and when any change occurred) may help account for the alternative hypothesis that it is marital status, and not school type, that better predicts college adjustment. Thus, you need to think clearly about reasonable alternative hypotheses and variables that may assess these hypotheses so that you can attempt to rule out the competing hypotheses!

● ●

SUMMARY

At this point you should have thought of a research idea and examined what has already been done in that area. By now you know the library and electronic resources your institution has available, how the interlibrary loan system works, how to search for journal articles through a number of different databases, and how to request articles that you cannot immediately download.

An important message in this chapter is the critical task of narrowing the gap between the variables that relate your research question and its predictions. As you have learned, your job is to eliminate mediating variables by narrowing the research question sufficiently to rule out the alternative explanations that are the most viable candidates. You cannot control every variable that may have an effect, but you can certainly pose your research question in a way that reduces the likelihood that one of these competitors provides a better explanation.

● ●

APPLY YOUR KNOWLEDGE QUESTIONS

In the event that you did not have time to do them earlier, here is the list of APPLY YOUR KNOWLEDGE questions in this chapter. Try them now:

1. Write down two or three potential research ideas that come out of your personal experience and two to three that come from recent television viewing or newspaper perusal.

2. Go to your own library, identify the Library of Congress call numbers for your area of interest, and see what reference books in that area are available to you.

3. Check out the current issues of two to three journals in your disciplinary area (anthropology, education, psychology, sociology, etc.). Look at the differences in article length, section headings in the article, number of authors, indication of grant support, and so on. In your discipline, what might be the equivalents to *P&MS* and *JPSP*?

4. Starting with your library's home page, find how many different ways you can access the *Journal of Social Psychology* through your library's electronic offerings.

5. Go to your library's home page and see what specific subject and research guides your library offers.

6. Go to the library online, find an article of interest in your area, read it, and write down five ways you could improve upon it.

WEB RESOURCES

There are a number of research methods workshops on the web that may enhance your knowledge of the topics in this chapter. Here is a list of these workshops and their web addresses:

Getting Ideas for a Study

Evaluating Published Research

Common Mistakes in Student Research

www.wadsworth.com/psychology_d/templates/
student_resources/workshops/resch_wrk.html

Research Design and Statistical Considerations

2

Introduction and Chapter Overview

Before you begin to collect data, it is crucial to sit down and think through whether the variables you intend to measure and the way you intend to measure them will answer the research question(s) you have posed. Often when students prepare research proposals, they have formulated their hypotheses, identified where they are going to recruit participants, decided upon research measures, and determined the order in which they are going to administer their measures or other aspects of their procedures. Yet they have neglected to give any thought to how they are going to analyze their data. Stop! Before collecting any data, you need to ask yourself whether the data you will collect can be analyzed in such a manner as to answer the research questions you have posed. Thus, the major question this chapter addresses is how to tell whether your hypotheses can be answered by your proposed research design. Carefully considering whether you will actually be able to answer your research questions can avoid major disappointment toward the end of the project, *and* such planning makes clear what kind of data analysis should be carried out when the time comes.

Students often wait until after their data are collected to consider what kinds of statistical analyses are appropriate. Sometimes this is too late. In this chapter, we will look at the relationships between the stated hypotheses, possible research designs, and the appropriate statistical approach for different types of research designs. No, this is not a review of your statistics course. Rather, the chapter concentrates on getting you to see the relationships between the way research questions (and hypotheses) are framed, the kind of data that need to be collected to answer these questions, and the appropriate approaches to data analyses. You will see how slightly different statements of the research hypotheses can lead to different research designs, and you will learn when you really *can* say something about cause and effect.

Hypotheses: Slight Changes with Big Implications

Any given topic can be examined in a number of ways, and the manner in which you state your hypotheses will determine your particular research design, whether you will be able to reach any conclusions about cause and effect, and the statistical approach you should adopt. Let's take an example. Imagine you are interested in the relationship between health and the environment. A good number of studies show a positive impact of nature on physical well-being (e.g., Kaplan &

Kaplan, 1989; Ulrich, 1981; Ulrich, Simons, Losito, Miles, & Zelson, 1991). Studies show that even vistas or views to nature through windows promote well-being (e.g., Kaplan & Kaplan, 1989; Ulrich, 1984; Verderber, 1986). As a student in college, in all likelihood you will have to limit your research project to the college environment. So, your next step is to focus your interest more narrowly—perhaps in terms of whether different kinds of student rooms, with different views to the outdoors, are linked to different levels of stress.

Study 1: Correlational Design

You can examine the relationship between the number of natural elements visible from a student's dorm room (i.e., the number of trees/bushes or other forms of nature visible from these rooms), and the degree of daily hassles (as a measure of stress) reported by the students on a measure like the Daily Hassles and Uplifts Scale (Kanner, Coyne, Schaefer, & Lazarus, 1981). Essentially, your hypothesis, based on the literature, is that there is a negative relationship between the number of natural elements visible out the window and daily hassles—the more nature, the lower the level of daily hassles. In this design, you are looking only at the *relationship* between variables. As the number of natural elements increases, does the level of daily hassles decrease? There is no cause and effect; no variables are manipulated. It is certainly possible that A causes B, B causes A, or that a third variable is involved. But as there are no manipulations or interventions, no determination of causality can be made. In fact, this kind of design has been labeled *passive* by Wampold (1996). There are no manipulations or interventions. In this study, the statistical approach you would use is the calculation of correlation coefficients, Pearson's *r*. Figure 2.1 illustrates the relationship in this study.

Study 2: Quasi-Experimental Design

You examine the same variables, but you assume that students (probably first-year students) have been randomly assigned to "condition"—and

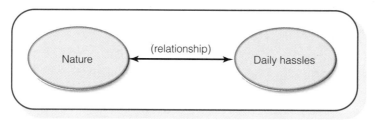

FIGURE 2.1 Correlational Design

you categorize students into those with views of nature (ignoring the number of natural elements, just whether they see them or not) and those without views of nature. If your college is one in which first-year students are spread throughout the residence halls, random assignment to those rooms is a reasonable assumption. Even if first-year students are housed together in specific dorms or in specific locations within a given dorm, there is a good chance that they have been arbitrarily assigned to those rooms. Then you might hypothesize that students who live in rooms with views to nature (whether one, two, or more natural elements) will have significantly lower daily hassles scores than students who have views to parking lots, other dorms, or garbage dumpsters (which is not uncommon). Here, too, the design has been labeled *passive* (Wampold, 1996) because you are not manipulating any variable. Bordens and Abbott (2002) call this a quasi-experiment using a quasi-independent variable (IV). Statistically, you are taking a random sample from two pre-existing groups (those with views to nature vs. those with views to the built environment) and doing a between-groups design (Figure 2.2 illustrates this relationship). The difference between Study 1 and Study 2 rests in whether you are looking at the general relationship between nature and daily hassles over a continuum (low to high), or focusing on groups, defined as those with or without views to nature. With only one independent variable (view condition) with two levels (nature or not), and one dependent variable (the hassles score), you would conduct a *t*-test to examine group differences. Still, you cannot make a judgment about cause-and-effect relationships because you have not manipulated any variables. If there are significant group differences, the results are suggestive, and the researcher might

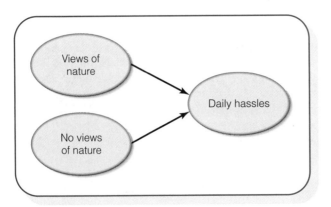

FIGURE 2.2 Quasi-Experimental Design

want to follow up with a real experiment, which is explained in the next example.

Study 3: Experimental Design

In this version, you do an actual experiment by manipulating variables. You could find those rooms in which students had a view of the built environment (views to other buildings, parking lots, or dumpsters) and add attractive plants to half the student rooms, selected at random. With a large enough population, you can make the assumption that the level of daily hassles is randomly distributed across these particular students, and you can add attractive plants to the windowsills of half of the population. After a specific length of time (e.g., three weeks), you could administer the daily hassles scale to students with and without these plants. In this version, you have actually manipulated a variable (the addition of plants or not), and you can now make some tentative conclusions about cause and effect. To evaluate the group differences, you would again do a *t*-test (one independent variable with two levels and one dependent variable). If there is a significant difference in the level of daily hassles reported by the two groups after the three-week period, you could venture the conclusion that plants have an impact on the level of daily stress. This design is no longer passive; you have an *experimental* design (Wampold, 1996) (see Figure 2.3). Although, as Wampold points out, you might use precisely the same kind of statistical test (e.g., a *t*-test) in both a passive and an experimental design (our Examples 2 and 3, respectively), there is a vast difference in the conclusion you are able to reach. In Example 2, there still is no ability to make a causal determination, whereas in Example 3, one can venture such a conclusion.

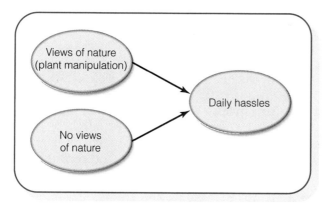

FIGURE 2.3 Experimental Design

Cause and Effect and Types of Research Designs

As the previous discussion indicates, unless you are randomly assigning participants to conditions and manipulating the levels or treatments of an independent variable or variables, you will be unable to reach any conclusions about *cause and effect* in your research. That's okay, but you need to be aware of the pluses and minuses of any given research design and determine whether you have the appropriate approach for the question(s) you are asking. If not, you need to either change the question(s) or change the design.

The inability to make causal inferences does not make your research invalid; it only limits or curtails the ability to say something definitive about the direction of effect and the influence of the variables you are studying. If you look back at the list of student projects at the beginning of Chapter 1 and carefully examine their titles, you will see that some of the titles promise more than the research design can deliver. For example, consider the following research project titles:

Cognitive Styles and Academic Major: Influence on
    Student-Professor Relationships

The Effect of Parenting Style on College Success

What you will notice about these titles is that each of them suggests the ability to determine causality in the research. This inferred promise is created through the use of such language as "influence on" and "effect of." Consider the research project title "Cognitive Styles and Academic Major: Influence on Student-Professor Relationships." The title of this project suggests that a student's cognitive style and academic major *influence* student–professor relationships. Now it may be the case that particular cognitive styles and/or academic majors are *associated* with different kinds of student-professor relationships, but being *associated with* is quite different from *influencing*. One reasonable hypothesis may be that students who major in studio art have close student-professor relationships because of the small class sizes in art studios. However, because of the nature of this kind of study, which is correlational (that is, we do not randomly assign students to either their majors or their cognitive styles), we will be limited to statements of association, not causation.

On the other hand, examine the titles of the student projects in the following list (taken from sections in Chapter 1), and consider the degree to which we can talk about causality.

The Media's Effect on Women's Body Esteem and Body
    Dissatisfaction: Effect of Brief Media Exposure

The Effects of the Neuroactive Steroid Pregnanolone as a Putative
    Modulator of Anxiety when Administered to Rats on an
    Elevated Plus Maze (EPM)

Accuracy of Memory Recall for Eyewitness Events

What each of these projects has in common is the manipulation
of levels of an independent variable and random assignment to condition. The ability to determine causality is perhaps least suspect in
the case of the research with rats on the elevated plus maze, but we are
still willing to consider the possibility of causality in the other projects. For example, in the project entitled "Accuracy of Memory Recall
for Eyewitness Events," the two student experimenters used confederates to stage an encounter with two conditions: "no violence" and
"minor violence." The minor violence condition involved a three-
minute argument in which arm grabbing of one student by another
occurred. In the no violence condition, the argument occurred without the physical contact. Students in the experiment, who were randomly assigned to one of these two conditions, answered questions
about what they had witnessed through use of a free narrative recall
and specific questions that required numerical responses. Results in
this study indicated significant differences between the two conditions in terms of remembering the content of the conversation, with
those in the minor violence group generating fewer answers that involved the precise language used by the confederates (St. Pierre &
Wong, 2003). When variables are manipulated, as they were in this experiment (exposure to minor violence or not), one can reach a conclusion about causality. Here, witnessing minor violence influenced
the degree to which participants were able to recall the exact words
(i.e., verbatim exchanges) in the confrontation they witnessed.

Many studies that students propose take the participants "as is";
that is, the students are not randomly assigned to a particular condition, although they may represent categories of students with different kinds of experiences. For example, in the proposed research study
from Chapter 1 involving the type of high school a student attended
and that student's adjustment to college (in the section entitled
"Reasonable Questions and the Problem of Mediating Variables"),
no one has been *randomly assigned* to high school type. This kind of
research essentially looks at the *relationship* between high school type
and college adjustment. As we discussed in Chapter 1, the "variable
space" between high school type and college adjustment is so large
(that is, the number of potential variables that could affect the relationship between those two factors is so large) that the measured relationship between the two undoubtedly will be quite small because of
the **mediating variables.**

A word of caution—because your participants (often other college students) are not rats from Charles River Laboratories, there may be background experiences that mediate or influence the relationships you seek to examine, even in research designs that we would label *experiments*. Consider a study where you are examining the effect of space available (in a room) on problem solving, and you plan to do this by randomly assigning three groups of students to research spaces that vary in square footage (25 sq.ft., 64 sq.ft., and 100 sq.ft.). In your random assignment to condition, it *is* possible that, by chance, all participants in one of your groups grew up in high-density apartment buildings and, as it turns out, are comfortable with higher social densities (i.e., more people in a given spatial area) than are people who grew up in single-family dwellings with separate yards. You can see that differential experiences of this sort (type of housing density growing up) may be related to performance on your task. Generally these kinds of problems can be addressed by having a sufficient number of participants in the study so that it is highly unlikely that people with a particular characteristic will all end up in one group. You might also try to do some pre-assessment of demographic characteristics that may be of relevance to your study. But it is hard to try to anticipate *everything* that might influence the outcome of your study, which is why it is such a good idea to talk to others about your ideas and hear the "what if?" and "have you thought about that?" questions that may help to strengthen your research. Often departments have research groups, usually run by faculty, that cover topics in that faculty member's area of interest (e.g., developmental, personality, social, cognitive). Beyond talking to your research methods instructor or graduate teaching assistant (if you have one), you can also discuss your research idea with the faculty member whose research is most closely aligned with the topic you have selected.

Your research methods instructor might want to schedule time for students to break into small groups to critique each other's research ideas and procedure. Other students are excellent at identifying aspects of the research design that might elude the researcher who often seems to have put on blinders or closed off consideration of variables that might affect the research outcome. One thing that other students can help identify is aspects of the potential research participants' background that may affect the outcome of the research. In our previous example on problem solving and room density, variables such as childhood housing type or even geographical location might be appropriate to assess.

The following sections discuss in more depth types of research approaches and their relationship to questions of causality.

REFLECT AND REVIEW

Why is quasi-experimental design so common in social science research?

APPLY YOUR KNOWLEDGE

With this brief introduction, see if you can take a research question and approach it from three different research designs: correlational, quasi-experimental, and experimental.

Make a list of the demographic variables that might commonly be used in research with college students.

Passive Designs

As mentioned previously, Wampold (1996) uses the term passive to describe research where no manipulation of variables occurs. He specifies two categories of passive design, correlational and between-groups. People often refer to the kind of between-groups design where we accept the grouping as we find it (that is, we don't randomly assign people to their groups) as quasi-experimental design. There may be very good reasons for selecting a quasi-experimental design. Usually the reasons involve the ethics of dealing with the participants or the fact that the groups of interest are naturally occurring and we couldn't possibly assign people at random to those groups. For example, it would be ethically unconscionable to tell people that a sibling had died (when this had not occurred) and study their grief reactions. Obviously, no Institutional Review Board (IRB) (see Chapter 5) would approve such research. Instead, we may approach this project by finding people (to form a naturally occurring group) who have lost a sibling and study their grief process over time. In the case of finding this naturally occurring group, there are other factors in the backgrounds of these individuals that may affect their grieving process. As we cannot control all of the relevant variables involved, this study *approaches* the idea of an experiment; hence we would call it a quasi-experiment. Often, because we may be using naturally occurring groups in quasi-experimental designs, these experimental approaches have greater **external validity** (generalizing to other populations) than true experiments. External validity involves the extent to which our findings may generalize to other populations and to the real world.

Correlational Research

Many of the studies proposed by students involve correlations; that is, they examine the relationships between variables, typically those that are measured on a continuous scale. Examples of such variables and some scales that measure them are depression, as measured by the Beck Depression Inventory (Beck, Steer, & Brown, 1996), and Environmental Preference, as measured by the Environmental Preference Questionnaire (Kaplan, 1977). Typically these are interval scales, which means that the numerical distance between each of the rating values is the same (i.e., in a 5-point rating scale, the numerical distance from 3 to 4 is the same as the distance between 1 and 2). An example of a correlational study would be examining the relationship between high school grade point average (GPA) and Scholastic Aptitude Test (SAT) scores. For each student in the study, there is a numerical GPA as there is a numerical SAT. We are asking whether there is a predictable relationship between the two variables. Do students who have high GPAs also have high SATs? Imagine that the answer is "yes" (although this is not necessarily a consistent finding) (see Bridges, 2001). Do we know why, based on that correlation? We do not. The relationship could be mediated by a limitless number of other variables, such as intelligence, family income, hard work, AP courses, SAT "prep" courses, number of books in the home, parents' educational level, and so on. We could certainly pursue these other variables if we extend our research, but the point is that although correlational research tells us if two variables tend to be co-related or associated, it gives us no explanation why.

One of my colleagues, Stuart Vyse, uses the following example in teaching the relationship of cause and effect to correlation. A graduate student colleague of Professor Vyse's found a relationship between marital conflict (assessed through a questionnaire) and observations of aggression in the couple's child on the playground at school. For any correlation that represents a real relationship, there are three causal paths. What are the causal explanations? A (marital conflict) causes stress in the child (or is imitated by the child), B. Or, a temperamentally difficult child (B), causes marital conflict (A). Or, poverty or another stressor (C) causes both A and B (see Figure 2.4).

You can see from this example that correlations open the door to a number of causal explanations. The determination of a *particular* cause and effect is not possible. So, returning to the initial question: Can your research design answer your research questions? Be sure that you are not asking more of the design than it can provide. Don't ask for a cause-and-effect answer when you can only assess relationships. If you are interested in determining cause and effect, your research design must involve the manipulation of the independent variable(s).

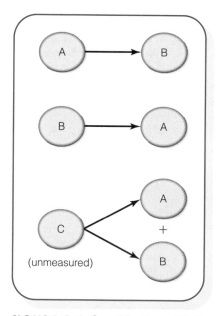

FIGURE 2.4 **Possible Causal Paths**

Recently, there was a lively exchange of e-mails on an Internet mailing list I follow, entitled Children, Youth, and Environments (CYE). One participant quoted an article from McHale, Crouter, and Tucker (2001), which reported that "time spent in outdoor play at age 10 was negatively related to school grades and positively related to conduct problems within and across time" (p. 1770). The header to the e-mail was "outdoor play 'causes' poor grades and conduct problems." As you can imagine, although this header was tongue-in-cheek, it highlights the problem of correlational data that are all too often interpreted causally, especially by reporters or laypersons, although even as a researcher it is easy to make such an inference upon initial consideration.

Observational Methods, Nonobtrusive Measurement, and Archival Research

We often have the conceptualization of research that it involves surveying people, interviewing people, exposing them to some treatment (e.g., new teaching techniques) or some other form of *interaction*. However, there are many forms of research that involve no interaction with the participants. Technically, when no direct consent is obtained from the individual him or herself (e.g., in the case of infants), participants are called subjects (American Psychological Association, 2001, p. 65).

Let's look at some examples that do not involve intervention.

Observational methods. In observational measurement, you use observational means to gather information about behaviors of interest, but with the goal that your presence does not alter the behavior you are observing. As an example, I once did some research at Norwich State Hospital, at that time one of three state psychiatric institutions in Connecticut (Devlin, 1992). My goal was to understand how patients and staff spent their time, and how much interaction there was. To that end, part of the study I designed involved behavior mapping, where a student assistant and I recorded the behaviors we saw during a 1-minute segment (done at 10-minute intervals for an hour at a time, twice a week). We used a small map of the psychiatric ward, on which we imposed a spatial grid and recorded the type of behavior that occurred. Specifically we recorded where on the ward the behavior occurred, the actor (staff or patient), and the behavior itself (e.g., sitting, walking, taking medication). Recognizing that our presence might have influenced the behaviors we observed, we spent weeks prior to the coding on the hospital ward, getting to know the staff and patients. Although we were visible as we coded, we hoped that the prefamiliarization would, to some extent, limit the influence on the behavior we observed.

Nonobtrusive measurement. In nonobtrusive measurement, there is no question about whether the researcher or observer has influenced the behavior of interest. He or she has not. An example of such nonobtrusive measurement comes from John Zeisel (1981) in his book on environment–behavior research. Zeisel devotes an entire chapter to "Observing Physical Traces," where, in a systematic manner, we look at "physical surroundings to find reflections of previous activity not produced in order to be measured by researchers" (p. 89). Often this examination of the physical traces takes place *after* the individuals who created the traces have left the environment in question. I think that a good example of such physical traces would be the chair arrangements in classrooms with movable seats. One could visit a given classroom (after class had concluded) on a regular basis to see whether the chairs remain in rigid rows or are rearranged in clusters or other small groups. Such arrangements might reflect some of the kinds of interactions that take place in the class. Another example might come from looking at the trash people put out to see whether they recycle, whether people display decals on their cars (and if so, representing what kinds of organizations), or even the kinds of clothes students leave behind (lose).

Archival research. In archival research, you are typically taking existing documents and examining some variables contained in these documents across time or condition. In a seminal archival study (remember Chapter 1) by Ulrich (1984) published in the prestigious journal *Science,* he contrasted the medical records of two matched groups of patients who had undergone gallbladder surgery: those who had a view of nature (deciduous trees) from their hospital window and those who viewed a brick wall out their hospital window. Ulrich compared these groups on a number of measures, including number of days of hospitalization, the number and strength of pain medication doses each day, and nurses' chart notes about the patient's condition. Results indicated a significant difference between the groups, with the "nature view group" having more positive evaluations on a number of these variables, including a shorter hospital stay and fewer moderate and strong doses of pain medication.

Another example of an archival study was an honors thesis by one of our students, Mindy Erchull (1998), who examined the content of educational brochures and pamphlets dealing with menstruation to make judgments about their technical accuracy, assumptions about family constellation, and representation of diversity. In this study, each booklet was separately evaluated by two coders to reach conclusions about whether the representation of information concerning menstruation had changed significantly, using 1980 as a dividing line (when toxic shock syndrome became an issue). These two examples (Ulrich and Erchull) give some sense of the wealth of archival information that is available and has the potential to become a fascinating and meaningful study.

Qualitative Research Designs

Qualitative methods involve trying to understand a particular phenomenon of interest without formulating hypotheses. Although qualitative methods are not yet commonplace, Smith (2003, p. 1) argues that there is an "explosion of interest" in qualitative approaches to psychology, as reflected in such indices as Ph.D. projects that use qualitative methods; conference, symposia, and workshops that feature qualitative methods; and the increase in qualitative articles that appear in journals that are peer-reviewed. In tracing the history of qualitative methods in psychology, Ashworth (2003) reminds us that psychology has always been interested in the question of experience, but the discipline has argued about how to examine that experience. Although some authors think that we returned to examining what was "inside" the black box when cognitive psychology replaced behaviorism as the dominant paradigm in psychology, Ashworth argues otherwise. He points out that cognitive psychology shares with behaviorism an emphasis on **positivism** (only those events that can be observed and tested reflect the truth of experience). As such, cognitive psychology similarly excludes the study of the individual reality that each person structures. The work of Husserl in phenomenology, Allport in idiographic psychology, and Mead in symbolic interactionism helped pave the way for the emergence of interest in qualitative psychology that we see today (Ashworth, 2003).

A qualitative approach usually involves open-ended or semi-structured interviews, which are typically tape-recorded and then transcribed. These transcriptions are then subjected to a series of analyses, beginning with the raw data and, step by step, moving to relevant text, repeating ideas, themes, theoretical constructs, theoretical narratives, and research concerns (Averbach & Silverstein, 2003). Averbach and Silverstein (2003) emphasize that qualitative approaches, such as grounded theory, are hypothesis generating, unlike quantitative approaches, which involve evaluating existing hypotheses. "Grounded theory derives its name from the fact that theoretical coding allows you to ground your hypothesis in what your research participants say" (Averbach & Silverstein, 2003, p. 7). The authors further comment:

> Qualitative hypothesis-generating research involves collecting interview data from research participants concerning a phenomenon of interest, and then using what they say in order to develop hypotheses. It uses the two principles of (1) questioning rather than measuring and (2) generating hypotheses using theoretical coding (p. 8).

Unlike quantitative approaches, random sampling is not a focus in qualitative research. Averbach and Silverstein (2003) used convenience sampling (finding relevant people who are available) and snowball sampling (asking people who participate to recommend others who might participate). "In effect, you stop increasing your sample when each new group of participants basically tells you the same story that previous groups have told" (p. 19).

In terms of a student research methods project, it would be possible to do a project in qualitative psychology; in fact, some professors may insist on a qualitative project, depending on their discipline. In situations where a qualitative project is not required, undertaking such a project becomes more feasible if the student can find a population of interest and restrict the number of questions that are asked (because of the time involved in transcribing the material and then coding and understanding it). Before deciding to do such a project, it might be helpful to at least read examples of projects that are considered qualitative in approach, even though the projects that are mentioned here were considerably more time-intensive than a single semester. Examples of projects include understanding fatherhood (Averbach & Silverstein, 2003), and the experience of chronic illness (Charmaz, 2003). Smith and Osborn (2003) give examples of research questions that have been asked within the framework of Interpretative Phenomenological Analysis (IPA), another kind of qualitative approach, including how people come to accept the death of a loved one, issues surrounding identity for someone (a donor offspring) who was conceived through the donation of a sperm or egg, and how gay men think about sex and sexuality. For research methods students, one could imagine a project that dealt with trying to understand what it meant to be a transfer student, or an international student, or a nontraditional student (for example, someone who has returned to college after a long absence). Students who return to college, often called RTCs, are generally older students who have interrupted their education in their twenties and return in their forties and fifties to complete their degree.

Averbach and Silverstein (2003) recommend that researchers pose six general questions about the phenomenon of interest, and "ask questions that take the research participants through their history with the phenomenon in question" (p. 16). Their term for this process is the **narrative interview.** In their Haitian fatherhood project, focus group interviews of four to five fathers were held, lasting about 60–90 minutes. For those students who want to learn more about the specifics of analyzing qualitative data, including computer programs that are available, I recommend Averbach and Silverstein's book *Qualitative Data: An Introduction to Coding and Analysis* (2003). In an appendix, this book also discusses qualitative data analysis (QDA) computer programs, particularly NVIVO, which replaced earlier versions called N5 and NUDIST. Information about NVIVO can be obtained from the distributor's website: www.scolari.com. For a one-semester project, it is probably better for a student to concentrate on hand-coding all of the material rather than using the computer approach, which involves a considerable amount of time and effort to master.

REFLECT AND REVIEW

What makes a research approach passive (in Wampold's terms), and what kinds of research questions can best be approached using a passive design?

APPLY YOUR KNOWLEDGE

Think of a qualitative question that you might use that focuses on college students as a unique group.

Between-Groups Design: Quasi-Experimental Design and Quasi-Independent Variables

In our example of high school type and college adjustment from Chapter 1, we may treat high school type as if it were truly an independent variable (as if people had been randomly assigned to their high schools), but we know that this is not the case. Our approach could thus be called a quasi-experiment. In the study, we may still use a statistical approach such as analysis of variance that involves looking at group differences (i.e., the adjustment levels of students from public vs. private vs. home schools), but any significant differences that are found cannot be interpreted causally. The fact that there are different levels of college adjustment that are related to high school type may be explained or caused by many other variables not under consideration. As a statistical approach, analysis of variance is pretty robust (i.e., it allows some violation of underlying assumptions), but we must still be cautious in the way we interpret any significant findings. In research, we often treat variables such as one's gender or race as if they were independent and randomly assigned to condition. These factors are obviously not. Variables such as race and gender are also usually referred to as quasi-independent.

Experimental Design

In some research methods courses, the instructors require that students design actual experiments (that is, no correlational research is permitted). In general, such research is more time-consuming, but it is also the case that students learn a great deal from designing an experiment. They learn to isolate a particular variable (like level of violence in our earlier example of eyewitness accuracy), and such research often forces students to think more deeply about the issue of hypotheses. Rather than simply predicting that a relationship will exist between two variables, an experiment requires that students think about the effects of different levels of an intervention, such as our room size example for studying spatial density mentioned earlier.

Research Designs: Issues of Sample Size, Power, and Effect Size

Sample Size

Part of your research design involves making some judgment about the number of participants you will need. As a rule of thumb, you need more subjects for most correlational research than you do for experimental research. Your need for a larger number of participants in correlational research is related to the variability you may find in the participants' responses regarding the constructs you are assessing (e.g., depression, environmental preference, etc.). When you do an experiment, you are essentially saying that "all other things are equal" with regard to the participants' background, and you are thus focusing on the effect that your manipulation of the independent variable will have. Determining the number of participants you will need is important for fairly evaluating your hypotheses. That is, you want to make sure that you don't miss an effect that is there (avoiding **Type II error**) as much as you want to make sure that you don't say that an effect is there when it isn't (committing **Type I error** and rejecting the null hypothesis by chance). The issue of sample size is intimately connected with the power of a research design.

Power and Effect Size

When people talk about the **power** of a study, they are referring to the study's ability to reject the null hypothesis (assuming it is false) and avoid making a Type II error. Remember that a Type II error involves failure to reject the null hypothesis when you should; that is, when there is a significant difference between group means. A study with sufficient power adequately tests whether there is actually reason to reject the null hypothesis. Power is the probability of rejecting Ho (the null hypothesis), assuming Ho is false. Another way of thinking about power is that power is an indication of whether it is worthwhile to conduct the experiment. Will you be able to find what you are looking for? Without sufficient power, and in the absence of a significant finding, you don't know whether you are missing a significant difference that is actually there.

What are some possible reasons that you might not have been able to reject the null hypothesis (assuming it was false)? One potential reason for novice researchers is a poor experimental design and other threats to **internal validity**. Internal validity, discussed in more depth later in this chapter, is concerned with whether your research project has integrity. Are you sure that your research design adequately measures or assesses what you say it does? Threats to the internal validity of your research occur when there are aspects of the way you conduct your study that may undermine your ability to measure your variables appropriately, such as the consistency with which you measure the variables. Examples of such threats are the experimenter unintentionally treating different groups of participants in a different way or equipment malfunction, such as an inaccurate timing mechanism on a computer. Another reason that you may not have been able to reject the null hypothesis is that there actually is no relationship between the variables in your study. A third reason is that there is a lack of power in your study.

In discussing the issue of power, Howell (1992) lists four factors that contribute to the power of a study: (1) the alpha level you set, (2) the true alternative hypothesis, (3) the sample size, and (4) the particular statistical test to be used. He goes on to comment that of these four, sample size is the simplest way to control the power of your study. Discussions about the need to calculate the power required to evaluate an hypothesis and the need to report effect sizes (Cohen, 1988) are becoming common in the social sciences. Increasingly, authors are asked to include estimates of effect size in their studies (Howell, 1992). Most statistical programs such as SPSS™ include an option for reporting estimates of power and effect size for a given analysis.

The concept of **effect size** is related to the concept of power, and effect size (d) is the degree to which the sampling distributions of the two means of interest (when Ho is true and when Ho is false) are expressed in terms of the standard deviation of the parent population. Simply put, d is the difference between means in standard deviation units. Conceptually, effect size is talking about just that: the impact (or effect) of the intervention you are interested in. If there is little overlap between the distributions of the populations from which the samples were drawn, the effect size is large. Cohen (1988) lists three levels commonly associated with effect size. A small effect size has a d of .20, a medium has a d of .50, and a large effect has a d of .80. The degree of overlap for these three is 85%, 67%, and 53%, respectively. These percentages make clear the idea that in a small effect, there is considerable overlap in the two distributions (85%), whereas in a large effect, there is considerably less overlap (53%). Although you may not be making determinations of power in a one-semester research project, knowing about these concepts is important for you to carefully consider how many participants will be appropriate to adequately assess your hypotheses.

Looking at other research in your area is a good way of getting a sense of the sample sizes that are used to detect meaningful differences. If you expect a relatively weak effect in the research you are doing, you will need more participants to detect that effect. Also, there may be ways to ensure that the independent variable you are using is as strong as possible, which will produce a greater effect size (see the comments about internal validity later in the chapter).

The following example from Howell (1992) helps to illustrate the relationship of sample size to power. Howell gives the example of a clinician whose hypothesis is that people who seek out therapy for psychological problems have higher IQs than those who do not. In the presentation that follows, the emphasis will be on the relationship between power and the number of participants, rather than on the specific mathematical calculations per se. Calculating the power in a sample size of 25 clients in order to be able to detect a difference in IQ of 5 points, the power is determined to be .38. Howell explains that power of .38 means that 62% of the time (1-power), you will be likely to make a Type II error (miss a finding that is really there). Obviously, missing a significant finding that much of the time is a problem. By increasing the sample size, you can increase the power. However, it may not always be easy to find the participants that you need. Howell next explores what would happen if the power in this example involving the clinician is set at .80 (so that you would only miss a finding 20% of the time). The calculation for power of .80 in this example yields the need for 72 clients. As he continues with this example, Howell demonstrates that a power of .99 would require almost 160 participants. If the experiment in question involved college students, 160 participants might not be a problem. However, in the case of needing 160 clients, it is a significantly more challenging task. This example illustrates that it may not always be possible to conduct an experiment with the power sufficient to adequately test the hypothesis in question, if the special kind of participants you need are not available.

Before moving on, let's review your understanding of power and effect size and take one more example where effect sizes were reported. Remember that one way to get a sense of the number of participants that may be appropriate for the variables you are studying is to examine the articles you have read on the topic and see the number of participants in the Method section. These articles may also list the effect size associated with a particular relationship. If you have a sense of the effect size in a given area of study from consulting the literature, you can even check tables that have been published that show how many participants are needed to detect a difference (reject the null hypothesis, assuming it is false), given a particular effect size. Cohen (1988) has published such tables.

One study reporting effect sizes (Devlin, 2004), looked at the relationship between men and women members of college sailing teams and men and women members of the general study body in terms of one aspect of spatial ability, mental rotation. The results indicated that, overall, men were better than women at the mental rotation task, and that college sailing team members were better than members of the general student body at the mental rotation task. The effect size associated with the difference between men and women was .11, whereas the effect size for the difference between sailors and nonsailors was .03. What do these effect sizes tell us? Think back to the categories of effect sizes (small, moderate, and large) established by Cohen (1988). In this study on mental rotation ability and sailing, the effect sizes are small, but, given the effect sizes, the difference between men and women on the mental rotation task is more convincing than the difference between sailors and nonsailors. The means for men and women on this task (21.7 and 15.7, respectively) are farther apart than the means for those of sailors and nonsailors (20.9 and 17.4, respectively).

● ●

REFLECT AND REVIEW

Explain why having sufficient power is important for a study. What is the most common way to increase power?

Research Design: Some Practical Issues

One of the very real problems in doing research at small colleges (or even at large colleges or universities where there are many people making demands of the subject pool—see Chapter 4) is the difficulty in recruiting enough participants to conduct meaningful research. Such pressure is very real, and it is felt by many segments of the research community (e.g., untenured faculty), lest research methods students think they are alone.

Not only is there competition for participants, but there is also the issue of budgetary pressures if there are costs associated with doing the research. Although in general more participants will give your experiment more power (i.e., the ability to detect whether an effect is present), participants take time—to recruit, and to collect their data, score it, and enter it for statistical analysis. More participants may also translate into greater expense, which can be particularly problematic in the case of using copyrighted instruments and scoring forms. A larger sample is obviously more costly in experiments in such areas as behavioral neuroscience, animal learning, and Magnetic Resonance Imaging (fMRI) research, in terms of animals, equipment, and/or pharmacological interventions. With regard to behavioral neuroscience, the number of rats required in any given experiment may be quite small (unlikely to be larger than 10 per cell, according to the behavioral neuroscientist in my department), but the cost is significant. In September 2003, 200-gram male rats purchased from the Charles River Laboratories cost $19.75 each. There are also daily costs related to food, water, caretaking, veterinary oversight, housing, lights, and security.

While in general it is true that having more participants will give you more power in your research, there is a trade-off between power and the time and resources you need to invest to obtain a given number of participants.

Factors to Consider

There are many factors to consider before finalizing your research design, from the fundamental nature of your design (i.e., whether correlational or experimental) to the ease with which you will be able to recruit participants. The following list offers a number of issues to evaluate.

1. Think ahead about the ease or difficulty of soliciting and obtaining data from participants.

If you have a subject pool in your department (see Chapter 4), is there a limit (typically there is) to the number of participants in the pool available to *you*? What other options for obtaining participants do you have?

2. If you are doing correlational research, make particular note of the numbers of participants that have been used in previous studies assessing the variables in which you are interested.

3. How many independent or quasi-independent variables do you plan to include? Let's take our example of high school type and college adjustment. Consider a number of versions of this study. In version A, you limit yourself to one quasi-independent variable, high school type, for which you have three categories: public, private, and home schools (all day schools, that is; not boarding schools). In version B, you add another category: private boarding school. That gives you four categories in version B. One rule of thumb for estimating the number of participants you need is 10 per cell (a minimum). At this point, you thus need 40 participants, 10 in each category, for version B of your study. Although 40 participants seems like a manageable number, remember that some of your categories may be much easier to fill (probably public school background) than others.

Now, consider adding another category of quasi-independent variable: gender. If we added gender to version A, we would now have 6 cells to fill. If we added gender to version B, there would be 8 cells to fill. Suddenly, our research project has become significantly more difficult in terms of the number of participants needed (60–80). And again, some of those cells will be much easier to fill (with participants who have the right combination of gender and high school type) than others. Therefore it is critical to determine which variables you really need to include in order to test your hypothesis(es).

4. Another question to ask yourself is whether you will be able to administer all of your measures at once (either through the mail or in person). In some studies, there are so many measures to complete that people need a break because they are fatigued. In that case, the study

is designed for two data collection sessions. A related issue is whether there can be group administration. In some cases, it is fairly straightforward to bring participants to a room and administer a series of measures in one sitting. Other studies require individual interviews or individually administered experimental manipulation (like the study about eyewitness testimony that involved a no violence condition and a minor violence condition).

5. Do your survey instruments or equipment cost money? Unfortunately, a positive answer to this question may mean that you can't do your "ideal" study but will need to reshape it based on financial considerations. Some students, although not many in my experience, are willing to pay for research expenses of more than $50 out of their own pockets. Others seek funding from the department or the dean's office, but generally deans and departments approve these requests only if they involve individual study or honors study projects, not a beginning research methods endeavor. Chapter 3 discusses measures that are commonly used in research in social science, their sources, and their costs (if any).

One of our students, Susan Dutton, actually solicited and obtained materials (crayons) from the Binney & Smith Corporation in her honors thesis study of the racial identity of children in integrated, predominantly White, and Black schools (Dutton, Singer, & Devlin, 1998). Binney & Smith provided a box of Crayola Multicultural Crayons for each of the 159 fourth-graders in the study. Without the support of the Binney & Smith Corporation, the cost of providing the crayons for each child might have forced her to alter her approach.

6. Consider the time of the semester and its likely impact on your ability to successfully collect data (see Chapter 4). If you wait until the week of Thanksgiving or spring break to collect data, you have a problem!

Kinds of Research Questions and Associated Statistics

At this point in your education, you probably have just one semester of statistics behind you. It is therefore not surprising that knowing what statistics are in order for a given project is still a challenge for you, as it is for most students. Yes, you are probably adept at manipulating computer programs like SPSS, but knowing what tests are appropriate to run is different from running them! Table 2.1 presents a summary of the different kinds of studies we have discussed and the statistical tests that accompany them.

TABLE 2.1 Research Design and Statistical Approaches: A Summary

Test	IV Data Type	# of IVs	DV Data Type	# of DVs
Chi Square (2x2)	Nominal Ex: men, women	1	Nominal Ex: car, no car	1
Ind. Samples *t*-test	Nominal Ex: men, women	1 (2 levels)	Continuous (interval) Ex: depression	1
One-way ANOVA	Nominal Ex: urban, rural, suburban upbringing	1 (more than 2 levels)	Continuous (interval) Ex: Precautionary Measures Scale	1
Factorial ANOVA	Nominal Ex: men, women; urban, rural upbringing	2 or more	Continuous (interval) Ex: Precautionary Measures Scale	1
MANOVA	Nominal Ex: men, women	1 or more	Continuous (interval) Ex: Env. Preference Questionnaire (has 7 scales)	2 or more
Correlation Pearson's R	Continuous (interval) Ex: GPA	1	Continuous (interval) SAT scores	1
Regression	Continuous (interval) Ex: Vocational maturity	1 (predictor variable, X)	Continuous (interval) Vocational indecision	1 (criterion variable, Y)
Multiple Regression	Continuous (interval) Ex: Vocational maturity; self-esteem	2 or more (predictor variables, X1, X2)	Continuous (interval) Vocational indecision	1 (criterion variable, Y)

Sampling Distributions

Before discussing some of the more commonly used statistical tests, it may be wise to review our understanding of the concept of sampling distributions, because sampling distributions underlie all statistical tests. When we conduct research we typically sample some members of the population of interest (e.g., registered voters). The data from the registered voters in any study we do will come from a much larger set of data (the data of all registered voters, or the population of registered voters). Think of the 2004 presidential election and the constant stream of political polls predicting which candidate was ahead in Ohio and Florida, the states that were judged to be critical to win the presidency. These polls rarely agreed, and each poll was accompanied by a "margin of error," the extent to which the pollsters calculated that the polling data could be in error. Many reasons prevent us from including every member of the population in such a poll, notably the time it would take to contact each individual and the money that would be involved in paying people to make such contact. Reaching people, especially in this era of cell phone use, also provides a challenge.

We thus resort to sampling to obtain an estimate of the characteristics of the population under investigation. Because of sampling error, the characteristics of your sample may not accurately reflect the characteristics that underlie the population. But statistical sampling distributions suggest that if you sampled over and over and over again, your sampling distribution would be normal. Each statistical technique we apply to our sample of data allows us to make an estimate of the characteristics of interest in the population itself. Thus, although we do not sample every registered voter, the techniques allow us to make predictions about the population of registered voters (and keep pollsters in business!).

Chi-Squares and *t*-Tests

At perhaps the most basic level, students are often confused by two of the simplest statistical tests, chi-square and *t*-test, and the circumstances under which each is appropriate. The appropriateness of using one or the other rests with the kind of data you are analyzing, categorical or continuous. **Categorical** or **nominal data** have no inherent order (e.g., the categories "men" and "women"), whereas **continuous** or **interval data** represent a continuum of equally spaced intervals. On a 5-point interval scale, the distance from 2 to 3 is the same as the distance from 4 to 5.

When a chi-square test is appropriate, both variables of interest are categorical in nature, such as gender (categories of men vs.

women) and having a car on campus (yes or no). The chi-square is an example of a **nonparametric statistic.** Nonparametric statistics make no assumptions about the distribution of scores in your sample. What confuses some students is that you can represent the categories with numerical values (men=1, women=2; having a car=1, no car=2). But consider for a moment the question of calculating a mean for either of these dimensions (gender or car availability). Would that make any sense? No. These categories represent nominal data, or data with no inherent order. In thinking about categorical data, obtaining frequencies is appropriate (e.g., how many men; how many women), but descriptive statistics like means are inappropriate. If you did a chi-square test in the situation of gender (men vs. women) as one dimension and car ownership (yes vs. no) as the other dimension, you would answer the question of whether the proportion of car ownership was different for men than women.

The popular *t*-test is a form of analysis of variance in which there is one grouping variable (independent or quasi-independent) with two levels, and one dependent variable (often a score, like GPA or anxiety, on some interval or continuous data scale). The grouping variable, like gender or treatment level, is categorical (and this is where the confusion with chi-square tests may arise), but the dependent variable is **continuous,** not categorical. To say that the dependent variable is continuous means that it is measured on a scale where there is some ordering (typically interval data, where the spaces between rating values is uniform—that is, the distance from the value 2 to the value 3 is the same as the distance from the value 4 to the value 5). A *t*-test would be an appropriate analysis for the question: Do men and women differ in their degree of anxiety (measured by an anxiety scale)?

One reason that students may be confused is that in our two examples, chi-square for car ownership and *t*-test for degree of anxiety, one of the variables (gender) is the same grouping variable for both examples, yet the tests that are appropriate are not the same. Remember, both dimensions must involve categories for a chi-square test to be appropriate, whereas the dependent variable must be continuous for some form of analysis of variance (of which the *t*-test is the most basic form) to be appropriate.

When examining group differences, as is the case in *t*-tests, groups (such as men and women; or people who grew up in urban vs. rural environments) are compared with reference to some output variable of interest, such as anxiety, depression, openness to experience, extraversion, or fondness for nature. As was discussed earlier in the chapter, we treat these groups as quasi-independent variables, because the assumptions about analysis of variance are robust; that is, they can take some "stretching."

REFLECT AND REVIEW

Explain the difference between categorical and continuous data. If both variable dimensions you are measuring are categorical, which statistic is appropriate: (a) *t*-test, or (b) chi-square? (B is correct.)

One-Way Analysis of Variance

A one-way analysis of variance is only slightly more complex than a *t*-test. It is the situation where there is one independent variable (the grouping variable), and one dependent variable (the outcome variable). So far, this sounds just like the *t*-test. The difference is that instead of just two levels of the independent variable, as is the case for the *t*-test, you have more than two levels of the independent variable (typically three or four). Let's take a comparative example. In our previous example for the *t*-test, we looked at the question of whether men and women differ in their level of anxiety. If we ask the question, do high school students, college students, and graduate students differ in their level of anxiety, we are now asking a question that can be answered with a one-way analysis of variance. The grouping variable in question, school level, has more than two levels, hence the use of the one-way analysis of variance and not the *t*-test.

Let's imagine that the result of the analysis indicates a significant difference ($p < .05$). Are we done? Not quite. With three levels of the independent variable, we don't know where the significant differences are—whether between high school and college, high school and grad school, college and grad school, any two of those, or all three of them! To answer this question, we then do a post hoc test, such as a Tukey's HSD (Honestly Significant Difference) Test, which will pinpoint where the significant differences lie (i.e., which groups reflect significant differences in their scores). Post hoc tests are discussed in more detail later in the chapter.

Analysis of Variance and Multivariate Analysis of Variance

Building on *t*-tests, as we have seen, research designs about group differences involve increasing levels of complexity, including adding more independent variables and more dependent variables (but still attempting to evaluate group differences).

Factorial ANOVAs and interactions. When you move beyond one independent (or quasi-independent) variable, you are dealing with factorial ANOVAs and will need to look at the possibility of interaction effects. Interaction effects reveal whether a grouping variable such as gender interacts with another grouping variable such as locus of upbringing (rural, urban, or suburban) in a manner that affects the behavior measured. In the case of a study with two independent variables, an interaction is the situation in which the effect of one variable (on the dependent variable or behavior measured) changes across the levels of the other independent variable. The effect of one independent variable on the dependent variable varies for the levels of the other independent variable.

For example, let's say that you were looking at gender and upbringing as they might interact with each other in terms of the behavior measured, the kind of precautionary measures (such as not walking in unlighted areas or never walking alone after dark) people take to protect themselves in cities (see for example Devlin, 2000). You might hypothesize that when visiting a large city (1) women take more precautionary measures than men, and (2) that people who were raised in urban environments take more precautionary behaviors than those raised in rural environments. You might further hypothesize (3) that there will be an interaction between gender and upbringing such that women who were raised in urban environments are no different than men raised in those environments with regard to their level of precautionary behavior. If your hypotheses were supported, the results would indicate a main effect for gender (women are more cautious than men), a main effect for upbringing (people raised in urban environments were more cautious than those raised in rural environments), and an interaction between gender and upbringing (women raised in urban environments did not differ from men raised in urban environments in terms of their precautionary behavior), although men and women did differ when raised in a rural environment. This interaction effect essentially modifies the strength of your main effects. What that means is that you can't simply say that women take more precautionary behaviors than men (Hypothesis 1) and that people who are raised in urban areas exhibit more precautionary behaviors than those raised in rural environments (Hypothesis 2). Those statements are modified by the finding from Hypothesis 3—that is, that men and women who were raised in an urban environment are not, in fact, different in the number of precautionary behaviors they employ.

REFLECT AND REVIEW

State the difference between a one-way ANOVA and a factorial ANOVA. How does the presence of an interaction effect change the interpretation of your main effects?

MANOVAs. Multivariate analyses of variance come into play when you have more than one dependent variable that may be related to other dependent variables you are assessing. Rather than running separate analyses of variance to evaluate each dependent variable, it is often prudent to attack the analysis in one fell swoop, assessing all of the related dependent variables in one analysis. The results of MANOVAs involve a number of levels. The first, and most comprehensive level, which is usually assessed with a Wilks's lambda value, indicates whether, overall, there is a significant linear combination of the dependent variables in terms of the independent variables. If there is, as indicated by the alpha level, you go on to examine the univariate effects (called univariate effects or between-subjects effects when the study involves group differences) for each of the dependent variables, separately.

Let's take a simple example where there is one (quasi)independent variable, say gender, and a series of related dependent variables, such as the seven scales of the Environmental Preference Questionnaire (EPQ; Kaplan, 1977). The EPQ has seven scales related to aspects of nature: Nature, Suburbs, Romantic Escape, Modern Development, Social, City, and Passive Reaction to Stress. Using a MANOVA (which involves one analysis), you avoid doing seven separate *t*-tests; hence you reduce the possibility of Type I error, or the possibility that any significant results you find are due to performing multiple statistical tests rather than to a true difference. If the results of your analysis indicate a significant multivariate effect (with the Wilks's lambda), this essentially means that, overall, there is some difference between men and women in terms of these seven EPQ scales. The significant difference need involve only one of the seven to produce a significant Wilks's lambda. You find out on which of the seven scales men and women differ significantly by examining the univariate Fs (which are essentially your typical ANOVAs). No post hoc analyses are involved in this example because the (quasi)independent variable has only two levels (men and women).

● ●

REFLECT AND REVIEW

How many dependent variables are necessary to use MANOVA? Explain how using MANOVA may reduce the possibility of Type I error.

The Bonferroni *t* correction. Although we try to avoid doing multiple tests (to reduce the possibility of Type I error), there are some circumstances that require multiple analyses with the same dependent variables. Typically this situation arises when you have very small numbers of participants (< 5) in some of your independent (or quasi-independent) variable categories. You might even have no participants at all in one or more of those categories. As an example, if you are looking at the factors of gender, class year, and upbringing (rural, suburban, or urban) on some dependent measures, like the seven scales of the Environmental Preference Questionnaire (EPQ; Kaplan, 1977), you might not have any juniors who are men and who also grew up in a rural environment. You would then have to do a series of analyses using the same dependent variables but with different groupings of the independent variables (gender and class year; gender and upbringing; class year and upbringing). Because the likelihood of committing a Type I error (saying a significant difference exists when it does not) increases with the number of tests you run, you need to correct for this possibility. You divide the standard alpha level (.05) by the number of separate analyses you ran (three in our example), to create a new and more stringent alpha level of .017 (3/.05 = .017). This more stringent alpha thus corrects for the increased likelihood of Type I error with multiple tests (Howell, 1992). Another situation in which you might employ a **Bonferroni correction** is when you have to do a large number of correlations.

Post hoc tests. When we have more than two levels of an independent variable, significant differences that emerge in data analysis need clarification. Imagine that we had measured people's preference for nature on a scale, and the grouping variable we used was whether people had been raised in rural, suburban, or urban environments. When there are only two levels (say rural and urban) and a significant difference exists, you can see what is happening by simply looking at the means for each group; one will be larger than the other, which tells you what you need to know. But if there are more than two levels, we need to know where those significant differences occur. On the variable of interest, preference for nature, are people raised in rural environments significantly different from those in urban environments and also from those in suburban environments? Or are they just different from those in urban (or suburban environments)? Or is it that people who were raised in urban environments are different from those in suburban environments? Post hoc tests, such as the Tukey HSD, will give you the answer to this question.

REFLECT AND REVIEW

With which of the following (quasi)independent variables would you use post hoc follow-up tests? (a) gender; (b) four age categories (11–15, 16–20, 21–25, 25–30); (c) car ownership (yes/no); (d) three upbringing categories (rural, suburban, urban)? (B and D are correct.)

Correlations: Statistics Involving Relationships, Not Group Differences

As was discussed earlier in this chapter, there is no possibility of determining cause-and-effect relationships with correlations; the researcher is simply trying to determine whether a relationship exists. As was mentioned previously with regard to selecting an experimental design, there are so many possible intervening variables between the two dimensions of interest that there is certainly no way to state anything about causality. Relationship is not influence.

In using correlations, the researcher is interested in whether there is a relationship between two variables of interest across the entire sample, not between groups; that is, the question the researcher asks is whether the dimensions covary—as one increases, does the other consistently increase (a positive correlation) or decrease (a negative correlation)? These dimensions are most often interval data—such as scores on a depression scale compared to scores on a scale of college adjustment. As the score on one dimension, say depression, goes up, does the score on the other dimension, college adjustment, go up? If so, the result would indicate a positive correlation between the two variables. Or, as is more likely the case in this example, as the score on one variable, depression, goes up, indicating greater depression, does the score on the other, college adjustment, go down, indicating decreasing college adjustment? This relationship would be a negative correlation. A third case is the situation where there is *no* predictable relationship between the two variables.

Regression. Regression is another, and in some ways a more specific approach to looking at the relationship between variables. In the case of correlation, if two variables are positively correlated, you know that as the scores on one variable go up, so do the scores on the other variable. Regression goes a step further, in a sense, by allowing you to *predict* the score on y, the second variable (DV), often called the criterion variable, by knowing the score on x, the independent or quasi-independent variable (IV), often called the predictor variable. Regression and multiple regression (see the next section) have many practical uses in such fields as industrial and organizational psychology, and education, among others. In a typical example, you may want to know the relationship between SAT scores and GRE scores, and in particular, with a given SAT score in math, what GRE score in math would be predicted.

REFLECT AND REVIEW

Explain why an analysis using regression might give you more precise information about the relationship between variables than is true for an analysis using correlation.

Multiple regression. In the world of work, employers may be interested in which of a number of employment screening devices (interview, intelligence test, recommendation) best predicts job performance. In this case, we have a series of predictor variables, and we want to know which of them predict job performance and whether one of these variables is much better at such prediction than the others (which might enable us to eliminate some of the screening steps). This example of looking at a number of predictors involves multiple regression.

In multiple regression, you are asking which combination of a number of independent or quasi-independent variables (IVs), typically called predictor variables, significantly predict the score of a dependent or outcome variable (DV), typically called a criterion variable. For example, one of my students was interested in the factors that predict vocational indecision (which is measured with a scale). She gave ninth-grade high school students and first-year college students a series of measures, including an ego identity scale, a self-esteem scale, a personality inventory, a scale of parent and peer attachment, a career exploration scale, and a vocational maturity scale (in addition to a vocational indecision scale). Vocational maturity has to do with whether people have clarity about and certainty of preference for an occupation. Her research question asked which of these variables helped to predict vocation indecision. Answering that question might provide useful information to high school and college career counselors in terms of directing their efforts with students who have a difficult time making vocational and career choices. Her research showed that the best predictor of vocational indecision was vocational maturity (Mikulinsky, 2002).

To try to understand more about the variance, she used a series of hierarchical regressions. In hierarchical regressions, you create conceptual blocks of variables, and enter them into the multiple regression equation. These hierarchical regressions showed that career-oriented variables (vocational maturity scale, VMS; vocational development scale, VDS; and career exploration scale, CES) predicted vocational indecision, as did a second block of variables, which included personality indices (self-esteem scale, ego identity scale, and personality inventory). Blocks that explained no additional variance were related to students' and parents' education and expected education (Block 3), to attachment to parents (Block 4), and to gender (Block 5). Appendix C gives an example of how her findings are numerically presented (see the examples of Regression and Multiple Regression).

Factor Analysis

In factor analysis, you are taking a series of items (these can be written items or in some other form, usually visual, like pictures), to determine whether the ratings of these items on some measure by your participants cluster in groups. These clusters or factors indicate that the ratings of one grouping of items differ from the ratings of another grouping of items. Are certain items rated the same (say at the low end of the scale) and others rated in the middle and still others rated at the high end of the scale across participants? Factor analyses require many participants (a rule of thumb is 10 participants for each item that will be part of your factor analysis). If you have 30 items, you can see the demand on participants (300). Other rules of thumb are that you need at least 100 participants for any kind of a factor analysis. Although students occasionally attempt factor analyses as part of their research methods projects, this approach might better be reserved for students with more statistical experience.

● ●

APPLY YOUR KNOWLEDGE

Without consulting Table 2.1, create your own chart that lists common statistical tests (chi-square, t-test, one-way ANOVA, factorial ANOVA, MANOVA, correlation, regression) and the characteristics of each (nominal or interval data, number of independent variables, number of dependent variables).

How to Analyze Open-Ended Questions: Cautionary Tales

Even when students are doing quantitative research, they often ask questions that are open-ended and are more qualitative in nature. In addition to gathering demographic information from their participants (such as gender, age, ethnicity), and administering established scales (see Chapter 3), students are often tempted to and *do* include open-ended questions in their research. Open-ended questions are those to which the participants write or verbalize their own response. An example might be the request, "Give me your reaction to the design of the new residence hall." One of my colleagues, Jefferson Singer, has a research program in the area of autobiographical memory. In his research paradigm, students are asked to generate self-defining memories and rate them on 12 emotions, on vividness, and on importance (see Moffitt & Singer, 1994; Singer & Blagov, 2000; Singer & Moffitt, 1991–1992; Singer & Salovey, 1993). Singer and one of his former students, Pavel Blagov, have developed an elaborate coding system for the classification of these self-defining autobiographical memory narratives. It is useful to recognize that analyzing open-ended responses of this sort involves a significant amount of time, energy, and expertise.

One of the students who worked with Professor Singer and with me on a honors thesis project combined quantitative and qualitative approaches. The project was entitled "Athletic Identity, Self-complexity, Self-defining Memories, and Vulnerability to Depression in Division I Basketball Players" (Bradley, 2001). In Bradley's study, she asked Division I basketball players at two different schools to first recall a self-defining memory. They then filled out a number of standardized questionnaires, including the Rosenberg Self-Esteem Scale (Rosenberg, 1965), the Athletic Identity Measurement Scale (AIMS: Brewer, Van Raalte, & Linder, 1993), and the Personally Expressive Activities Questionnaire (PEAQ: Waterman, 1993). After filling out these measures, participants read a hypothetical vignette involving inadequate playing time and performance failure in basketball. After reading this, participants then completed the Profile of Mood States Questionnaire (POMS: McNair, Lorr, & Droppleman, 1992).

In the self-defining memory task, participants were asked to create a self-defining memory. To understand this concept, they were given criteria for a self-defining memory and were told (adapted from Singer):

> To understand best what a self-defining memory is, imagine you have just met someone you like very much and are going for a walk together. Each of you is very committed to helping the other get to know the "Real You." You are not trying to play a role or to strike a pose. . . . In the course of conversation, you describe a memory that you feel conveys how powerfully you have come to be the person you currently are. It is precisely **this memory**, which you tell the other person and simultaneously repeat to yourself, that constitutes a **self-defining memory** (Bradley, 2001, p. 66).

This kind of open-ended query produces a significant amount of data, which must then be coded according to either a pre-existing scheme or one that you create yourself. In the case of Bradley's study, she and another rater independently coded the memories in terms of thematic content (whether they involved sports or not) and emotional tone (whether positive or negative).

A number of issues related to this kind of research should be apparent. One is the fact that coding of material takes "others," and it takes a great deal of time. That is, to make sure that the researcher or someone else isn't "reading too much into the data," independent raters need to evaluate the written material. First, you have to decide on the categories that are going to be used for rating, and then you have to create an operational definition for each category, and then you have to have at least two people independently score the narratives according to these operational definitions. These steps are clearly time-consuming.

As another example, a student and I had people look at 35 slides of physicians' waiting rooms and rate (1) how comfortable they thought they would be in these waiting rooms, and (2) the quality of medical care that they thought they would receive in these environments (Arneill & Devlin, 2002). For each slide at the bottom of the page, a space was provided for the participants to write a few words to explain their ratings (e.g., they liked the warm, homey feeling of the place, or they didn't like it because it looked too dark, too cramped, or too out of date). Ultimately, we used factor analysis to generate categories of slides that "hung" together. Then, we had to interpret what was actually being communicated by the slides in a given category; that is, we had to answer the question, "What do these slides have in common?" At that point, we read through all of the responses people had written down to slides that belonged to a given category. Generally, you begin to try to understand the reasons behind people's ratings by reading through all of the responses and jotting down some phrases or descriptions that seem to occur with modest frequency.

In this particular example of the use of open-ended responses, the task is to come up with descriptions of the categories or factors produced in the factor analysis. In the research in question, there were five categories of rooms that emerged in response to the task of rating the slides for the quality of care people thought they would experience in the waiting rooms. We labeled these factors: Ordinary and Plain; Unusual-looking; Homey Victorian; Attractive Lighting; and Colorful and Neat.

As you can see, open-ended responses can be used in a variety of different ways in research, but they are very much a starting point and require significantly more time to analyze than do quantitative responses. The amount of time involved was a point that was also made earlier in the chapter with regard to doing qualitative research projects. In any open-ended response that you want to use in your research, essentially the same steps are involved. The differences lie in the length of the material to be analyzed and the complexity of the rating schemes.

More discussion about the creation of open-ended and other kinds of questions is covered in Chapter 3 on measures.

Qualitative Research and Statistics: Kappa as a Measure of Agreement

In research such as the qualitative responses discussed earlier, at least one other person has to read through the categorizations and then you have to calculate the degree of agreement. Has Rater Number 2 put item 3 (a picture or a phrase) in the same category as Rater Number 1? Whatever judgment you make about an item's membership in a category, your individual "say so" is not sufficient. Someone else has to demonstrate that the classifications are reliable. So, recognize that open-ended responses likely will involve more steps than having people check off pre-existing attributes. In the example cited earlier involving physicians' waiting rooms, you might want to consider doing a small **pilot study** first. In a pilot study, you test out your manipulations or measures on a small number of participants. In our example, you would use a pilot study to create a list of attributes, and then include those attributes for people to rate (that is, whether the particular waiting room they were looking at possessed any of the listed qualities) rather than having them write down their own responses. In that situation, you would avoid the need for categorizing qualitative responses.

But suppose you do need to categorize responses or create groups based on a subjective judgment. Let's imagine that you were categorizing people into groups based on hair color: brown, black, red, and blonde. There probably wouldn't be much question about the validity of your groupings. But what if you wanted to group people into the following hair colors: brown, reddish brown, and brownish red? At this point, we might not be willing to accept your judgment. In the situation where you have nominal categories (no ordering), and you need to make sure that your judgments are valid, you would use another judge or rater. The measure of agreement between the two judges in known as **Cohen's kappa** (Cohen, 1960). The advantage of Cohen's kappa over a straightforward determination of the number of cases in which you and your fellow judge agree is that Cohen's kappa takes into account or corrects for the degree of agreement that would occur by chance alone. The ratio that Cohen's kappa produces is usually lower than the number you would get without the correction for guessing. Although we will not review the formula for kappa (which can be found in more advanced undergraduate statistics books), it is important for you to recognize that categorical groupings of the kind we just discussed (where your judgment alone is not sufficient to convince someone of the validity of your groupings) will involve the work of someone else, and you need to plan for that.

General Concerns about Research Designs: Internal Validity

Whatever the nature of your research design, there are certain general concerns that must be addressed, such as whether some factors either within or beyond your control undermine what you are trying to test or explore in the study. The following sections address some general concerns about **internal validity.**

Internal validity is concerned with whether your research project has integrity; that is, are you sure that your research design adequately measures or assesses what you say it does? Did your independent variable (IV) really *cause* the change observed in the dependent variable? "Threats" to the internal validity of your research occur when there are aspects of the way that you conduct your experiment that undermine your ability to measure your variables in a consistent manner. One of my colleagues describes threats to internal validity as anything that provides an alternative explanation (that is plausible).

Many factors can influence whether your research project adequately tests the hypothesis you have stated. Some of these factors include the role and actions of the experimenter, the pre-existing beliefs or attitudes of the participant, whether the instruments that participants use have some faults or malfunctions, whether the materials that participants respond to contain any biases or omissions, and whether your research design adequately controls for variables that could present competing hypotheses. Threats to internal validity may even come from events outside the laboratory (Adair, 1973). For example, what if you were assessing the kinds of fears that college students have, and, midway through a month of data collection, a plane crash involving a commercial airliner occurred in the region? Might this event alter the pattern of student responses? As you can see, factors related to internal validity present an enormous challenge to the researcher. With specific regard to the behavior of the participant, some people use the general category of **demand characteristics** to cover aspects of the experiment that may influence or elicit (hence the idea of demand) particular behavior from the participant. Demand characteristics involve the participant's response to some unintended and uncontrolled aspect of the way the experiment is run.

The Behavior of the Experimenter

Researchers often communicate their expectations about the outcome of their research, either subtly or not so subtly. A famous and controversial example of this is the debate over facilitated communication (Bebko, Perry, & Bryson, 1996; Jacobson, Mulick, & Schwartz, 1995;

Mostert, 2001, 2003; Weger, Fuller, & Sparrow, 2003). Jacobson et al. (1995, p. 750) describe facilitated communication as follows:

> Facilitated communication (FC) is a method, or group of methods, for providing assistance to a nonverbal person in typing letters, words, phrases, or sentences using a typewriter, computer keyboard, or alphabet facsimile. FC involves a graduated manual prompting procedure, with the intent of supporting a person's hand sufficiently to make it more feasible to strike the keys he or she wishes to strike, without influencing the key selection (Mulick, Jacobson, & Kobe, 1993). In practice, manual prompting is maintained indefinitely, posing the hazard of influence by the assistant (usually termed a *facilitator*).

Virtually all of the facilitators believed their clients were doing the typing, not them. Yet every blind test in published studies has shown that the facilitator was doing the typing, which points to the power of belief and self-deception (S. Vyse, personal communication, January 16, 2004). There has been a heated debate about the validity of facilitated communication, as you might well imagine, especially as it involves the delivery of treatment to people with disabilities, the credentials and training of those who deliver the service, and so on. In clients whose disabilities were increasingly complex, Jacobson et al. (1995) worried about the inconsistency in the quality of the service that was delivered and the fact that such service was delivered by people without appropriate professional credentials.

Although the example of facilitated communication may be at one end of the spectrum, it is not difficult to see how someone's commitment to a given hypothesis leads to inadvertent behavior that influences the outcome of the research such as head nodding and other paralinguistic utterances (i.e., umhmmms). Concerns of this sort have led to various kinds of research designs such as blind and double-blind studies to address the issue of the experimenter's influence on the outcome of the research.

Blind and Double-Blind Research Designs

Although we think we can remain unbiased in our approach to research, an unbiased perspective is particularly difficult when we are conducting our own studies. To avoid letting biases influence the way the study is conducted, you can take a number of steps. In a **single-blind experiment**, the participant in the study does not know whether he or she is receiving the treatment or not. A typical application of a single-blind approach involves an intervention, such as a drug, and a placebo (which looks identical to the drug, but has no

FIGURE 2.5 Single- vs. Double-Blind Experiments

pharmacological effect). A more elaborate approach, often used in medical research, is the **double-blind experiment** (Figure 2.5 summarizes these two approaches). In the double-blind approach, not only are the participants "blind" to whether they are receiving the intervention or not (i.e., drug vs. placebo), but the person who administers the drug is also blind to the testing conditions. Someone other than the person giving out the drugs labels the placebo vs. active drug conditions in an innocuous way (e.g., alpha and gamma). The person administering the conditions is thus kept "blind" about which condition is the bona fide treatment, thereby contributing the second, or double-blind aspect to the study. This kind of stringent approach is important to use when the stakes are high (e.g., testing a new cancer drug), and people's belief systems (those of the participant *and* the person administering the drugs) may have a role in the efficacy of the treatment.

Pre-Existing Beliefs or Attitudes of the Participant

Although you may not have experienced this reaction yourself, it is not uncommon, when hearing that someone is "in psychology" or is a psychologist, for people to exclaim, "I don't want to be psychoanalyzed!" What this comment reflects is the stereotype that psychologists psychoanalyze people. That is, this response suggests people think that all psychologists do clinical work, and moreover, that they are disciples of Freud! Of course, this is hardly the case, but the point illustrates the concept of a **schema** (Neisser, 1976). People have cognitive representations of the way they think the world works, and those representations, or schemas, structure how we perceive any given situation. As has been stated about perception as a transaction, it is a "two-way street" (Ittelson, 1962). Not only do we detect actual stimulus properties of a given object or situation, but our own expectations also play a role in that detection process. Even though first-year students are probably the most naïve in terms of the expectations or schemas they have about what happens in research, increasingly students have taken courses in psychology in high school and come to college fairly well-informed about the nature of psychological research.

Ideally, we would like to have people participate in research who have no preconceived notions of what is going to be asked of them. Unfortunately, we are dealing with humans who have schemas of the way the world works. They may think that certain kinds of behaviors are expected of them because they are in a research laboratory (for example, that it is inappropriate to challenge the experimenter about any aspect of the research). Also, students who have taken no courses in the social sciences differ in their level of naiveté or sophistication (as well as in their skepticism and hypotheses regarding deception) from those who have taken such courses.

In his book entitled *The Human Subject: The Social Psychology of the Psychological Experiment,* Adair (1973) explains in some detail how participants may not be naïve at all and may uncover the hypotheses under investigation and respond with "insight rather than naiveté" (p. 19). When participants formulate hypotheses about what they think the experiment is testing, such behavior may threaten the internal validity of the experiment because the participant is, in all likelihood, altering his/her behavior to conform to his/her idea of what the experimenter wants. What if the participant thinks that experimenters are always trying to trick and deceive people and formulates a hypothesis related to what he or she thinks the experiment is *really* about? Certainly this kind of schema will interfere with the purpose of the experiment, whether it actually involves deception or not.

What can you do about this? One of the points Adair (1973) makes is that "the experimenter is half of this social interaction, and his contribution to the data must be assessed or controlled" (p. 65). In certain circumstances, it may make sense to tape-record the instructions participants receive; in more extreme cases, you may need to resort to a blind or double-blind experimental design.

> Since unintentional influence is based on the subtle performance and role attribute cues the experimenter provides the subject, an investigator may prevent expectancy effects by removing the experimenter or minimizing his contact with the subject. This could be accomplished by automating the presentation of instructions, the collection of data, or the entire experiment, or by keeping the experimenter ignorant of the treatment conditions and thus ignorant of the appropriate cues to transmit. Each of these techniques is effective. (Adair, 1973, p. 61)

Cover Stories

As we have just discussed, participants often bring with them expectations about what researchers do during experiments, such as an expectation that they will be deceived. Research participants may therefore be vigilant about assessing whether what the researcher says the experiment is about *matches* what the participant is asked to do. Often, if participants correctly guess the purpose of the experiment, they might alter their responses in such a way as to either support the hypothesis or possibly even to undermine it. For this reason, it is often important in research involving social behavior to provide a **cover story.** A cover story is an explanation of why participants are being asked to do particular things that is plausible but that may mask or cover the underlying purpose of the research.

Let's take an example. One recent student was designing an experiment to compare people's attitudes toward women after being exposed to sexually suggestive movie videos or to a romantic comedy (each group would be exposed to a different condition). The only dependent variables or measures she initially proposed using focused on sexual aggression and the acceptance of rape myths. It would probably be obvious to bright, MTV-watching undergraduates what the study was trying to measure. To improve the internal validity of the research, a number of changes were proposed. One change was to add a cover story that stated that the researcher was interested in cinematography and scene composition across different types of categories. A second aspect to reinforce the cover story was to repeatedly state at the beginning of the study that different groups of people would be looking at different types of film categories. A final change was to actually add measures designed to assess cinematography to those that assessed attitudes toward women. In this way, the dependent measures would more accurately match the purpose of the research as stated in the cover story.

Manipulation Checks

Not only is it wise to employ a cover story if you need to mask the true purpose of your research, but you also need to know whether the manipulation of your independent variable was convincing to the participants. Through questions or behavioral assessments, **manipulation checks** provide a way to assess whether the participants perceived the different levels of your independent variable in the way you intended. For example, Heilman, Wallen, Fuchs, and Tamkins (2004) investigated the reactions of women's success in a male gender-typed job. They thought that when information about the women's success was ambiguous (ambiguous condition; performance data were not available), women would be rated as less competent than when the performance data were available (clear condition; data available). Therefore, a critical manipulation in the experiment was the differentiation between the ambiguous condition and the clear condition. Did the participants perceive these two conditions in the way the researchers intended? In this study, the researchers used a manipulation check to make sure that participants had perceived the two conditions as the researchers intended. To accomplish the manipulation check, they asked participants "How successful has this individual been in the current job?" (Heilman et al., 2004, p. 418). Participants' responses indicated that the manipulation had worked because only one participant in the clear success condition failed to say that the target woman was "very successful," and all save three participants in the ambiguous condition claimed they could not make the judgment with the information they had been given.

If a manipulation check indicates that the participants did not perceive your experimental manipulation as you had intended, you need to redesign your experiment! In order to avoid that unfortunate outcome, you should test the effectiveness of your experimental manipulation through a small pilot study before proceeding with full data collection.

Variation in Your Procedure

Threats to the consistency of your procedure can occur in a number of ways, including working with a partner. For example, if you are working with a research partner, and your partner is presenting material to some participant groups and you to others, questions always arise about whether your presentation was the same as your partner's. To address such concerns:

1. Tape-record the instructions to participants so that everyone hears the same thing.
2. Counterbalance the order of presentations by gender, if you and your partner create a mixed sex dyad.
3. Videotape scenarios that people may assess (instead of having confederates act out the scenario each time).

Sampling Issues

Another kind of variation in procedure, in a sense, is when participants drop out (thus creating the possibility of bias in your sample). Usually what you then do is compare the demographic and other background characteristics of the people who drop out against the characteristics of those who continue. You do this comparison to demonstrate that the sample of participants that continues is representative of these characteristics. Or you can compare the sample that continues to the characteristics of the population as a whole. This approach would be possible if you are dealing with a college community where your Office of Records and Registration (the registrar's office) has such data available.

Another threat to internal validity comes from biases that may exist in what you *think* is random sampling. For example, imagine you are looking at the effects of type of upbringing (urban, suburban, or rural) on some dependent variable like environmental preference, as measured by the Environmental Preference Questionnaire (EPQ; Kaplan, 1973, 1977). What happens if a group of friends who are all taking Introductory Psychology and are in the participant pool (see Chapter 4) sign up for the same experiment at the same time? Further, what if these friends knew each other before college and all grew up in the same kind of environment (e.g., high-density urban environment)? If their background (kind of environment in which they were raised) differs in a meaningful way from the backgrounds of students who sign up for the same project at a different data collection session, the internal validity of your hypothesis may be threatened. As mentioned previously, a large enough sample and some pre-assessment of background characteristics typically addresses these problems.

Function of the Equipment

In addition to the role of the experimenter(s) and issues of sampling, the equipment that is used may also present a problem. A straightforward example of malfunctioning equipment, which then may affect participants' responses in a manner that undermines the validity of your research, is a slide projector bulb that burns out. Such an event will interrupt the flow of the experiment, and when the participants resume their slide ratings, the responses they give may be different in some way (because they are annoyed, eager to leave, etc.). Another example of such difficulty is computer malfunction. In some research a student and I conducted (Devlin & Bernstein, 1997), the computer was supposed to time out if a participant had not pressed a response within 99 seconds. But upon looking at the data, it was clear that some participants had latencies to touch a computer screen of over 200 seconds, which indicated some problem with the computer program (i.e., the timeout function had not operated). Although you cannot anticipate every possible malfunction that might occur, it is important to be as prepared as you possibly can (e.g., extra projector bulbs or even extra pens or pencils if students neglected to bring them).

Biases and Omissions in the Materials or Measures

Although Chapter 3 will cover these issues in more depth, let me just comment briefly about how mistakes in your materials can create threats to internal validity. If you are generating some of your own questions in a survey (for example, some of your demographic or background questions), the way in which you word these questions can create a bias. If you are doing research about satisfaction with student housing for example, find the difference between asking a question like this:

1. How much do you like your current residence hall? (Please circle your response on the following scale):

   Not at all   A great deal

      1   2   3   4   5

and this:

2. Please rate your residence hall on the following scale:

   Do not like   Like it
     it at all   a great deal

      1   2   3   4   5

In Example 1, the use of the word "like" in the "stem" or lead-in to the question may set up an expectation that students should, in fact, like their residence halls. In the second example, the evaluative component (the student evaluation of the residence hall) is contained only in the response options, not in the stem of the question itself. Example #1 is just one of many that illustrates how easy it is to "lead the witness."

Another example of problems with materials has to do with omission, or things we may leave out. Even experienced researchers have this problem. In one example I know well, students and a group of elderly citizens from the local community were asked to rate slides of physicians' waiting rooms on a number of dimensions (see Arneill & Devlin, 2002, p. 350). "Through an oversight," the rating form for the last slide was not included when the citizens in the community did their ratings. As a result, all of the data for slide 35 had to be dropped from the study. This example simply suggests that it is a good idea to check all of your materials before you actually collect data in any session.

Events in the Wider World

You should also recognize that events outside the laboratory can influence participants' responses to your experiment (Adair, 1973). At times, entire research agendas are intentionally centered on such external events, such as the flashbulb memory debates that deal with such phenomena as assassinations (Brown & Kulik, 1977), the Challenger tragedy (Neisser & Harsch, 1992), and the San Francisco earthquake (Neisser et al., 1996). Usually, however, unexpected events disrupt research plans.

Imagine that you were going to do research on the perception of safety at night on your campus and the week you planned to collect data there is an assault. The research of Tversky and Kahneman (1974; Kahneman & Tversky, 1973) also emphasizes the kind of heuristics people use in making decisions and the fact that variables such as the recency and vividness of information can influence its cognitive availability—and make its way into the laboratory. After the events of 9/11, people were more likely to initially attribute any accident or major problem that occurred (e.g., the power grid blackout of the summer of 2003) to terrorist activity. Depending on the nature of your research, such uncontrollable events can present a problem. If such an event may have an impact on the responses of your participants, you may be better off delaying the collection of data, if you have that option.

Summary of Threats to Internal Validity

- Demand characteristics
- Beliefs/attitudes of participants
- Variation in procedure
- Sampling issues
- Equipment problems
- Omissions in measures
- Effectiveness of cover story
- Effectiveness of manipulation (manipulation checks)
- Influence of events in the wider world

Internal Validity and Control of Variables

As has been discussed throughout this chapter, different kinds of experimental designs lend themselves to different degrees of inference about causality. At one end of the continuum we have correlational research, where there is no possibility of determining cause and effect. At the other end of the continuum is experimental design, where, because we have manipulated variables, we are in a better situation to make claims about causality. Somewhere along the continuum are quasi-experimental designs where we examine group differences without random assignment to condition. Whatever research design we select, however, it behooves us to establish as much control as we can over the possibility that our data can be explained by alternative hypotheses. Alternative hypotheses are hypotheses *other* than the one(s) we have posited that could also explain our data.

How do we establish this control? In the case of correlation, we ask "what else could explain this" questions and see if we can assess those alternatives. We also need to make sure that these alternatives don't do a better job of explaining the relationship we have hypothesized than the variables we originally selected. As has been discussed in this chapter and in Chapter 1, we can also establish more control by focusing on more specific aspects of behavior that have a narrow conceptual coverage. When you use broad concepts like intelligence or adjustment that might be linked to many other variables, you have a situation where the response to any significant correlation may be "so what?" Very little variance is likely to be explained by correlations that involve these broad constructs. Think more specifically!

Even in cases that involve experimental or quasi-experimental design, the "think specifically" advice is relevant. As an example, I once did some longitudinal research that involved the relationship between a survival skills training program for college freshmen and their adjustment to college as seniors (Devlin, 1996). Although there were significant findings in this research, there were also problems, like participants dropping out (called **subject mortality**). More troublesome was the fact that I was doing precisely what I have just said *not* to do: linking a particular variable/intervention (a four-day survival skills workshop) to a very broad concept (college adjustment measured during the senior year!). But what rescued the research was that the study also examined attitudes toward nature over the course of the college career, a variable much more closely linked conceptually to the original survival skills workshop. The attitudes toward nature were measured by the Environmental Preference Questionnaire (Kaplan, 1977), which uses a number of scales to determine the extent to which people prefer being in such situations as woodlands and wilderness, how much they like to escape from suburbia, and so on. Again, try to investigate the relationship or effect of variables that have some reasonable likelihood of being connected to each other in a direct manner.

General Concerns About Research Design: External Validity

External validity deals with the concept of whether, and the degree to which, the findings of your experiment may generalize to other populations and to behavior outside of the laboratory. In general, all other things being equal, experimenters want to have the best of both worlds: a tightly controlled experiment (which usually means a laboratory experiment) with a high generalizability of results and a high degree of external or ecological validity of the method. However, all other things are hardly ever equal (!), and the research community differs in the extent to which it favors generalizability over ecological or external validity (Banaji & Crowder, 1989). For example, in research on what is called everyday memory or ecological memory, Neisser and his colleagues (Neisser & Hyman, 2000) make a strong case for what can be learned by studying memory in natural contexts. As you might imagine, a strong argument about the importance of experimental control has been mustered by the other camp (Banaji & Crowder, 1989). For the beginning researcher, what is important to recognize is the ideal goal: striving to gain as much control as possible over the variables in question while at the same time taking into account ways to extend the results to the wider world.

With regard to the kinds of projects undertaken by students in a beginning research methods class, concerns about external validity give you all the more reason to plan a study for which college students *are* the target population (see Chapter 1). In that way, you are less likely to have to defend criticisms that your results will not generalize (as is the case if you are using college students to reach conclusions about some other target group, like managers in a company).

REFLECT AND REVIEW

Explain internal and external validity and the ways in which researchers can increase them.

SUMMARY

This chapter has covered the fundamentals of research design, with a particular emphasis on the implications of design for reaching conclusions involving cause and effect (experimental design) vs. being limited to statements of relationship (correlational and quasi-experimental designs). Qualitative research designs, observational methods, and archival research have been discussed as alternatives to the experimental approach. You have learned that the kind of statistics you use relates to the type of data you have, and that it is important to think through your statistical analyses before collecting any data. If you pose your hypotheses in terms of group differences, you need some groups! Finally, not only is research design about participants and apparatus/materials, and procedure; it is also about increasing internal and external validity and ruling out alternative hypotheses.

APPLY YOUR KNOWLEDGE QUESTIONS

In the event that you did not have time to do them earlier, here is the list of APPLY YOUR KNOWLEDGE questions in this chapter. Try them now:

1. With this brief introduction, see if you can take a research question and approach it from three different research designs: correlational, quasi-experimental, and experimental.

2. Make a list of the demographic variables that might commonly be used in research with college students.

3. Think of a qualitative question that you might use that focuses on college students as a unique group.

4. Without consulting Table 2.1, create your own chart that lists common statistical tests (chi-square, *t*-test, one-way ANOVA, factorial ANOVA, MANOVA, correlation, regression) and the characteristics of each (nominal or interval data, number of independent variables, number of dependent variables).

WEB RESOURCES

There are a number of research methods and statistics workshops on the web that may enhance your knowledge of the topics in this chapter. Here is a list of these workshops and their web addresses:

Experimental Methods

Reliability and Validity

True Experiments

Confounds—Threats to Validity

www.wadsworth.com/psychology_d/templates/ student_resources/workshops/resch_wrk.html

Choosing the Correct Statistical Test

www.wadsworth.com/psychology_d/templates/ student_resources/workshops/stats_wrk.html

Sources of Measures

● ●

3

Introduction and Chapter Overview

In real time many of the tasks discussed in this book (developing a research question, selecting a research design to evaluate that question, and selecting or developing scales or instruments that measure your stated hypotheses) occur in parallel, but an artificial sequence must be imposed in a book. The results of a search for measures or instruments may lead you to modify your research design, and sometimes aspects of your research question itself. These modifications are more likely to occur for the novice researcher.

At some point fairly early on, you will have to determine your variables of interest (e.g., interpersonal intelligence, task-oriented leadership), and the degree to which it is possible to measure them. On the one hand, you have a theoretical idea, like leadership. The **conceptual criterion** is the abstract standard of that idea of leadership, which you are trying to measure, but can never fully reach. Your goal is to identify an existing measure of that idea, a measure that you find in the literature or one that you create yourself (more on that later). This *measure* of the idea is your actual measure; it is what you give your participants. You want to have as much overlap as possible between your theoretical idea, leadership in our example, and your actual measure, so that the actual measure comes as close as possible to the conceptual criterion or standard.

This chapter will concentrate on practical ways to increase the overlap between the conceptual criterion and your actual measure. The chapter will provide practical ways to identify useful measures and ways to obtain these measures. You will learn the advantages and disadvantages of obtaining measures that other people have developed and the criteria for evaluating the quality and usefulness of a measure. These criteria include the measure's **validity** (does it measure what it says it measures?) and its **reliability** (does it produce the same results over multiple administrations?; do all of the items measure the construct in question?). Criteria for use may also include the length of the instrument and the difficulty of the items. The chapter will also make clear the pitfalls of developing your own measures and the kinds of questions (typically demographic or background) that are reasonable to generate yourself. You will learn how to calculate the **internal consistency** (e.g., Cronbach's alpha) for a measure. The greater the internal consistency of a measure, the greater the extent to which each item is measuring the same construct. Internal consistency is an important reflection of the quality of a measure.

You will learn how to locate and obtain measures and the importance of obtaining complete scoring instructions. The chapter will discuss the kinds of scoring issues that sometimes arise (like items that are reverse scored). A Resource Guide at the end of this chapter will also provide you with a list of commonly used measures and their sources.

What Measures or Instruments Do

At this point in your project, you have identified a research problem and generated some tentative hypotheses. But how are you going to evaluate these hypotheses? What kind of data will you use to evaluate the hypotheses? You want data that reflect the constructs (e.g., leadership, intelligence, hand–eye coordination) that are central to your hypotheses. As an example, perhaps you are interested in the relationship between the kind of support fathers give their daughters and whether the daughters continue to play sports in college (and on what level). Now it may seem fairly straightforward to determine whether a college student plays sports in college. You might ask a series of questions beginning with whether she plays sports in college (yes/no) and if so, about whether she is on a varsity, JV, intramural, or recreational team. But how are you going to measure the support a father gives his daughter?

In general, the more abstract a construct or idea is (like leadership or personality), the more difficult it is to measure that construct. It is generally much more straightforward to measure constructs such as reaction time, where the **operational definition** is almost self-evident. An operational definition exists when the variable you are interested in is defined by the operations that are used to measure it. If a student wants to do a research project to measure success in college, I might ask the student "What is your operational definition of success?" I am asking the student to think about how he or she plans to measure success, such as using GPA or the number of semesters a participant has been on the dean's list.

The diagram in Figure 3.1 (Muchinsky, 2003, p. 58) illustrates the problem we all face as researchers. We have an abstract standard, or **conceptual criterion**, such as our view of intelligence, but we need a way to measure it. The bottom circle represents the **actual criterion**, or the measure that we ultimately use to try to quantify or assess the essence of that construct.

The degree to which these two circles overlap is called **criterion relevance** (Muchinsky, 2003). The part of the conceptual criterion that your measure "misses" is called **criterion deficiency** (that is, you failed to measure *all* of the construct); the part of the actual criterion that your measure includes but *should not* is called **criterion contamination** (i.e., that aspect of your measure that is tapping or assessing something *other* than the conceptual criterion). Your measure is thus

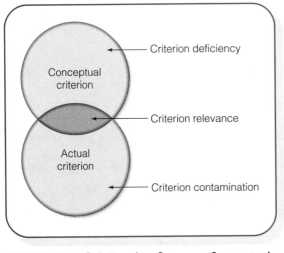

FIGURE 3.1 Relationship Between Conceptual
              Criterion and Actual Criterion

Source: Adapted from Muchinsky, 2003.

being contaminated because you are assessing something other than the concept you seek to measure. Your goal, as a researcher, is to achieve the greatest degree of overlap possible between those two circles. Generally, the more abstract the concept is (such as leadership or intelligence), the more difficult it is to measure successfully (i.e., to obtain a high degree of overlap between the conceptual criterion and the actual criterion).

REFLECT AND REVIEW

Explain why you need a maximum overlap between the conceptual criterion and the actual criterion. What happens when there is very little overlap?

Locating Measures or Equipment

After deciding on your research question and your research design, the next challenging task is locating the equipment or measures you want to use. At the end of this chapter, there is a Resource Guide with a list of some of the more typically used measures and scales in different areas of social and behavioral science (e.g., personality, social interactions, racism, women's issues) and a few representative tasks from neuroscience. The comments here focus on the general strategies you can use to obtain measures in any domain of behavioral science.

The Literature

Let's return to the example mentioned earlier in the chapter, the study looking at the relationship between the kinds of support fathers give their daughters and whether the daughters continue to play sports in college. When you began reading the empirical literature in your topic area, as a way to generate a research question, you probably looked at more than 25 articles that dealt with your topic area or were somehow related to your topic area. In the example used here, you may have read about parent–child or father–daughter relationships, and you also may have looked at the literature on motivation in sports. As was mentioned in Chapter 1, at the time you locate and read the articles, it is a good strategy to make a list of commonly used measures or equipment in a particular area. What you want to record are those measures that appear with some frequency in the literature of your topic area(s).

In the articles you read, some section of the article described the methodological approach taken in the study. In the discipline of psychology, this section of a journal article is called the Method, and it has three subsections: Participants, Apparatus (or Materials), and Procedure. In other behavioral sciences, the terminology is similar. For example, in the *American Sociological Review*, the section of the article in which the methodology is described is called Data and Methods; in the *Journal of Educational Research*, it is called Method, as is it in the *Journal of Experimental Education*. In the *Journal of the Scientific Study of Religion*, you find Data and Methods, whereas the *Journal of Anthropological Research* has a number of approaches, depending on the article. One article might call the section Materials and Methods, whereas another article in the same journal may call it Methodology.

The section that describes the Apparatus or Materials is an excellent place to begin your search for appropriate materials to use in your study. Pay close attention to measures or equipment that appear frequently in the literature in your area of interest. Repeated use of a measure or piece of equipment may indicate that it is highly regarded and/or thought to validly measure a construct of interest. For example, one of the most commonly used measures of self-esteem is the Rosenberg Self-Esteem Scale (Rosenberg, 1965). It consists of 10 items. As another example, the Vandenberg and Kuse (1978) Mental Rotations Test has become one of the commonly used measures of spatial ability.

Statistical Qualities of the Measure

In the Apparatus/Materials section, the author will provide some description of the equipment or measures he or she employed in the study. Although the extent of this information will vary, you can usually find the name of the author and the date of publication of the measure, or the manufacturer of a piece of equipment. If it is a scale, the article will typically provide the number of items in the scale and quantitative indices of **validity** (to what other indices the measure is related) and **reliability** (such as test–retest reliability and internal consistency). As discussed earlier in the chapter, the validity of the measure is the extent to which the scale measures what the author claims it measures. Often validity information for a scale involves its positive correlation with other measures of the same construct, and its negative correlation with constructs with which you would not expect it to relate. For example, if you have a measure of anxiety, you would not expect people who score high on that measure to also score high on a measure of calmness.

Regarding reliability, keep a lookout for statements of internal consistency such as **Cronbach's alpha.** This measure of internal consistency, which varies between 0 and 1, is an index of the extent to which each item on a scale correlates with every other item on the scale. The closer to 1, the better. When you are selecting among a number of different measures of the same constructs (e.g., three different measures of anxiety), one criterion you will use to make that selection decision is the measure's internal consistency. You want to find measures that have an internal consistency of at least .70. On occasion, you will select a measure with subscales where the Cronbach's alphas of one or more of the individual subscales fall below .70. Although that scale is not ideal, you may still select it because averaged across the subscales, the alpha is reasonably close to .70 and/or because there are other aspects of the scale that argue for its use.

In the example of father support and a daughter's participation in athletics in college, the students who conducted this research project selected the Parental Involvement in Activities Scale (PIAS)/(Anderson, Funk, Elliot, & Smith, 2003) to assess the father's involvement in his daughter's activities. The scale has two subscales; one measures father pressure and the other measures father support. The Cronbach's alphas for the two scales were .84 (pressure) and .85 (support).

A second measure, the Participation Motivation Questionnaire (PMQ)/(Gill, Gross, & Huddleston, 1983), was used by the students to assess the motivations behind participation in sports at the college level. The questionnaire has eight subscales of motivation, with Cronbach's alphas for the students' study ranging from .55 to .84.

A note about calculating Cronbach's alpha. Although you use a published index of internal consistency, like Cronbach's alpha, to select your measure, it is also important to know that you can calculate the alpha for your own study after you collect your data. It is important to calculate the Cronbach's alpha for your own study, because it will be one indication of the internal validity of *your* research. It is not a problem if the Cronbach's alpha of your data is higher than the published Cronbach's alpha. However, when the Cronbach's alpha for your own data is more than five or so points *lower* than the published Cronbach's alpha for the measure you are using, then that lower value may represent some problem with the way the participants responded to the measure. For example, the participants may not have taken the task seriously, they may have mismarked items, they may not have read the items carefully, and so on. The Cronbach's alpha for your own data can thus tell you if at least this part of the project went as planned! The method for calculating the Cronbach's alpha for your own data will be explained more fully later in this chapter.

Length and Difficulty of Items

Other aspects of scales for you to consider are the length of the measures and the difficulty of the items in the measures. Remember that your participants are volunteers, and there is a limit to their willingness to help out, even if they obtain research credit for participation. How many questionnaires do you plan to use? What is the length of each questionnaire? Some measures have hundreds of items, like the widely used measure of personality, the NEO PI-R (Costa & McCrae, 1992), which has 240 items and 3 validity items. Some measures may require a level of reading proficiency that your participants do not possess, although this drawback is unlikely if your research involves college students. Such a problem with item difficulty is likely to occur if your study involves individuals for whom English is not a first language or individuals with limited education.

So, when you are doing your literature review, keep track of these issues; the length of the scale may have some bearing on the fatigue your participants will experience, especially if your research design involves multiple measures. And certainly you will want to use measures that have good reliability and validity to maximize the degree of overlap between the conceptual and the actual criteria.

Although there is no hard and fast rule for the number of items you can expect people to complete, if filling out your materials takes more than 45 minutes, you might consider eliminating one or more of the measures. How do you know if your survey takes this long? Try it out! Better yet, have a friend take the survey at "normal" speed, and this will give you some indication of the time commitment you are asking of people. I have had colleagues who ask students to complete up to 10 autobiographical memories at one sitting. The danger in asking this much of participants is that they may begin to fabricate material just to finish the task (anonymous student, personal communication, March,

2004). A set of materials that is too lengthy may threaten the internal validity of your task, the extent to which the research process actually evaluates the proposed hypotheses (see also Chapter 2).

Summary of Factors in Selecting Measures

- Use in the literature
- Length
- Reading level and item difficulty
- Reliability (internal consistency)
- Validity
- Time to complete

REFLECT AND REVIEW

At this point, you should be able to define **validity** and **reliability.** What does a high Cronbach's alpha tell you about a measure? Name three criteria you might use to select a measure for use in your research.

APPLY YOUR KNOWLEDGE

Skim two or three articles in social science journals in the library to see the range of Cronbach's alphas reported in the articles.

Instructions for Scoring

Even when you obtain a measure for use, you are not finished. You need to know how to score the measure. Some measures include a subsection of items that are not scored (e.g., Bem Sex Role Inventory; Bem, 1974); many measures include items that are **reverse scored** (e.g., Rosenberg Self-Esteem Scale, 1965). When an item is reverse scored, the value of the item is exchanged, or reversed, with its parallel value at the other end of the numerical scale. For example, if for a given item the response choices are 1 (low) to 5 (high) and the item is reverse scored, the participant who records a "2" will now have a "4" in its place. Reverse scored items are discussed again in the section on Data Entry in Chapter 6.

Names of Measures

The name of a measure is generally meant to communicate the construct it seeks to assess. So, for example, we have the Rosenberg Self-Esteem Scale (1965), which is a measure of self-esteem, and the Vandenberg and Kuse Mental Rotations Test (1978), which is a test of mental rotation ability, a form of spatial cognition. There are also scales such as the Taylor Manifest Anxiety Scale (Taylor, 1953), which measures anxiety.

However, these names or labels may communicate information about the measure that set up unwanted expectancies. Often, you do not want participants to know precisely what you are assessing because it may change the nature of their responses in a more socially desirable direction. **Social desirability** occurs when participants modify their responses to present themselves in a more favorable light. To avoid this kind of demand characteristic, you may want to change the name or label of the measure before you type up your heading or title. A demand characteristic involves an aspect of the research process, including the behavior of the researcher, which unintentionally influences the participant's responses (see also Chapter 2). Thus, if you are giving a self-esteem measure, you might want to change it to a Sense of Self measure; an anxiety measure might become on Outlook on the World measure.

Measures of Social Desirability

Most people want to be perceived as upstanding individuals who do the right thing. If people have prejudices, and we all do, they may not want to reveal them for fear of being labeled as some kind of "-ist" (sexist, racist, ageist, etc.). Because we want to be perceived in the best possible light, we may "edit" our answers on any given scale to present ourselves more favorably (or at least in a manner that we perceive as more favorable).

If you are concerned about this problem in your research, you may want to include a measure of social desirability and then use the responses from that measure as a covariate in your analyses. That is, you may want to take account of whether people's social desirability responses vary with their responses to the construct in question.

As an example, consider another project from the research methods class in 2004. In this experiment, three student researchers assessed students' reactions to sexist jokes. Eight jokes were rated on a

5-point scale in terms of funniness (1=not funny and 5=very funny) and offensiveness (1=not offensive and 5=very offensive). In addition, half of the participants were told that they would have to stand up and report their ratings to the other participants in the group and half were not given those instructions. In fact, neither group actually had to read their responses aloud.

Social desirability may be an issue in this situation where the jokes reflect sexist humor. Consider the following joke from the study: Question: Why do brides wear white? Answer: It is important for the dishwasher to match the refrigerator and the stove. Participants presumably would not want to appear biased against women by rating this joke as humorous. But there certainly might be some variability in the extent to which people feel that they need to modify their answers in a socially desirable direction. To account for these differences in the degree of social desirability that people employ, the students incorporated a social desirability measure, the Balanced Inventory of Desirable Responding (BIDR)/(Paulhus, 1991), in their research. The researchers could then take into account the degree to which people generally respond in a socially desirable manner, and then use the social desirability score as a covariate in their analyses. That is, they could assess the degree to which judgments of humorousness and offensiveness were responded to in a manner related to the social desirability score. Not all research requires the inclusion of social desirability measures (most reaction time experiments would not, for example). But if your research focuses on socially sensitive topics, you might consider including a social desirability measure. In addition to the BIDR, the Marlowe-Crowne Social Desirability Scale (Crowne & Marlowe, 1960) is commonly used.

Availability: How to Obtain the Measure
The Article Itself

The next issue is whether the scale or measure is available in the article itself. Sometimes you are in luck and the complete scale and directions for scoring are included in the article. Typically this happens when the author is introducing a new measure. For example, when I developed a Precautionary Measures Scale (Devlin, 2000), the 19 items and directions for scoring were included in an appendix at the end of the article. The article also included information about the internal consistency of the scale, which had a Cronbach's alpha of .89.

If the measure is not included (and often it is not), look for the reference to the measure when it is described in the article (typically in the Method section, under the subsection Apparatus or Materials).

Identify that reference in the article's reference section. The next thing you want to do is track down that referenced article, and see whether the scale or instrument was included in that earlier article. Thus, just as a literature review requires a lot of backtracking to obtain articles that are mentioned in the reference section of earlier publications, so, too, does searching for the location of measures in their complete form.

But what if the scale you need is not published in any of the articles, even in the original? What then? Your next step might be to e-mail or phone the author of the original article in which the scale was mentioned to see if the measure is available from that individual. A good place to look for the author's contact information is on the first page of the article, usually at the bottom with the statement "Correspondence about this article should be addressed to _____." If the contact information is not available, you might track down the author by consulting professional directories in the discipline in question, like the membership directory of the American Psychological Association. That directory is now online for the use of its members, and you can work with your faculty sponsor, who may be a member, to track down the needed information.

Further, in this day of Internet access, you could do an Internet search entering the author's name, and the search would probably yield a link to the author's web page, which provides another means of contacting the individual. With respect to measures that have been used for decades, it is also possible that the author of the measure is deceased. If that is the case, I would recommend e-mailing or calling one of the authors of a more recent publication in which the scale has been used. You could ask the author in this recent publication how he or she obtained the measure. My experience has been that academics are generally very willing to help out undergraduate students.

Department Authors and Professors

Another good source of measures that you may seek resides in your own department. Ask your professors about the measures and pieces of apparatus they have available. They may even have personally authored a measure you want or designed a piece of equipment you need. Some departments keep a file of frequently used scales, which they make available to students as appropriate. The appropriateness of use depends on the training of the student. For example, many clinical measures, such as the intelligence tests, and projective tests, such as the Rorschach, require specific advanced training that undergraduates will not possess. Therefore, a number of widely recognized measures may actually be "off limits" for undergraduate projects.

But many professors have copies of scales, appropriate for under-graduates, that the professors often use in their own research. Thus, asking faculty members (or graduate students, if your department has them) is another potential way to obtain scales.

Books of and About Measures

A number of books contain measures for use in research as well as critiques of measures. These include the *Encyclopedia of Psychological Assessment* (Fernandez-Ballesteros, 2003), *Measures for Clinical Practice* (Corcoran & Fischer, 2000), *Test Critiques Compendium* (Keyser & Sweetland, 1987), and *Unpublished Experimental Measures* (8 volumes) (Goldman & Mitchell, 1996). Chapter 2 includes a section on such resources.

Ideally you would select measures based on their use in the literature; that is, you want to use those measures in your research that have been identified in the literature as appropriate for a given area, commonly employed, and with good internal consistency, demonstrated reliability, and so on. On occasion, it may not be possible to use a particular measure. Most commonly in my experience, a measure is out of reach because there is a fee charged for its use and/or because the researcher does not have the appropriate training to use the instrument (which happens most typically with clinical measures).

● ●

REFLECT AND REVIEW

At this point, cite two reasons for using pre-existing measures and name three different kinds of sources for locating measures.

● ●

APPLY YOUR KNOWLEDGE

In your own college library, locate a book that contains measures for use in social science research.

The Drawbacks to Using Pre-Existing Measures

Thus far in our discussion, there have been only positive aspects of using existing measures. It takes a considerable amount of skill and effort to develop a scale and establish its validity and reliability. So why would a researcher develop his or her own measure? There are three fundamental reasons to develop your own measure. One reason might be that there is no existing measure to assess a particular construct. The second reason might be the financial cost involved with purchasing a measure for which a fee is charged. The third reason might be that you are not professionally qualified to use an existing measure.

Assessing New Territory

The first reason students may develop their own research scales deals with the lack of a pre-existing measure. For example, one recent group of students in a research methods class studied students' awareness of the extent of diversity on campus. For this project, they developed a series of questions to assess the extent to which an individual had been exposed to situations involving diversity. Searching through the literature, they could not find examples of existing scales that met their needs, and they thus set out to develop their own scale. Examples of the questions they generated are "I went to a diverse daycare or early intervention program" and "My high school's curriculum consisted of an array of ethnically diverse authors." This scale consisted of 11 rated items and a twelfth item, a request to "define diversity." Participants responded to the 11 items using a 5-point Likert scale of "strongly agree" to "strongly disagree."

In another example of creating a new scale, a second student in this research methods class did an experiment in which she presented an ambiguously abusive parenting scenario to participants and varied whether the race of the mother and child was mentioned and, if so, whether it was Black or White. To evaluate participants' reactions to the scenario, she created her own Concern Scale (which she labeled a Reaction Questionnaire in the experiment). The Concern Scale consisted of 10 items such as "How concerned do you feel for the child in this situation?" The Cronbach's alpha for her new scale was calculated to be .72.

Developing Your Own Scale and Measuring Its Internal Consistency

Yes, it is possible to develop your own scale, if you do not find existing instruments that target your construct of interest. Although it is possible to develop such a new scale, it is not easy to produce a measure with acceptable internal consistency on the first try! To develop your own scale, you first do some brainstorming about the kinds of behaviors or beliefs that you think reflect the construct of interest. For example, the students who developed their own diversity experience scale made a list of the ways in which they thought people might receive exposure to diversity, using their own experiences as a starting point.

Once you have exhausted your own ideas about a topic or construct, ask other people you know who may have experiences different from your own. When I developed my scale of precautionary measures (Devlin, 2000), I started with my own experience of traveling to New York City and the "precautions" I usually take (like not wearing a lot of jewelry or crossing the street if I think someone is following me). I then spoke to my brother, who resides in Manhattan, about his precautionary behaviors in the city.

After generating a series of items, you can have a pilot group of participants answer the items and then calculate the internal consistency of the measure. You do this by setting up a data file (presumably in a statistical package like SPSS) in which the score for each item for each participant is recorded (rather than just a scale total), and then a **reliability analysis** is run. This reliability analysis yields information about which items are actually detracting from the reliability of the scale. You can then delete the items that detract from the reliability and rerun the reliability analysis to boost the Cronbach's alpha. When I developed the Precautionary Measures scale, I started with 42 items and actually ended up with only 19. These 19 items yielded the highest Cronbach's alpha for the scale (.89). For each reliability analysis, SPSS provides the user with a list of the Cronbach's alpha for the scale, if any given item were deleted. This information allows you to eliminate a given item that is pulling down the reliability. You keep eliminating items and rerunning the reliability analysis until the highest possible alpha has been reached.

Developing your own scale is possible, but it takes a considerable amount of effort.

Advice for Writing Instruments Yourself

Among the best articles I have found about how to pose questions for scales is Schwarz's (1999) article entitled "Self-reports: How the questions shape the answers." Through clear examples, Schwarz shows how the format of questions and response choices affect the answers that participants provide. Schwarz's recommendations apply equally well to the development of a new scale as to the formatting of demographic items that you write to accompany an existing scale. If you are going to write your own measures or many demographic items, I strongly suggest that you read the complete article by Schwarz (1999). What I comment on now are some of his major points, but by no means is this an exhaustive list.

One of the primary messages in Schwarz's article is that the structure of your questions, and not just their content, provides important information for the participants in your study. Unless you carefully plan this structure, what the respondents understand and what you intend may be quite different. As Schwarz notes (p. 103), "respondents do their best to be cooperative communicators." Schwarz goes on to explain the assumptions made by participants (p. 103):

> Consistent with the assumptions that underlie the conduct of conversation in daily life, they assume that all contributions of the researcher are relevant to the goals of the ongoing exchange, and they take these contributions into account in arriving at an answer. Unfortunately, as researchers we are often not fully aware of the information that our questionnaires—or our experimental procedures . . . —provide, and hence miss the extent to which the questions we ask determine the answers we receive.

One of the points Schwarz clearly demonstrates is that you often get very different responses to open-ended vs. closed question approaches. Furthermore, response scales offer clues to participants. Schwarz gives an example of whether people consider themselves successful, using a scale of not at all successful to extremely successful. In one version, the response anchors go from 0 to 10; in the other version they go from −5 to +5, the same numerical distance in absolute terms. In the first version, only 13% of the respondents indicated points in the 0–5 range, whereas in the second version that percentage was 34% (−5 to 0). Schwarz explains that in the first scale (0 to 10) participants consider the scale to be unipolar, whereas in the second scale, they perceive that the scale has bipolar properties. In the first scale, the range from 0 to 5 may indicate the absence of outstanding accomplishments; in the second, the lower six points of the scale (−5 to 0) may reflect demonstrable failures. This example vividly illustrates the role that scale range can play in shaping our responses. In addition to the role that the scale ranges play, participants also pick up clues from the researcher's affiliation, and the context in which the questions are embedded, particularly what questions have preceded an item.

Another formal aspect of the questionnaire structure to consider is frequency alternatives. Schwarz points out that people use their knowledge about the world, such as the distribution of events in terms of the frequency with which they happen (common vs. rare events), to understand a scale. Thus, the middle value in a scale is usually interpreted as typical or usual. Further, the ends of the scale are considered extremes of a distribution. If a respondent looks at a scale and discovers that an option he/she planned to circle is at the end of the continuum (because it represents the frequency with which he/she engages in a event, like checking e-mail), that person may alter his/her response to bring it in line with what he or she perceives to be the "norm" (as reflected in the scale distribution).

Schwarz presents research to support the conclusions that response alternatives will have more impact under certain circumstances: (1) when a behavior is not well represented in memory, and (2) when a behavior is not well defined. To combat these problems, Schwarz recommends that researchers ask frequency questions using an open-ended approach for the response format. An example would be "How many times a day do you check your e-mail?" _____ times per day. He points out the importance of specifying the units of measurement (i.e., _____ times per day) for the question. This specification is important, he argues, to limit vague answers such as "quite a few." In Schwarz's judgment, the worst choice for frequency alternatives involves the quantifiers "sometimes," "often," "frequently," and so on. What those words mean depends on the respondent's subjective standard, which obviously varies from individual to individual.

Writing demographic items. Although developing a reliable scale is usually beyond the scope of a research project done in a single semester, the researcher who is administering a survey will undoubtedly want to obtain some information about his or her population. This information is usually referred to as **demographics.** Demographic information includes such characteristics as the age, sex, and race of the participant. Other items that are commonly used include the individual's relationship status (i.e., single, married, etc.), income level, and the individual's religion.

With regard to asking about sex, a common method is to print the variable name and the choices as follows:

Sex: M   F

Usually there are instructions to the participant to "Circle the appropriate response for each item." While the format of the demographic item Sex is straightforward, other categories may not be so easy.

As a rule of thumb, it is better to obtain the most specific information possible, which can later be collapsed into categories if the researcher desires. For example, I recommend that you ask for age as follows:

Age: _____

In this example, the participant writes in his or her age, rather than circling a category such as:

16–20

21–25

26–30

and so on. In this example of age categories, the use of age spans may obscure important group differences that occur *within* a category, rather than between categories. As we have seen, Schwarz (1999) gives sound reasoning for this open-ended approach when he describes the role that structure can play in biasing the participant's response for any given question.

Race/ethnicity. Asking about this issue is important in terms of being able to describe the characteristics of your population and whether your sample is representative. For example, you may be recruiting participants through a department participant pool or through appealing to classes or by setting up recruiting tables in the student union, and so on. If your study involves a college population, you want to be able to demonstrate that it is representative in a variety of ways (e.g., by race, by sex). You can certainly obtain the percentages at your institution in terms of race and sex by going to your Registrar's Office or your Admissions Office; sometimes this information is even available in the college catalogue or on its website.

How you ask about Race and Ethnicity is a moving target, and one possible approach (although certainly not the only one) is to list the category choices as:

Caucasian/White

African American/Black

Hispanic/Latino(a)

Asian/Asian Pacific

Native American

Other _____

However, increasingly, people may be of mixed races and/or ethnicities, and for that reason using an open-ended approach may be preferable.

Race/Ethnicity: _____

A cautionary note about open-ended questions. It is important to keep in mind that the age group of your participants may influence whether you are able to use open-ended questions or not. For example, if you are using sixth graders, an open-ended item labeled Race/Ethnicity may not be understood by this age group.

Regarding religion, it is probably preferable to provide the following option:

Religious affiliation: _____

Leaving religious affiliation open-ended means that the individual can provide the most precise answer, which may include "none."

Family Income is an item that presents certain challenges, because participants, particularly if they are students, may not know their family income. You could provide a list:

_____ less than $10,000

_____ $10,001–$30,000

_____ $30,001–$60,000

_____ $60,001–$90,000

_____ greater than $90,000

(Also, note that the categories are non-overlapping; that is, one category ends with -,000 and the next begins with -,001).

However, at the institution where I teach, that particular list of options will create a **ceiling effect** in the data. A ceiling effect means that most people will cluster at the upper end of the scale, so there is little distribution of scores (think of an example of a memory test where almost everyone remembers all of the items; you have the problem of a ceiling effect). In our example it means that most of the population will be at the upper end of the income scale, so that you do not have a good distribution. If you are looking at group differences or doing a correlation, you are unlikely to get significant results when a ceiling effect exists. The opposite condition is called a **floor effect**, where everyone clusters at the bottom, e.g., everyone gets almost all the answers wrong on the memory test or, in our example, is at the bottom of the income scale.

Before creating an income scale such as the one in the preceding list, it is advisable to do some homework about your population and look at census data or, in our case, institutional data, to determine the range of income choices you will need. You can probably obtain such data from the Office of Financial Aid at your institution. Now, you may ask "Why not simply create an open-ended question: "Family Income: _____"? Although this is another option, participants often report that they don't know where to start when thinking about Family Income, and the categories may provide some guidance for them, although Schwarz (1999) would undoubtedly favor the open-ended question approach.

As with every part of your project, you need to keep in mind the characteristics of your population that may influence their ability to complete your study in an accurate way. A central issue is whether they understand what information you are requesting. When in doubt, ask beforehand. Do a small pilot study. As mentioned in Chapter 2, a pilot study is a study where you test out the effectiveness of your manipulations or measures on a small number of participants.

Creating Your Own Scale: Item Format

In the scale on precautionary measures that I developed (Devlin, 2000), participants were asked to "Rate the likelihood that you would take these steps on a scale ranging from 1 (not at all likely to do that) to 5 (definitely likely to do that)" for each of the 19 behaviors in the scale (e.g., avoid eye contact with strangers). Beyond content, there are issues of format to consider when you develop your own scale. Among the issues to consider are the number of anchors and the stem itself.

In general, using 5 to 7 anchor points works well. When there are too few points (e.g., 3), you may not get enough of a distribution to reveal group differences that exist. When there are too many points (e.g., 12), people's responses tend to become unreliable because there are too many choices. From 5 to 7 choices also matches what is known about the limitations of human information processing (Miller, 1956). People can assimilate from 5 to 7 points of information.

Odd or even? What's the difference between giving a respondent 5 or 6 choice points? An odd number of choice points provides the opportunity for a middle or neutral response. If people genuinely feel neutral about the question you are asking; that is, they feel neither positive nor negative, or neither agree nor disagree with a statement on a 5-point scale, then it may make sense to provide them with that option. Such an option requires an odd number of choices.

In the case of 6 points, you are either on one side or the other; if you want to force their choice to the positive or negative side, or to agree or disagree, an even number of options may be the route you want to take.

The stem itself. The stem is the part of the question that presents the question's content. Consider the following options:

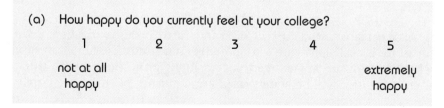

(b)   How do you currently feel at your college?

1	2	3	4	5
not at all happy				extremely happy

What is the difference? The first example "leads" the witness or has embedded in it an implicit assumption (that you do, in fact, feel some degree of happiness at the college). The second example does not lead; the anchors provide the options. The first example has a kind of demand characteristic; the participant reading it may think that the researcher *seeks* a report of happiness.

Pilot testing. I always recommend that you pilot-test any questions you have written. Test them on a sample of people who are like your participants. If you are using college students, run a pilot test of college students. Take into account whatever feedback the people in your pilot test give you. Revise accordingly. If the members of the pilot test don't understand, have questions, or point out errors or problems, fix them! Don't assume that participants will understand the meaning of a word as *you* understand it. Remember where we began the chapter; the more abstract a concept (like leadership or charisma), the more difficult it is to measure, and the more variable its interpretation.

● ●
REFLECT AND REVIEW

Explain what Schwarz sees as the advantages to questions with open-ended response formats.

● ●
APPLY YOUR KNOWLEDGE

Draft your own demographic questions to assess: class year, geographic upbringing, and political orientation.

Fees

A second reason students on occasion turn to designing their own measures is cost. There are a good many commonly used measures for which fees for use are charged. Increasingly, professionals who think their measures may be widely used are requiring payment for copies of the questionnaires and surveys, answer keys, scoring templates, and so on. There are a number of publishers of measures used in research and assessment. Some examples include Mind Garden (www .mindgarden. com), EdITS (www.edits.net), Psychological Assessment Resources (www.parinc.com), and Consulting Psychologists Press, now CPP (www.cpp.com/company/index.asp).

Among other instruments, EdITS publishes a number of personality measures, including the Comrey Personality Scales (CPS), 180 items that measure eight personality dimensions plus two validity scales. According to EdITS, the CPS is appropriate to assess "normal socially functioning individuals" and is "useful in educational and business settings" (EdITS, 2000, p. 8). The test is reported to take 35–50 minutes. A package of 25 reusable test booklets is $23.00. A packet of 50 hand-scoring answer sheets is $15.00, a package of 50 profile sheets is $13.00, the manual and handbook of interpretations is $25.75, and so on (price information retrieved from www.edits.net/CPS.html on 7/23/04). You can see the dimensions of cost related to the size of your study. Several times a year, EdITS publishes a newsletter describing updates about its offerings, research using the measures it publishes, and so on.

Another publisher with products such as the State-Trait Anxiety Questionnaire, the Ways of Coping Questionnaire, and the Bem Sex Role Inventory, among others, is Mind Garden (Mind Garden, 2001 also www.mindgarden.com). Let's take the Bem as an example. The Bem Sex Role Inventory (BSRI) is a widely used measure that assesses the degree to which men and women endorse masculine, feminine, androgynous, or undifferentiated gender role characteristics. A Manual/Sampler Set is $30 and a Duplication Set is $120. With this $120 purchase, you can reproduce the instrument (a maximum of 150 copies) for personal and non-commercial use for one year (information retrieved 7/23/04).

Other well-known sources of tests include Psychological Assessment Resources (PAR), which publishes such widely used measures as the NEO PI-R, a measure of personality by Costa and McCrae (1992), and Consulting Psychologists Press (CPP), which offers many measures in organizational development and career planning. CPP offers such measures as the Maslach Burnout Inventory, which assesses the stress people feel in their human service and educational jobs, and the Position Analysis Questionnaire, which identifies job components and their importance.

If you look in the catalogues of firms that produce and charge for testing materials, there is usually a statement regarding the use of tests for research. If you write or e-mail the company and outline your proposed study, you may receive permission to use the test for a reduced fee. If the test is copyrighted and published in a test catalogue, the best course of action is to write to the publisher and request permission to use a given test in research. I also recommend that you contact the author of the scale directly, who may provide you with the scale without any charge.

Qualifications for Use

In addition to lack of an adequate measure and cost, the third factor that may push you to design your own measure is your lack of qualification to use an existing measure. For example, in the PAR catalogue (2003), each measure has an associated Qualification Level. The NEO PI-R, for example, is listed as requiring Qualification Level B or S. Qualification Level B, the less stringent of the two, requires a degree in psychology, counseling, or a closely related field from a four-year college or university that is accredited. In addition, the user must have coursework in test interpretation, psychometrics, educational statistics, or closely related areas. As you can see, undergraduates could not use such measures on their own. In certain circumstances, a student's professor may purchase the materials and supervise the student in the use of the materials, as might happen in the case of an honors thesis or advanced Individual Study. It is important for you and your faculty adviser to sit down and go over the measures you want to use and their appropriateness given your level of education.

If you want to read more about the ethical issues surrounding test use and professional standards, consider work by Eyde (Eyde, Moreland, & Robertson, 1988; Eyde & Primoff, 1992; Eyde, Robertson, Krug, Moreland, Robertson et al., 1994), the American Educational Research Association (1999), Bersoff (2003), and Robertson (1992).

The Resource Guide at the end of the chapter provides a list of commonly used measures and their sources.

• •

SUMMARY

This chapter has given you the tools you need to identify and select existing measures that you might use in your research. You now know the criteria for selection such as internal consistency, length, and difficulty. You also know the logical places to look for measures, including journal articles, your department resources, the author of a given scale, and test publishers. If the need arises, you can also even create your own scale and calculate its Cronbach's alpha. Further, you know Schwarz's (1999) recommendations for the construction of questions and response choices and you can write sound demographic items.

APPLY YOUR KNOWLEDGE QUESTIONS

In the event that you did not have time to do them earlier, here is the list of APPLY YOUR KNOWLEDGE questions in this chapter. Try them now:

1. Skim two or three articles in social science journals in the library to see the range of Cronbach's alphas reported in the articles.

2. In your own college library, locate a book that contains measures for use in social science research.

3. Draft your own demographic questions to assess: class year, geographic upbringing, and political orientation.

WEB RESOURCES

There are a number of research methods workshops on the web that may enhance your knowledge of the topics in this chapter. Here is a list of these workshops and their web address:

Reliability and Validity

Specifying Constructs

Surveys

Designing a Survey

www.wadsworth.com/psychology_d/templates/
student_resources/workshops/resch_wrk.html

Resource Guide to Commonly Used Measures

General Sources of Measures

These directories and source books provide the names of measures, a description, and their sources.

Directory of Unpublished Experimental Measures (Vols. 1–3) (Goldman & Mitchell, 1996).

Encyclopedia of Psychological Assessment (Vols. 1 & 2) (Fernandez-Ballesteros, 2003).

Measures for Clinical Practice: A Sourcebook (3rd ed.). Vol. 1: Couples, Families, and Children (Corcoran & Fischer, 2000).

Measures for Clinical Practice: A Sourcebook (3rd ed.). Vol. 2: Adults (Corcoran & Fischer, 2000).

Practitioner's Guide to Empirically Based Measures of Anxiety (Antony, Orsillo, & Roemer, 2001).

Practitioner's Guide to Empirically Based Measures of Depression (Nezu, McClure, Ronan, & Meadows, 2000).

Test Critiques Compendium (Keyser & Sweetland, 1987).

Fees: General Note. In all instances where there is a statement that fees are charged, you may want to contact the author to see if it is possible to use the scale without charge.

Personality and Clinical Psychology

NEO PI-R. Five major domains of personality are measured (Costa & McCrae, 1992); 240 items. Fee charged. Available from Psychological Assessment Resources, Inc.; evaluator must meet APA guidelines.

NEO Five Factory Inventory. Shortened version of the NEO PI-R; consists of 60 items that measure the five domains of adult personality; openness, conscientiousness, extraversion, agreeableness, and neuroticism (Costa & McCrae, 1991). Fee charged. Available from Psychological Assessment Resources, Inc.; evaluator must meet APA guidelines.

Big Five Inventory. Another standard measure of personality (John, Donahue, & Kentle, 1991). Contact the authors.

Rosenberg Self-Esteem Scale. Measures self-esteem with a 10-item scale (Rosenberg, 1965, 1979). Available from the author.

Moos Family Environment Scale. Measures 10 dimensions of family environments using 90 items (Moos & Moos, 1994). Fee charged (Consulting Psychologists Press, Inc.).

Beck Depression Inventory. Assesses the level of depression in an individual; 21 items (Beck, 1978). Contact Dr. Aaron Beck's office (215-898-4100 or marinell@mail.med.upenn.edu) for research-related questions and to ask permission to use the scales in research.

Zuckerman Sensation Seeking Scale. Assesses the degree to which people seek stimulation (Zuckerman, Kolin, Price, & Zoob, 1964; Zuckerman & Link, 1968).

Multiple Affect Adjective Check List (MAACL-Revised). Anxiety, depression, and hostility are measured using 132 items. Can be used in terms of Today or In General (Zuckerman & Lubin, 1965). Fee charged (EdITS/Educational and Industrial Testing Service).

The State-Trait Anxiety Inventory (STAI). The STAI is a frequently used measure to assess anxiety in adults; 40 questions (Spielberger, Gorsuch, & Lushene, 1970). Fee charged. Available through Mind Garden.

Profile of Mood States (POMS & POMS Short Form). The POMS uses 65 adjectives to measure dimensions of affect or mood (McNair, Lorr, & Droppleman, 1992). Fee charged. Available through EdITS.

Sixteen Personality Factor Questionnaire (16PF). This is a comprehensive profile of personality with 16 main scales (Cattell, Eber, & Tatsuoka, 1970). Fee charged. Available through EdITS; appropriate qualifications required.

Hassles and Uplifts (HSUP). HSUP measures respondents' attitudes about daily situations defined as hassles and uplifts (Lazarus & Folkman, 1989). Fee charged. Available through Mind Garden.

Spence and Helmreich Attitude Toward Women (ATW)-Short Version. This 25-item measure assesses individuals' attitudes toward women (Spence, Helmreich, & Stapp, 1973). Available in the article.

Eysenck Personality Inventory (EPI). The EPI has 57 questions, which measure extraversion-introversion and neuroticism-stability. There is also a Lie Scale to help determine which respondents are answering in a socially desirable manner (Eysenck & Eysenck, 1968). Fee charged. Available through EdITS; appropriate qualifications required.

Social Psychology

The Bem Sex Role Inventory (BSRI). Developed by Sandra Bem (1974); commonly used measure to assess gender roles. Sixty items (40 scored) assess masculinity, femininity, androgyny, and undifferentiation. Fee charged. Available through Mind Garden.

Marlowe-Crowne Social Desirability Scale (M-C SDS). Scale with 33 items commonly used to assess whether participants have a tendency to respond in a socially desirable manner (Crowne & Marlowe, 1960). Available in the article.

Balanced Inventory of Desirable Responding (BIDR) Version 6 – Form 40. There are two subscales: self-deceptive positivity and impression management. A person who exhibits self-deceptive positivity will give reports that are honest, but exaggerated in a positive direction (Paulhus, 1991). Consult the article.

Self-Efficacy Scale. This 30-item measure, with two subscales (general self-efficacy and social self-efficacy) assesses expectations about self-efficacy independent of specific situations. Contact the lead author (Sherer, Maddox, Mercandante, Prentice-Dunn, Jacobs, & Rogers, 1982).

Social Avoidance and Distress Scale (SAD). The 28-item scale measures anxiety in social situations. Available in the journal article (Watson & Friend, 1969).

South Oaks Gambling Screen (SOGS). The primary use of this 20-item scale is to identify pathological gamblers (Lesieur & Blume, 1987). Available from the authors.

Modern Racism Scale. Seven items measure overt racism (McConahay, 1986). Available from the author.

Implicit Association Test. A computer-implemented reaction time test to assess implicit racism (Greenwald, McGhee, & Schwartz, 1998). Available online at: https://implicit.harvard.edu/implicit

Athletic Identity Measurement Scale (AIMS). Ten items measure the degree to which an individual possesses an athletic self-concept (Brewer, Van Raalte, & Linder, 1993). Contact the lead author.

Kenyon's Attitude Toward Physical Activity Inventory. In a revised version (Mathes & Battista, 1985), nine dimensions of attitudes toward physical activity are assessed. Consult Mathes and Battista's article.

University Residence Environment Scale (URES). Ten dimensions are used to assess the social climate of university residence halls (Gerst & Moos, 1972; Smail, DeYoung, & Moos, 1974). Fee charged. Available through Mind Garden.

Parental Authority Questionnaire. Sixty-item survey (30 per parent); scale measures parental authority from the child's point of view (Bari, 1991). Contact the author.

Core Alcohol and Drug Survey. This 22-item measure assesses alcohol and drug use and is widely employed in research with college students (Presley, Meilman, & Lyerla, 1993). Fee charged. Available from the Core Institute.

Women's Issues

Body Esteem Scale. Twenty-four items assess body esteem (Mendelson & White, 1982); can be used with children. Available in the article.

Body Shape Questionnaire. Thirty-four items assess satisfaction with one's body shape (Cooper, Taylor, Cooper, & Fairburn, 1987). Contact the authors.

Eating Disorder Inventory (EDI). Eight subscales, 64 items, can be used to differentiate those with normal dieting behaviors from those with severe disorders (Garner, Olmsted, & Polivy, 1983). Fee charged (Psychological Assessment Resources, Inc.).

Eating Attitudes Test (EAT). This 40-item test is used to assess behaviors indicative of anorexia nervosa (Garner & Garfinkel, 1997). Contact the authors.

Eating Attitudes Test (EAT-26). Shorter version of the 40-item EAT, this 26-item test is used to assess and diagnose eating disorders (Garner, Olmstead, Bohr, & Garfinkel, 1982). Fee charged. Available from Psychological Assessment Resources.

Figure Preference Rating Scale. People's feelings about their body shape and size and their attitudes toward eating are measured using drawings of figures that people rate (which body shape you want to look like, which one you think the opposite sex finds attractive, etc.) (Furnham & Baguma, 1994). Contact the authors.

Menstrual Joy Questionnaire. This questionnaire (Delaney, Lupton, & Toth, 1987) consists of 10 questions about positive experiences related to menstruation. Contact the authors.

Moos Menstrual Distress Questionnaire (MDQ). Characteristics of a woman's menstrual cycle are assessed on eight factors using 47 symptoms (Moos, 1968). Fee charged (Western Psychological Services).

Menstrual Attitudes Questionnaire. Developed by Brooks-Gunn and Ruble (1980), this questionnaire is divided into five subscales and contains 33 items. Contact the authors.

The Sociocultural Attitudes Toward Appearance Questionnaire (SATAQ). This 14-item measure assesses familiarity with the ideal of being thin and the degree to which that ideal is endorsed (Heinberg, Thompson, & Stormer, 1995). Contact the authors.

Health Psychology

Multidimensional Health Locus of Control (MHLC). The scale contains three dimensions of health behavior that measure the beliefs one has about control of one's health. The three subscales (six items each) are Internality of Health Locus of Control, Powerful Other Locus of Control, and Chance Locus of Control (Wallston, Wallston, & DeVellis, 1978). Contact the authors.

Animal Behavioral Measures

The following list gives some commonly used measures in behavioral neuroscience. The best way to learn about these measures is to contact the professor in your department who conducts research in behavioral neuroscience. As is true of research with human participants (see Chapter 5), research with animals must be approved by the official group on your campus that monitors the use of animals in research. This monitoring group is often called the Institutional Animal Care and Use Committee (IACUC).

Tail Flick Measure of Pain Sensitivity

Morris Water Maze Test for Spatial Memory

Elevated Plus-Maze Test of Anxiety

Social Interaction Test of Anxiety

Forced Swim Test for Depression

Rotorod Test of Motor Coordination

Obtaining Your Subjects

4

Never Appear on Stage with Animals or Children

Introduction and Chapter Overview

An old vaudeville axiom, sometimes attributed to W. C. Fields, suggests that one should never appear on stage with animals or children. A word to the wise: students who have but one semester to devise, conduct, and write up a research project should generally avoid using children (or animals) as subjects!

Obtaining participants for your study is a challenge, whether you are using a departmental subject pool, a convenience sample on campus, or people in the surrounding community. This chapter deals with recommendations for the types of approaches that typically work in recruiting participants. As you read in Chapter 1, as a college student you are advised to focus on topics within your domain of experience and to enlist the participation of those who can provide the answers. Most often, those people will be other college students.

In addition to explaining how to recruit other college students from department subject pools, this chapter discusses doing research in the field and using **vulnerable populations.** Vulnerable populations are populations for whom extra care about participants' rights must be exercised. Examples include children, prisoners, and fetuses. Research with vulnerable populations and research in the field both present a challenge for a one-semester research project.

Ethical and practical issues associated with incentives for participation, including monetary compensation, are also discussed. The chapter ends with a series of 12 tips for conducting research in the field. The tips, labeled "Dustin's Dozen," are recommendations from a graduate student who had great success recruiting participants in the field, from train stations to laundromats.

Once You Have Your Idea, Then What?

Once you have formulated your research idea, there are a number of steps that you will perform in parallel. These include obtaining your measures or apparatus, refining your procedure, and obtaining your participants. Each of these is important, but the one that seems least within the researcher's control at times is obtaining participants. No one is required to participate in research (see Chapter 5 for a discussion of the ethics of research participation and the Institutional Review Board process). Given the voluntary nature of research participation, you may need repeated attempts to obtain a sufficient number of participants to test your hypothesis(es). Assuming for the moment that you are in a college environment, there are typically a number of options open to you.

As was discussed in Chapter 1 on developing ideas for research, it makes sense to conduct a study that is related to something you are interested in and with which you may have some experience. Topics that lend themselves to research by college students include family relationships, achievement, adjustment, developmental issues, dating, and so on. College students also make excellent participants for research on perception and cognition, and they certainly are ideal for research involving advances in technology and use of the Internet.

It makes little sense to do research on topics for which college students are a substitute rather than the target population itself. For example, consider resume studies about hiring people with particular qualifications, where the college students put themselves in the shoes of the potential employer. Although there may be reasons you would design a study that did use college students to review applicant qualifications (e.g., to examine what qualifications college students think employers seek), you would not want the students to be substitutes for a population beyond your grasp (e.g., Fortune 500 employers).

Subject Pools

Many undergraduate colleges and universities, even those without graduate programs in psychology, have subject pools (Landrum & Chastain, 1999). These pools are established to provide participants for the research projects done by faculty, honors thesis students, and others doing research in a psychology department. Often the pools are composed of students in courses where there is a requirement of participation in research (or an alternative activity). Although these subject pools exist, Sieber (1999) points out that they have been "grandfathered" in from a regulatory standpoint and would not in all likelihood comply with federal regulations if proposed today. That is, there is an inherent antagonism between the idea of voluntary participation and a requirement of participation for course credit. As Sieber (1999) points out, the alternatives to research participation need to be appealing if they are really going to qualify as genuine alternatives. Among the appealing alternatives she cites are watching a movie or a demonstration. Unfortunately from the students' perspective, it is far more common to hear about writing a short paper as an alternative (Sieber, 1999). Perhaps instructors fear that if the alternative is too attractive, students will be less inclined to participate in research projects! The participants in the subject pools are usually students in the introductory psychology course who are required to take part in a certain number of projects (or project hours) or in alternatives to research to complete the course (see Chapter 5 for a discussion about the ethics of subject pools).

Formal guidelines exist to help the researcher make decisions about appropriate steps to protect subjects who participate as a result of a course requirement. The American Psychological Association's Code of Conduct (American Psychological Association, 2002) states, "When research participation is a course requirement or an opportunity for extra credit, the prospective participant is given the choice of equitable alternative activities" (Principle 8.04b, p. 1069). Researchers must also "protect the prospective participants from adverse consequences of declining or withdrawing from participation" (8.04a, p. 1069). Further, Principle 8.06(a) of the APA code (p. 1070) states, "Psychologists make reasonable efforts to avoid offering excessive or inappropriate financial or other inducements for research participation when such inducements are likely to coerce participation." It would be inappropriate to require a 15-page paper as an alternative to an hour of research participation or to lower students' grades if they did not participate in research (e.g., by awarding more credit for research participation than for alternative activities). Also, when extra credit is given for participation, some reasonable upper bound needs to be established so that students are not participating merely to offset poor performance in another part of the course (a kind of grade coercion).

How Subject Pools Function

There are a number of different ways in which subject pools are run. Some departments allot research hours at the beginning of a semester and may give the student doing a research methods project (who is low on the totem pole) very few if any of the total number of hours available. The largest numbers of hours are typically allotted to those higher up on the list (i.e., faculty and graduate students). In other departments, subject pool hours are allocated as they are requested, but there is also a limit on the total number of subject hours someone can have (as a percentage of all of the hours available). Usually there is a Subject Pool Coordinator whose job it is to determine the number of hours that will be available and communicate with those who request the hours about the extent to which these requests can be met.

Due to the increasing demand for research participants and the inability of the introductory psychology subject pool to meet all the needs, especially at small colleges, some departments have moved to a system where courses beyond the introductory sequence also require research participation or offer extra credit for research participation. In my own department, there are times when we restrict the introductory psychology subject pool to faculty, graduate students, and honors thesis students because of the large number of research proposals from those constituents. When that restriction occurs, we use a second research bulletin board that is open to students in other classes (e.g., methods classes, social psychology) who need participants for research. To earn extra credit, students in other classes can participate in this second pool. If, near the end of the semester, there are not enough projects for the introductory psychology students to meet their course requirements through the primary subject pool, they can then participate in the projects of students in other courses that are listed on this secondary board.

The Timing of Your Request

There often seems to be a mismatch between the timing of students who seek to fulfill their research hours and students who seek participants to complete their studies. Often, the mismatch forms an inverted U-shaped curve. In the beginning of the semester, when the researchers are not yet organized, there may be students who want to fulfill their hours but have few projects to select. Then, near the end of the semester, when most researchers have obtained their subjects, there may be students who still have research hours to fulfill and, again, few projects available. On occasion I have also seen the opposite circumstance at the end of the semester: many student projects (especially from the research methods course), and few introductory psychology students with research hours left to complete. Therefore, if you are going to use the subject pool, it is wise to post your request well before mid-semester and also to avoid the period around major vacations or breaks (e.g., Thanksgiving in the fall; spring break in the second term). Moreland (1999) notes that in his experience most students wait until the end of the semester to complete their research hours and also comments that few people seem to participate around vacations (or mid-terms). In the data he has kept, about 9% of the students use some alternatives to satisfy the research credit requirement.

Beyond the pragmatic reasons for starting early, there may be reasons for an early start that are related to the quality of your data. Some studies indicate that those who participate late as opposed to early in the semester have different personality characteristics, for example more exhibitionism (see Landrum & Chastain, 1999, for a review).

Advertising/Pitching Your Research and Setting an Appropriate Tone

Are there more and less successful ways to ask students to participate in your research, particularly if these are students-at-large rather than those in the subject pool? Yes. First of all, avoid being a beggar (the "please-help-me-I-won't-graduate-otherwise" approach). You can grab students' attention and interest by focusing on the content of the research with a topic such as "Students' Internet use and academic achievement" or "Athletic participation and college adjustment." Whatever your chosen topic, you can appeal to the students' interest in contributing to a body of knowledge.

Doing research is hard work, especially when you collect data in person. You want your participants to take it as seriously as you do. *You* set the tone for the research subject to approach the task with the seriousness it deserves. Sometimes behaving in a professional manner is a problem for student researchers who are interacting with their peers. But if this professional tone is not established, how valid are the data that are collected? Martin (1985, pp. 186–187) suggests that the researcher be present, prompt, prepared, polite, private (regarding the data), and professional. This is good advice, and we might invoke the golden rule of researchers: Do unto participants as you would have other experimenters do unto you!

Sensitive Topics

There are particular issues that surround research on sensitive topics such as sexuality (Wiederman, 1999), and adolescent sexual behavior is a topic of interest to college students doing research. For example, at a recent psychology conference that our department sponsored, there were a number of projects that focused on the topic of sexuality. One in particular, "Sexual behaviors relating to attitudes, contraception, drug use, religion, relationships, gender, attractiveness, and fear of STDs and pregnancy at Connecticut College over three decades" (Schon, 2003), was the fourth in a series of studies done on sexuality at Connecticut College, begun by Professor Bernard Murstein over 20 years ago (Murstein, Chalpin, Heard, & Vyse, 1989; Murstein & Holden, 1979; Murstein & Mercy, 1994).

With regard to sensitive topics such as sexuality, the problem with alerting participants to the topic of the research at the recruiting stage is that subjects may self-select, lending bias to the sample. Wiederman (1999) describes a process in which participants are not initially alerted to the focus of the research until they appear for the study. Potential participants are then given the opportunity to withdraw and find an alternative if they do not wish to participate. Those who do not participate are given 30 minutes of credit, the minimum at his institution for participants who travel to the test site. To avoid the possibility of coercion at this point, because people may feel pressure not to admit that the topic bothers them, they are informed that they can behave as if they were filling out the questionnaire, and then turn it in blank when they leave the test site. The anonymity of the questionnaires protects their choice (i.e., to fill it out or leave it blank). Using this process, he reports that only about 1% of the students either leave the site or submit a blank questionnaire. Another approach to sensitive topics such as sexual behavior is to use a randomly distributed mail survey to college students, but again, people may discard the questionnaire if they find the topic objectionable.

Keeping Track and Planning Ahead

With as many as 30 projects going on in a given week, participants may have difficulty remembering where a given project is taking place (and when). Some departments have a book of projects that is kept by the department secretary or administrative assistant. All researchers log in their projects (and project titles) in this book, and students who have forgotten where they are supposed to be (which room in the building or on campus) can check in the log.

The department secretary or administrative assistant is also usually helpful in telling students the process for (1) reserving rooms to collect data, (2) ordering equipment that may be necessary (e.g., document projector, LCD projector), and (3) photocopying materials (he/she often knows whether the campus print shop is cheaper than Staples or Kinko's). For that reason, it is also important to plan ahead for "disaster" with regard to equipment and gaining access to locked rooms after hours. Also make sure that you understand how to use an LCD projector or its equivalent if you are using a computer to project material. With regard to equipment, have "extras" on hand. For example, if you are using a slide projector, have a second projector bulb. It is also helpful to conduct research at a time when campus media services technicians are available to help with malfunctioning computer equipment. Also, there are generally one or two faculty in a department who are particularly knowledgeable about technology, and it is a good idea to get to know them. In terms of entry to locked rooms, I have even written notes to the campus security force to request permission for a particular student researcher to be granted access to a data collection room if that room happens to be locked when the student arrives.

Credit slips. Students who participate in research for credit (either as a course requirement or for extra credit) typically need some verification of their participation. This verification is generally called the "credit slip." Ask your subject pool administrator if there is a form used by the department or develop your own if none is available. The credit slip should contain the following information: name of researcher, name of project, name of participant, and date and time of participation. The researcher then signs the credit slip and gives it to the student participant. It is also important for the researcher to have a "sign-in" sheet so that each student who participates in his/her experiment is accounted for, and the sheet provides a means of checking participation if questions arise later (e.g., a lost credit slip).

Departments also typically have a policy for no-shows (see next section). Often students who are no-shows are required to participate in a greater number of research hours (or alternative activities).

No-shows. As a researcher, it is exceedingly frustrating to schedule a session for 15 people and have only 9–10 (or fewer) appear. Estimates for no-shows range from about 10% to 24% (Butler, 1999). Butler conducted research to examine the reasons students are no-shows for studies. Among the reasons students cite for missing experiments are a lack of motivation, memory failure, conflict with another (important) activity, illness, and navigation (they could not find the room). The most frequently cited reason was forgetting.

One clear message that emerges from Butler's research is that reminding participants about their research appointments will help, and other studies support this recommendation (Butler, 1999). Butler reports that in a study of no-shows at area dentists' offices, patients who were reminded of their appointments with a telephone call had a significantly lower no-show rate (at 3%) than those who did not receive such a call (at 20%). In research with undergraduates using three conditions (mail, telephone, and control), those reminded by mail had a no-show rate of 14%, by telephone 12%, and in the control group, 28%.

Although these methods help reduce no-shows, a significant number of students cannot be reached through these methods, and Butler describes another approach that departments (researchers) may want to adopt. On the first day of classes where participants will be part of a subject pool, students are asked to provide their name, address, and telephone number on an index card. These cards are then alphabetized and kept by the departmental secretary. Researchers can use these cards to contact subjects ahead of time to reduce no-shows. Some large institutions, such as the University of Pittsburgh, even have subject pool hotlines, which participants can call if they are going to be late for a research project or have to cancel altogether (Moreland, 1999).

As a means to determine whether participants are being treated according to APA and other ethical guidelines, and to assess whether the research experience has been a meaningful one, departments often distribute forms that evaluate the researcher and the research experience. These forms include such questions as whether the participant was treated courteously, whether the project was explained in enough detail to permit the participant to make a decision about participating, whether the participant was debriefed, and whether the participant's questions were answered (see Sieber, 1999, pp. 53–54 for a list).

REFLECT AND REVIEW

How can you improve the data completion rate for participants who signed up for your research?

APPLY YOUR KNOWLEDGE

Find out if your department has a subject pool and, if so, how it functions.

The Ins and Outs of Data Collection

Where You Collect Data

In addition to asking students to come to laboratory or classroom spaces to complete research projects, students often solicit subjects in such places as the library and the student center. Many of our students have had very good success by setting up a table near the entrance to the library (in the main foyer) with a sign advertising their research project. The library staff permits this (and even provides the table), and such a location gives researchers access to all four class years. Often students want to take a break from their library work and are eager to think about something else for 15 minutes rather than the assignments they have due. A similar procedure (i.e., setting up a table) has been used with success in the student center near the entrance to student mailboxes. Activity areas or gathering places on your campus are probably good locations to collect data.

Scheduling/Time of Day, Days of Week

As students, if not professors, increasingly shrink the college week, with fewer classes taken or offered on Fridays (and certainly not Friday afternoons), researchers must determine the most effective and efficient times for collecting data. Researchers have to navigate around the other commitments subjects have, including sports, jobs, meals, day and evening classes, studying, and TNEs (i.e., Thursday night events/parties). Almost like the work week, Mondays and Fridays have problems with absenteeism, and student researchers are advised to concentrate on collecting data Tuesday through Thursday. Often, soliciting participants over a range of times is advisable to avoid a sampling bias. For example, if you schedule data collection for 4:30 in the afternoon during the spring semester, you will in all likelihood miss all student athletes who play spring sports. Most students with whom I have spoken find that offering a range of sessions at 4, 5, 6, and 7 p.m. over different days of the week covers most bases. Some students find that scheduling research sessions immediately following the end of introductory psychology labs works well. The lab students can simply remain in the room and complete the research session. Also, as discussed previously, the time of the semester in which one collects data makes a difference.

Attrition

In designing their studies, students should be aware that multiple sessions contain the possibility of attrition. When students have to return for follow-up sessions, either because it is part of the experimental design or because the questionnaires/materials are too long to complete at one sitting, the issue of attrition comes into play. Although we are focusing here on one-semester projects, consider the following longitudinal example (Devlin, 1996). This study examined the impact of a first-year student orientation, in the form of a camping trip that included outdoor challenges (e.g., rock climbing), on the formation of friendships throughout the college career. Data were collected at four points in time, before and after the camping-trip experience, at the end of the first year, and at the end of the fourth year. By the final point of data collection (the end of their senior year), 46.7% of the original sample did not return their surveys. Although approximately 10% were no longer available (i.e., had transferred, graduated early, or dropped out of college), this is a problem for the researcher because of the potential bias it creates.

Attrition is a serious problem in longitudinal studies (Miller & Wright, 1995), and attrition rates can be as high as 50% (Menard, 2002). Attrition results in "a potential threat of bias if those who drop out have unique characteristics such that the remaining sample ceases to be representative of the original sample" (Miller & Wright, 1995, p. 921). This is known as **attrition bias.** As longitudinal assessment may be a type of research design that is increasing in some areas (Goodman & Blum, 1996), it is important to monitor the effects of participant attrition. Although the statistical approaches to addressing attrition are beyond the scope of this book, the approaches one can take to avoiding attrition apply to many areas of participant recruitment and retention. Much of the advice researchers have given for longitudinal projects applies to the student's one-semester multiple session project.

Robles, Flaherty, and Day (1994) talk about the following tactics they used to engage participants in a study of the effects of prenatal substance use on pregnancy and infant outcome: telephone calls to establish rapport, letters, visits to the home, and a home assessment. They also included paid transportation and child care for siblings. They further employed such tangible incentives as a gift for participants' children near a holiday or an additional $5 to complete the interview. An incentive judged less tangible was telling the participant that the information in the study would contribute to a better understanding of child development. One of the clear themes in this approach is the importance of good communication, frequent contact, and trying to make participation in the project as easy as possible. These same principles can be adopted by student researchers. The authors also stress the important themes of respecting the participant and establishing trust.

In their research with the homeless mentally ill, Hough, Tarke, Renker, Shields, and Glatstein (1996) state "Recruitment and retention of research participants is a major concern in any mental health research concerned with outcomes of treatment or changes over time" (p. 881). They also offer advice that could be applied to student researchers. The themes they discuss in engaging this population are similar to those discussed previously: the approach must be client-centered, involving unconditional respect. Hough et al. provide a list of incentives that are used, beginning with interpersonal trust. They also list trust in the research team, appeals to altruism (producing information that may be useful), the novelty and interest of participating in research, and a number of other variables, including money. In addition to a modest cash payment of $10 or $20, food vouchers, cigarettes, a cup of coffee, or a sandwich "can help cement a relationship and encourage enrollment" (Hough et al., 1996, p. 884). Similar advice regarding respect and the importance of relationships is made by Coen, Patrick, and Shern (1996).

For retention itself, Hough et al. (1996) discuss **anchoring**, phone tracking, mail tracking, agency tracking, and field tracking. Of specific relevance here is the idea of anchoring. Anchoring means initially obtaining as much information as possible about the person's usual whereabouts, or the identity of those who would know about the person's whereabouts. Now this may seem unrelated to college student projects, but the similarity is the idea of obtaining the index card information we discussed earlier.

Another useful point comes from a study of healthy minority women in a longitudinal project (Gilliss et al., 2001). In discussing what approaches worked, the women who participated in the study said that what attracted them was the endorsement from trusted agencies, in particular their church and their child's school. The relevance here is finding someone and/or some agency or institution to endorse the project, and that is one reason why it is a good idea to have your sponsor's name and affiliation on the informed consent document (see Chapter 5 regarding informed consent documents).

In studies involving multiple research sessions, the student can thus look for advice to the procedures used in longitudinal research. Mason (1999) notes that the general rate of completion for [longitudinal] studies in clinical treatment is around 80%, with more attrition typically observed in studies involving youth. Mason provides a list of strategies for reducing attrition including creating a project identity (with logos, letterhead, etc.), creating meaningful networks among agencies (to help keep track of people), and rewarding participants consistently (he mentions that cash incentives are very effective in retaining participants). He also mentions the use of food, the convenience of the location, and the use of comfortable environments (such as a coffee shop). He recommends to start tracking early, using the simplest and most cost-effective methods of tracking first (e.g., telephone directories), and to keep follow-up interviews brief. With regard to student projects, there are a number of useful implications, including calling participants in advance of their research appointment (start tracking early), using a convenient location (such as a room in the centrally located library), and providing comfortable surroundings (a student lounge as opposed to a formal classroom).

REFLECT AND REVIEW

Which of the tactics for reducing attrition might apply even if you are not using multiple sessions or a longitudinal design?

Payment and the Ethics of Payment

Double Dipping

Typically, introductory subject pools have restrictions that do not permit payment for a number of reasons. One reason is that payment creates the situation known as "double dipping," where students receive credit *and* financial remuneration. Another problem is that paying students in the subject pool may set up a competition among researchers, and many student researchers may not be in a position

(1) to pay participants, or (2) to compete financially with faculty who may have research funds to pay participants.

For undergraduate research, there *may* be occasions where payment is necessary to solicit a sufficient number of participants. However, most departments still hold to the prohibition against double dipping, and participants must be sought from sources other than the subject pools. Projects for which payment may be appropriate usually involve multiple sessions so that the participants have to come back a number of times. I have also seen lotteries used successfully in these circumstances, so that participants who complete a given number of sessions are eligible for a drawing of a gift certificate to a local store. In a longitudinal study involving runners, Rudy, Estok, Kerr, and Menzel (1994) found that using money was more effective in retaining participants than were prizes imprinted with the study's logo.

Student researchers sometimes offer food (e.g., pizza, candy) as a token of appreciation for participation, but again, there is a difference between saying thank you for participating in this way vs. offering pizza as an incentive for participating (e.g., a signup poster that reads "There will be pizza if 15 people sign up for this session"). If students are participating for research credit, many departments prohibit offering what seem to be innocuous incentives such as food for recruiting purposes.

Ethical Concerns

Beyond the specific double-dipping problems involved with paying participants in the subject pool, more general ethical issues have been raised about paying individuals for participation in research. "The literature of research ethics contains only fragmentary analyses of moral guidelines for paying research subjects" (Ackerman, 1989, p. 1). "For decades, many investigators have paid subjects for participating in research studies, and this practice remains one of the most controversial methods of recruitment" (Dickert & Grady, 1999, p. 198). Although Dickert and Grady's statement applies more generally to clinical research, the payment of participants in any kind of research raises issues. "No consensus has emerged on when and in what manner it is ethical to pay subjects" (Dickert & Grady, 1999, p. 198). They point out that no mention of payment appears in the Federal Common Rule, the regulation that guides the review of research on human subjects (see Chapter 5 for a discussion of Human Subject Institutional Review Board issues). From the models of payment they review, the authors recommend the adoption of the wage payment model, which "operates on the notion that participation in research requires little skill but does require time, effort, and the endurance of undesirable or uncomfortable procedures. This model adopts the egalitarian position that subjects performing similar functions should be paid similarly" (Dickert & Grady, 1999, p. 199). It is also important to recognize that when individuals participate under circumstances when they are financially compensated, there is a real possibility that the sample will be biased (that is, payment may differentially attract participants).

Some research involves substantial payments, with the sums increasing the further out the research extends (Sullivan, Rumptz, Campbell, Eby, & Davidson, 1996). In a study of low-income women who had experienced some type of abuse, each woman was paid $10 for her initial interview, with increasing sums for the 6-, 12-, and 18-month follow-ups, culminating in a $100 payment for the 24-month follow-up. Financial remuneration is also common in research on the mentally ill homeless (Hough et al., 1996). "In research on HMI populations, it is generally accepted that cash payment is a very important incentive" (Hough et al., 1996, p. 884).

In general, this issue of payment is most often discussed in terms of clinical research, and one of the real concerns is that people will be persuaded to take risks (e.g., participate in clinical drug trials) they otherwise might not choose because remuneration is involved. "Concern about payment focuses on the voluntariness condition" (Ackerman, 1989, p. 1). Ackerman (1989) notes that some writers recommend the limitation of remuneration to incidental expenses like travel, in the process limiting the likelihood that someone will participate simply because of the possibility of profit. Macklin (1989) also makes the point that withholding payment until the end of a study may be coercive, because the participant's feeling of freedom to withdraw from the research may be compromised.

Payment raises a number of problematic issues, and research indicates that participants themselves may not support payment (Russell, Moralejo, & Burgess, 2000). In particular, the participants took a dim view of participation that was specifically presented as an incentive, as opposed to compensation for what were considered more legitimate reasons such as travel expenses, injury, and payment for time and effort (the idea of the wage model suggested by Dickert and Grady, 1999). In their recommendation, Russell et al. make some suggestions based on the comments of their participants, in particular the notion that recognition for time and effort may be appropriate, and that this recognition need not be financial. "Less than 45% of the subjects in this study, unpaid volunteers, agreed with paying research participants" (Russell et al., 2000, p. 130). Thus, whether dealing with introductory students or participants in clinical drug trials, payment for participation in research is a hotly debated issue.

Other Ways to Obtain College Students

Introductory psychology students tend to be first- or second-year students, and the research you have proposed may require all four classes or some other student characteristic or student body representativeness that is not possible to obtain through a subject pool. There are a number of options at this point.

Campus Newsletters or Daily Postings

If your campus has a newsletter or other form of communication (either paper or computer based), it may also be possible to place an ad there.

Campus Groups

Another successful way of obtaining subjects may be to approach a campus office (e.g., the Office of Student Life) to see if personnel in the office might support your research, or at least facilitate it. As an example, one of my students was interested in the relationship between residence hall vandalism, substance use, residence hall climate, gender, and athletic participation. These are topics of interest to Student Life administrators, and they permitted him to piggyback his survey onto the administration of the Core Alcohol and Drug Survey (Presley, Meilman, & Lyerla, 1993), which student life personnel were already planning to ask students to fill out at residence hall meetings. Out of an on-campus population of 1,514 that semester, his study yielded 688 usable questionnaires, and the respondents were representative of the campus at large in terms of gender and class year (see Brown & Devlin, 2003). Again, it pays to make early inquiry of campus offices about any potential survey projects that might offer the opportunity for students to piggyback their research.

Mail Surveys

Students who distribute surveys by mail may do so in a number of different ways. If a researcher wanted to sample a quarter of the student population, he or she might target every fourth name in the student directory, for example. Some campus post office policies permit students to stuff student mailboxes themselves. If this approach is not possible, you might be able to obtain mailing labels for every fourth student from the campus office that handles student records. You could then affix the labels with the students' names and post office box numbers to your surveys and have the post office staff stuff the mailboxes. Surveys addressed by name may be more likely to be read rather than immediately discarded. Investigate what the campus post office distribution policies are at your institution.

Many students use the campus mail to distribute their surveys. I can remember that in the early 1990s, before our department emphasized student research as much as it currently does, a research project that used the vehicle of campus mail might have a fairly good return rate. But without taking the kinds of steps recommended by writers such as Dillman (2000), a high return rate is unlikely today. During the spring semester at our institution, when the research methods students are doing their data collection projects, the student post office is often littered with discarded questionnaires that students dump in the wastebasket (or even on the floor). What steps can be taken to increase the return rates for mail surveys?

Consistent with our theme of communication, the cover letter is critical in convincing someone, especially a stranger or a student you don't know, to complete and return your survey (Dillman, 2000; Leong & Austin, 1996). The cover letter should stress (1) the importance of the research, (2) an explanation of how the recipient was selected (randomly or otherwise), and (3) a description of the privacy of the recipient's responses (e.g., whether the survey is anonymous or the steps being taken to protect the confidentiality of the respondent) (Leong & Austin, 1996).

Return rates and reminders. A minimal procedure described by Leong and Austin (1996) involves sending out your survey with an informative cover letter and, if you are mailing off campus, a postage-paid addressed return envelope. This mailing is followed two weeks later by a postcard, which is sent to everyone, thanking participants if they have already returned the questionnaire and urging them to do so if they have not. Many students will be conducting their research on a campus where mailing costs can be avoided, but they can still use the informative cover letter, an addressed return envelope, and a reminder card. In a meta-analysis of incentives used for mail surveys, Church (1993) reports that providing the incentives (either monetary or nonmonetary) upfront leads to greater participation than waiting until the research is concluded.

On college campuses, the mail survey may make more sense than the telephone survey in terms of protecting the identity of respondents. Dillman (2000) emphasizes that distributing surveys and responding to them involves social exchange theory, and that the "actions of individuals are motivated by the return these actions are expected to bring, and in fact usually do bring, from others" (p. 14). He argues that rewards, costs, and trust are critical to the success of the endeavor. The **tailored design method** he describes evolved from an earlier approach (TDM; total design method), which was essentially a one-size-fits-all approach to survey design and administration. In the tailored design method, the "tailoring" involves the approach to "survey sponsorship, population, and content" (p. 26). Dillman's (2000) book is an excellent resource for students who plan to send out mail surveys.

Internet Surveys and Software

Internet surveys are an increasingly popular form of collecting data, and there are a number of different approaches one can take. Some of these approaches restrict themselves to the student's campus environment or to known e-mail lists or discussion groups. Others create a website to which people can go to participate in an experiment. An example of such a site is the widely used Implicit Association Test (IAT) formerly at Yale and now located at Harvard and called Project Implicit (https://implicit.harvard.edu/implicit). This test measures the association of target concepts with an evaluative attribute (e.g., flowers vs. insects/pleasant and unpleasant) and has been used to examine a wide variety of emotionally charged issues such as racial attitudes and attitudes toward obese individuals. The home page of University of Washington Professor Anthony Greenwald, one of the developers of the IAT, (http://faculty.washington.edu/agg/iat_materials.htm), provides implicit association test material and a variety of other useful links to this line of research.

Although the technological details involving e-mail and Web-based surveys are beyond the scope of this book, there are a variety of excellent resources you might consult, including a chapter in Dillman (2000) and an entire volume by Birnbaum (2000).

Companies that provide software to create your own online surveys are proliferating, and a number of these companies offer affordable packages for student (and faculty) use. For example, a number of students and administrators at my institution have used SurveyMonkey (www.surveymonkey.com) to create Internet surveys that are e-mailed to students. SurveyMonkey is considered an inexpensive and straightforward approach to online surveys. It has a number of features including tracking who has responded to the survey so that e-mail reminders can be sent only to the non-respondents. The user interface is considered to be straightforward and easy to use. The current fee charged by SurveyMonkey is $19.95/month. For that amount, you get up to 1,000 responses per month, an unlimited number of surveys, and an unlimited number of questions. There is even a "Basic" subscription that is free, but it is limited to 10 questions and 100 responses per survey, although that level of feedback may be sufficient for some student projects. On its website, SurveyMonkey lists 34 software competitors, and how SurveyMonkey compares to each in terms of pricing and features.

Although these e-mail and Web-based approaches are attractive, they have some drawbacks that need to be recognized. Among the attractions are lower costs associated with paper, postage, data entry, and so on. The Internet also opens up the possibility of international respondents, and the time to respond is also significantly less than using snail mail surveys (Dillman, 2000). But at the same time, Dillman also states, ". . . the security and confidentiality issues associated with electronic technologies raise entirely new issues of trust that must be considered, but have not been adequately addressed by researchers" (Dillman, 2000, p. 353). A number of fundamental points are made by Dillman and others including the question of sample representativeness and response bias (Dillman, 2000; Lenert & Skoczen, 2002). Some very elderly individuals notwithstanding, certain age groups such as the elderly, and racial groups such as minorities, are less likely to participate in electronic research (E-research). It has also been noted that the Web-based approach, although convenient in many respects such as scoring, is not always superior in completion rates (Cronk & West, 2002).

Dillman (2000) discusses a number of problems dealing with the representativeness of data one may get from Internet-based surveys. One problem is that a relatively small percentage of the U.S. population has computers. Although the number is increasing rapidly, the distribution of computers across the population is by no means random. Dillman states ". . . there is no possibility for listing general populations and drawing a sample in which nearly every adult in the U. S. population has a known nonzero chance of being selected for participation in a survey" (p. 355). For this reason, it would be a mistake to generalize from the data collected in an Internet survey to the population at large. Dillman also notes that simply because large numbers of people respond to an Internet-based survey does not mean that the coverage is representative. To use an Internet survey approach, you need to be doing research on an audience that has access to computers, such as professional groups, university employees, people who purchase computer equipment, and so on. Even for those who have computer access, a survey that is too technologically sophisticated may also bias who responds. As Dillman summarizes, ". . . e-mail and Web surveying of the general public is currently inadequate as a means of accessing random samples of defined populations of households and/or individuals" (p. 356).

If you do undertake E-research, Nosek, Banaji, and Greenwald (2002) offer excellent advice about the ethics, security, design, and control of such research. They note that E-research presents methodological challenges that are not present in typical lab research, including "treatment of participants, the security of the data that are transmitted and obtained, and the internal and external validity of the data" (p. 162). Nosek et al. also point to the ethical issues E-researchers face including the "absence of the researcher, uncertainty regarding adequate informed consent and debriefing, and potential loss of participant anonymity or confidentiality" (p. 162). Another good source of information is an article by Simsek and Veiga (2001) in which they discuss steps researchers can take to improve the quality of the data they receive through Internet and intranet (within one organization) surveys. Among the aspects they mention are the importance of the introduction, including sponsorship, use of prior notification and follow-ups, incentives such as coupons for an online gift, the impact of questionnaire layout and design, and the possibility of using **remailing software** for anonymity. Remailing software, available in the public domain, serves as a means of message transmission rather than information storage. "Remailer computers are set up to receive incoming electronic mail, strip the messages of the sender's identifying information, and forward them anonymously to recipients . . ." (Simsek & Veiga, 2001, pp. 230–231).

Although Dillman (2000) notes that e-mail is less dynamic and flexible than web-based surveys in terms of such issues as the need for extensive skip patterns (i.e., when you need to skip to another question that is typically further along in the survey based on some response you have given), e-mail surveys are more likely to be of use to the student who is doing a one-semester project. E-mail surveys are fairly easy to compose and distribute, and Dillman (2000) recommends following many of the same principles as he states for mail surveys (e.g., the importance of good communication). With regard to one of the major concerns, security, you can save responses separately from the e-mail addresses and any other identifying information contained in the header of the e-mail (Nosek et al., 2002).

If you are targeting a particular group, it is also possible to take advantage of a group discussion board or an e-mail list to advertise your study. For example, I belong to the Environmental Design Research Association (edra), and students often contact the edra website to request help with projects related to environment and behavior or to solicit participation in their research. An example of a related group is the Children Youth Environments network (CYE-L), which is also student-friendly and supportive of student requests. Figure 4.1 summarizes the different sources that can be used to obtain participants.

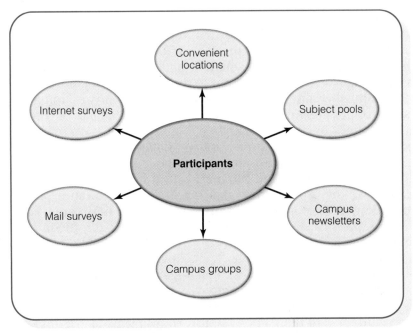

FIGURE 4.1 *Sources of Participants*

REFLECT AND REVIEW

What are the advantages and disadvantages of Internet-based research?

APPLY YOUR KNOWLEDGE

Generate three format issues that may affect both the willingness to participate in and the accuracy of Internet-based research.

Real People: Research in the Field

Yes, it is possible to do research with "real people" (i.e., those who are not part of your student body). Although it is possible, it isn't easy. However, some students have had great success, typically when they have a connection to the population they are sampling.

Connections

One of the most prudent pieces of advice is to make use of connections that you have. For example, one of my students did a project examining the job satisfaction of men vs. women who work in teams. What made this research possible for her was that a relative owned the company in question. Another student looked at communication issues in research and development teams at a local pharmaceutical company. One of our adjunct faculty worked at this company and was interested in the topic, lending the student's project the official support it needed for company approval.

However, connections do not always overcome what are seen as drawbacks to the topic you are studying, as was the case in another project that involved people's reactions to the experience of sexual harassment on the job. In this case, although the student in question had access to the population (her parents worked at the company), someone higher up in the organization vetoed the project out of concern related to the topic. This person's reaction was that having employees fill out questionnaires dealing with sexual harassment might lead to more sexual harassment complaints (i.e., prompted by scenarios in the questionnaire, people might be motivated to file complaints about behavior they found unwelcome or that they thought created a hostile working environment). What this last example illustrates is that the topic itself is of particular importance in persuading "real people" to participate in the research. Topics that might be considered sensitive, such as sexual harassment or rule violation (e.g., theft), may be less likely to be approved in the real world.

Making a Contribution

Another aspect of your research that helps open doors is studying something that is of particular interest to the school, company, organization, and so on. For example, if the impact of after-school enrichment programs is something that a local school is interested in learning more about, it is possible that the school's administration might be more willing to have a student (supervised by a faculty member) gather data on such a project.

"Cold Call"

It is also possible, although more difficult in my experience, to gather data in places where you have no connection. A good example of this is a student who collected data from hundreds of people while they were waiting at a local train station. People typically have some "time on their hands" in this situation, and after asking the local Amtrak counter people and Amtrak police if he could hand out questionnaires while people were waiting, and receiving their permission, this student had great success (see Dustin's tips at the end of this chapter). In

this kind of situation in particular, it is helpful to have official identification from your institution (a laminated badge that you can hang
around your neck or at least show to people), so that people will be
less wary about participating. This is also a situation where good communication skills and a friendly approach can significantly increase
the likelihood that people will participate. Having supplies (clipboard
and pencil) for them to use is also a good idea.

Returning to the theme of communication, which is important in
all aspects of research, it is also helpful to be polite and to communicate your identity. For example, one of my students says that he has
great success saying the following: "Excuse me, can I interest you in
filling out a brief crime survey for my master's thesis project at
Connecticut College?" He reports that this approach works significantly
better than simply saying, "Excuse me, can I interest you in filling out a
brief crime survey?" The first approach doesn't differ substantially but
creates an identity for the researcher who is not an employee of a marketing firm but is trying to advance his education. He reports that the
more personalized approach has an approximately 70% cooperation
rate (D. Wielt, personal communication, Spring 2003).

Bureaucracy

In general, the greater the degree of bureaucracy of an organization,
the more difficult it is to gain permission to conduct research with
that organization. A good example of this in my experience is the Department of Motor Vehicles (DMV). As we all know, a lot of waiting occurs at the DMV. In many respects, it is an ideal place to gather data—
people have little to do while waiting and a broad sample of the
population is involved. In one particular instance, a student had received tentative permission from a local supervisor to collect data, but
that permission was later revoked when the supervisor checked at the
state level.

If you are dealing with commercial sites, it generally helps to approach businesses that are owned by locals rather than by a regional
or national chain. For example, one student reports approaching the
proprietors of local laundromats to ask permission to solicit subjects
there while people were waiting for their laundry. All three of the proprietors agreed, but when he asked the manager of a laundromat
chain, he was turned down.

Vulnerable Populations/Service Learning

Many students now do internships or service learning in their local
communities, and these affiliations may provide the opportunity to

do research on a variety of populations, including those who are categorized as vulnerable (e.g., children) by federal regulations to protect human subjects (see Chapter 5). With any population where the student is both an intern and a (potential) researcher, issues of confidentiality and the nature of the relationship may be problematical. For example, suppose that you are doing an internship in a group home for adolescent girls with behavioral problems and you learn that many of the girls there have histories of being abused sexually. You become interested in studying the family conditions that are associated with such abuse and want to interview the girls as part of a research project. Questions would be raised about the appropriateness of doing research with a population you are serving, and the IRB review (see Chapter 5) would undoubtedly raise serious questions. I have seen students do research with vulnerable populations such as these young women when the facility was large enough to permit the student to use a different segment of the population. One example would be in a prison where a student might be able to survey a different pod or unit. Another example would be in a large residential facility as opposed to a small group home. However, gaining permission to do research in facilities such as prisons involves a considerable amount of paperwork and length of time—as much as a year.

Ethical Issues in Multiple Relationships

Regarding these interwoven relationships, the American Psychological Association's Ethical Principles of Psychologists and Code of Conduct (APA, 2002) offers some guidance, including Principle 3.05 Multiple Relationships. Principle 3.05 states, "(a) A multiple relationship occurs when a psychologist is in a professional role with a person and (1) at the same time is in another role with the same person" (p. 1065). In our example of service learning, the student is in the roles of intern and researcher. It also states, "Multiple relationships that would not reasonably be expected to cause impairment or risk exploitation or harm are not unethical" (p. 1065). Thus, although such dual roles may be permitted, the student who wants to conduct research and continue to provide service has to very carefully navigate these issues involving the ethics of multiple relationships.

Children

Although it is not advisable to conduct research with children for a one-semester project (because of the length of time involved in obtaining the appropriate permissions), it may be possible if you plan ahead and if you have the kind of connections discussed earlier. One of the hurdles is that participants must be past the age of consent (often 18) in their state to agree to participate in research without the permission of a parent or guardian. Still, if you want to attempt such research for a one-semester project, one strategy that has been successful is to approach your old school(s). If you have a good relationship with a teacher, he/she might be willing to help you obtain the appropriate permissions and be an advocate for your project with the "gatekeepers" (i.e., principal, superintendent). Like many colleges where students obtain teaching certificates, our college has affiliations with local elementary and secondary schools, and there have been a number of fruitful research collaborations between the college and these schools. Using a cross-sectional approach, one student compared the career decisiveness of students at a secondary school in the ninth and twelfth grades, and at our college with first-year and fourth-year students. To accomplish this, she first spoke to the head of the secondary school to gain her permission, and then attended a parents' information meeting about the school year to introduce her project and hand out informed consent documents at this meeting. To increase the response, she also had students take informed consent documents home for their parents to sign at two subsequent points in time. The students themselves (those for whom parents/guardians had returned consent documents) filled out informed consent documents before participating in the project (see Chapter 5 for more discussion about informed consent). Regarding research in schools, Sieber (1992) suggests the following:

> Avoiding coercion is especially important in school research, where peer and authority pressures are especially salient. To assure that each child's participation is truly voluntary, the researcher must implement the following objectives:
>
> 1. Minimize the coercion implicit in a request to participate from parents, teachers, or other adults.
> 2. Minimize peer pressure and fear of ridicule for not participating.
> 3. Keep any reward for participating small and not valuable.
>   (p. 122)

Other connections involving children include sports or artistic or religious activities. One student taught gymnastics after school and gained permission (through a process similar to the one described previously for obtaining permission from parents or guardians) to evaluate the effectiveness of two different approaches to teaching a cartwheel to her students. Other examples of groups that might be approached are Brownies/Cub Scouts and Girl/Boy Scouts, soccer teams, swimming classes, and so on. For any of these populations, a personal connection is almost always a prerequisite for a student project.

Sources of Participants in the Real World

- Your connections
- Offer to solve a problem (make a contribution)
- Cold call
- Transportation centers; laundromats
- Service learning

REFLECT AND REVIEW

In the research process, what special precautions are taken to protect the rights of vulnerable populations?

The Convenience Sample or Using Your Friends as Research Subjects

A **convenience sample** is just that, a sample that you gather conveniently, rather than randomly or in some other methodologically rigorous way. Generally, it is not advisable to use your friends as your research participants. They may suffice for pilot testing of a measure in terms of reading comprehension or for cognitive and perceptual experiments, but otherwise, they are biased in particular ways because they are, after all, your friends. They may have similar personality characteristics and backgrounds, and familiarity could undermine experiments on a variety of different topics, including social cohesion (Leong & Austin, 1996). In a word, they are not representative.

Dustin's Dozen: Tips for Collecting Data in the Field

I have compiled the many useful suggestions from one of our graduate students, Dustin Wielt, into a list of do's and don'ts for collecting data in the field. Dustin's MA project was a study of the attributions people made about murderers as a function of the murderer's criminal history, psychiatric history, and social status. Over the two months he collected his data (a sample of over 300 participants), his major collection point was the local Amtrak train station.

1. Dress decently. As Dustin says, don't dress like a "bum." If you are a male student, wear a shirt tucked in and a belt. Don't wear a baseball cap facing backwards. Basically, if you are negotiating with a business owner about whether you can collect data at his/her establishment, dress appropriately. And dress appropriately when you collect the data, of course!

2. The inverse correlation. There seems to be an inverse correlation between the likelihood of gaining permission to collect data at a facility and the height of the hierarchy. For example, Dustin asked permission of the local Amtrak police and the Amtrak counter personnel to distribute questionnaires at our New London train station. They granted permission, with the caveat that if anyone complained, he would be asked to leave. Then they "shook" on it. This agreement worked very well. But when Dustin pursued gaining permission from the much larger train station in New Haven by calling the number of an Amtrak official there, the response was "no." The higher up you are required to go to get permission (and the less likely you are to do it in person), the less likely it is that the permission will be granted. This same experience was replicated in seeking permission from the local owner of a laundromat ("yes") vs. from the manager of a chain of laundromats ("no").

3. Avoid "No Solicitation" locations. As a matter of policy, establishments that have "No solicitation" signs posted are less likely to agree to your research.

4. Carefully select your "first ask" of the day. As your first "ask" of the day, try to identify someone who seems likely to cooperate with you. As an example, Dustin found that women who were reading books were likely to agree to participate. If they said "yes," the people sitting around them became curious and were more likely to agree. If the first person you ask who is sitting in a group says "no," it is less likely that others will then have the courage to say "yes." Dustin estimated that on average, about 60% of those he first asked said "yes" immediately, and if they asked a question about the research, another 10% said "yes."

Although there will be difficulties, the train station has turned out to be a good data collection source. In Dustin's sample, he had an age range of 18–84, and the sample was almost normally distributed in terms of age. There was also racial and socioeconomic diversity, and a fairly good gender split (53% women, 47% men). There may be other ways in which this sample is not representative (people who take trains may be different in certain respects than those who do not), but it is a reasonable place to start.

Although he did not implement it, another strategy Dustin considered was the use of a confederate who could be approached first to say "yes," thereby establishing a climate of cooperation. In the two months that Dustin collected data at the train station, he had only two or three people who were asked twice to fill out the questionnaire, so the number of repeats was quite low and a confederate could be helpful in this situation with a high turnover of people.

5. Personalize your "pitch." Ask the individual for participation in your project, as opposed to simply asking for participation. It is harder to turn someone down when you are turning down the individual as opposed to a representative of a large organization.

6. Be mobile. Rather than putting yourself at a desk or in a stationary position, which strangers may be reluctant to approach, move around the facility. If you are collecting data at a train station, a laundromat, or some other facility, put your questionnaires on a clipboard and approach people for their help. This approach works much more effectively than waiting for people to approach you.

7. Approach people with a respect for their personal space. Stand about five or six feet away when you first ask people to participate. If they agree to participate, you can move closer to hand them the clipboard. Dustin recommends having about 10 clipboards available (in a backpack or tote) to hand out, then "reloading" them with fresh questionnaires so that materials are always available. He provided pens (which he retrieved) for all participants. He placed the debriefing form, face down, at the end of the questionnaire so that it was immediately available to participants when they finished the questionnaire. Make sure that the informed consent information in the introduction to the study is printed in large enough type so that people can read it easily.

8. Be ready to assist those with low reading levels. Dustin found that a good number of people for whom English was a second language or for whom reading at a sixth-grade level was a problem frequented the laundromat. Although he asked people if they had any questions before they started filling out the questionnaires, on occasion people asked him for definitions of words (one example is the word "generous"). At this point, he offered to read the questionnaire to this particular individual, and she agreed. Questionnaires can be designed for a minimum reading level, and certain word processing programs have reading-level indicators. For example, MS Word has such an option. If you look under Tools, then under Spelling and Grammar, you can click on Options. Under the Grammar section of the Options, you can click on "Show readability statistics." After the spelling and grammar check is complete, an assessment of the reading level of the material you have highlighted will appear. You can also pilot your materials by asking a number of people to read your questions and comment on the appropriateness of the reading level for your target

population. Although questionnaires can be designed for a given minimum reading level, it is still the case that the researcher may need to assist participants. When this happens, the researcher then will need to make a decision about the validity of the data (because people's responses may change in a socially desirable direction) and whether these data should be included in the analyses.

9. Limit the length of your survey. Dustin estimates that a 10–15 minute questionnaire is the maximum length that will work, especially in places like train stations where people are waiting, but may not arrive too much in advance of their trains. He also said that the day before Thanksgiving was his most successful data collection session, where he collected over 100 questionnaires as people began their holiday travel. Trains were running 10–15 minutes late all day, so that even those who had planned to arrive just a few minutes before the train's scheduled departure had "time on their hands."

10. Be sensitive to the day of the week and time of the day. Dustin found that weekends were better than weekdays for cooperation, as weekend travelers were more likely to be traveling for pleasure as opposed to business. Business people traveling on Monday mornings were the least cooperative.

At the laundromat, the best time to approach people was the moment after they had put their clothes in the dryer (rather than when they were folding clothes, etc.).

11. Safeguard your personal information. Dustin recommends listing the department's phone number rather than your home or dorm number as a contact number on the debriefing sheet. This is a matter of safety. He was once called at 3:30 a.m. by someone who was drunk and disoriented. This person wanted more information about the study but was clearly in need of other kinds of assistance.

12. Be ready for challenges. Challenges to research may come in many different guises. Some people may want to engage you in a lengthy conversation, and you need to extricate yourself and move on. Others may criticize your research because they know something about questionnaire construction or the topic you are studying. The best advice is to remain polite and continue to state that they are under no obligation to fill out the questionnaire, and so on.

Final Words

Although some authors have stated, "Subjects are at risk when student researchers are at the helm" (Kallgren & Tauber, 1996, p. 20), student researchers are capable of doing impressive work. When you collect data in the field, personal rejection will come, but don't be discouraged. It is also worth noting that collecting data in person is emotionally and physically taxing, and you need to pace yourself. There may even be some days where you can't face it, but if you start early in the semester, you can succeed.

● ●

SUMMARY

In this chapter you have learned the ins and outs of obtaining participants, from departmental subject pools to locations in the field. You have seen the importance of what you say in how you introduce your topic to participants, the timing of the request during the semester, how to keep track of participants, including credit slips and no-shows, and steps to minimize attrition. Heavily populated sites on campus have been suggested as locations to recruit participants, and the fundamental aspects of mail and Internet surveys, including ways to protect participants' privacy, have been introduced. The hurdles you face when using vulnerable populations such as children have been identified, as have ways to address these hurdles, such as use of personal connections. The chapter concluded with Dustin Wielt's excellent suggestions for collecting data in the field.

APPLY YOUR KNOWLEDGE QUESTIONS

In the event that you did not have time to do them earlier, here is the list of APPLY YOUR KNOWLEDGE questions in this chapter. Try them now:

1. Find out if your department has a subject pool and, if so, how it functions.

2. Generate three format issues that may affect both the willingness to participate in and the accuracy of Internet-based research.

Ethics and the IRB Review Process

I'm from the IRB and I'm Here to Help You

Introduction and Chapter Overview

Human Subjects Institutional Review Boards (IRBs) are institutional groups that review any research done with human subjects, whether on or off campus, whether funded or not, whether conducted by students, faculty, or staff. In making sure that the researchers meet specific ethical guidelines, IRBs protect researchers as well as participants.

This chapter provides a thorough understanding of the purpose and history of the Human Subjects Institutional Review Board and the steps that are typically required to prepare a proposal for IRB review. There are different levels of review, depending on the parameters of the research (e.g., whether a vulnerable population such as children is involved; see also Chapter 4). The chapter explains these levels of review so that you can assess how much time your proposal's review is likely to take. Please note that in this chapter, the sections on the history of the IRB tend to use the term "human subjects" when describing all research. According to the *APA Manual* guidelines (see Chapter 7), that phrase is now limited to research where there is no direct informed consent from those who participate (e.g., from infants). The phrase used for research involving consent is "human participants."

The documents needed to submit a proposal for IRB review are explained, and sample **informed consent** and **debriefing** statements are provided. Informed consent involves explaining the research and stating the participant's rights so that he or she can decide whether to participate. After the participant has completed the tasks that the research involves, a debriefing statement provided by the researcher explains the specific hypotheses and purpose of the study in more depth. Institutions differ in the extent to which they have templates or standard paragraphs for the IRB documents that they require. Always check with the IRB chair of your institution to determine the format of the materials you will be asked to submit.

Although this chapter focuses on research with humans, institutions where research is done with animals have committees to evaluate, approve, and monitor the use of such animals. This group is often called the Institutional Animal Care and Use Committee (IACUC). Guidelines for research with animals can be found at the website of the Association for Assessment and Accreditation of Laboratory Animal Care International at http://www.aaalac.org. One of the options on their home page is "Reference Resources," which lists links to animal care guidelines in the United States.

A Personal Reflection

When I was in elementary, junior high, and high school, I attended what I fondly refer to as a "guinea pig" school. This small facility was a laboratory school, connected to a major university. In addition to a fairly traditional curriculum, students at the school participated in research projects and annually took intelligence tests administered by the university's graduate students who presumably were honing their clinical skills. We fondly referred to these intelligence tests as "birthday games" because they were usually scheduled around a student's birthday.

However, I vividly recall a research project in the fifth or sixth grade of which I have less than fond memories. The project involved deception and basically examined the role of peer influence. Students, interviewed individually, were asked to name their best friend and then were asked how they would handle the discipline for a student who had committed some "crime" (stolen something or broken some significant rule). After a short break, these students were again interviewed individually, only to learn that their best friend supposedly had made a disciplinary recommendation significantly different from their own. In fact, all students were told that their friend's judgment was significantly different from their own, independent of the actual judgment that the best friend had made. The question of interest was whether one would, under these circumstances, change one's mind.

I think that the reasons for the deception (part of debriefing) were explained later, but I continued to feel uncomfortable about the deception. The experience has made me appreciate the role an Institutional Review Board can play in protecting the rights of research participants, especially the rights of children.

What Is the IRB and Why Does It Exist?

At an educational institution, the Human Subjects IRB or Institutional Review Board is a group whose charge it is to protect the welfare of individuals who participate in research projects proposed by any member of that institution. The IRB consists of at least five individuals, one of whom is not related to the institution.

Frankl (cited in Williams & Ouren, 1976) states that prior to 1950, no federal or state statutes had been established to protect human subjects in research. However, in a series of legislative acts since then, and gaining momentum in the 1970s, the federal government has established and refined its mechanisms for protecting the welfare of human subjects. In 1974, the Federal Government passed the National Research Act (Public Law 93-348) and established the National Commission for the Protection of Human Subjects of Biomedical and Behavioral Research (Office for Protection from Research Risks [OPRR], 1993). This group issued a report in 1978, known as the **Belmont Report**, which described the principles that were to be followed in the ethical treatment of human subjects. By 1981, the government codified the regulations from the Belmont Report as **Title 45 Part 46 of the Code of Federal Regulations** (Landrum, 1999; Pattullo, 1984). In this book, this code will be identified as 45 CFR 46. In 1991, the government adopted a Federal Policy for the Protection of Human Subjects, known as the **Common Rule** (OPRR, 1993).

The National Research Act required universities and colleges who receive federal funds and conduct research with human subjects to establish such an IRB review committee. In reality, most larger colleges and universities, whether or not they have these federal funds, have established IRBs to review research projects with human subjects. In so doing, they work to protect the safety of research participants, improve the quality of research that is done, and address issues of liability. However, Kallgren and Tauber (1996) note that many smaller colleges, because they do not have federal research funds and therefore do not fall under the legal mandate, do not have an IRB to review undergraduate research. They are of the opinion that all institutions would benefit from using IRBs.

History of IRBs

The Nazi experiments during World War II, the subsequent Nuremberg Military Tribunal, and creation of the **Nuremberg Code** are often identified as the impetus for establishing the federal code to protect human subjects. Emanating from the Nuremberg Trials that judged war criminals, the Nuremberg Code consists of 10 major points that describe principles in the ethical treatment of human subjects. And although research in the medical community (in the form of clinical trials for medication or experimental surgeries) has received a good deal of attention, the social and behavioral sciences also have contributed to society's concerns about research with human subjects.

In the medical community, a number of scandals have come to light, including the Tuskegee experiments that lasted 40 years, from 1932 to 1972. In the Tuskegee Syphilis Study, poor Black men were recruited for the study to follow the course of the disease. However, the study continued even after the discovery that penicillin treated the disease effectively. This decision to continue the research essentially denied the participants a cure. If you want to learn more about this scandal, the book *Bad Blood* (Jones, 1981) is a good source.

In the social and behavioral sciences, Stanley Milgram's obedience-to-authority research at Yale (Milgram, 1974) is often mentioned as violating ethical principles, and certainly raises issues about the use of deception in research (Fisher & Fyrberg, 1994). In this research, which arguably would not receive IRB approval under current standards (Gillespie, 1999), volunteers from the New Haven community participated in what they were told was an experiment about learning. As "teachers," they were to deliver electric shocks to "learners" if the learners did not answer correctly. These shocks were increasingly stronger as "learners" supposedly made more errors, and much to the surprise of Milgram and others who had hypothesized what would happen in advance, a significant number of the "teachers" in one of Milgram's conditions delivered shocks at a very high level to "learners" who continued to make errors. At the conclusion of the research, the "teachers" were told about the true purpose of the research (to study obedience), and that no shocks of any sort were delivered to the "learners" (who were confederates in the experiment). Although only a small percentage of subjects (1.3%) indicated that they regretted their participation when asked in a one-year follow-up of the research (Milgram, 1974), Milgram's study continues to raise questions about the appropriateness of research involving deception.

Another study that raised an enormous public outcry was Laud Humphreys's (1970) research on what is called the "tearoom trade." Tearoom sex is the name given to fellatio in public restrooms. For those who might be wondering, the origins of this phrase from the homosexual lexicon are unknown, according to Humphreys (1970). For Humphreys's doctoral research in sociology (which was supported by research grants from the National Institutes of Mental Health [NIMH]), he attempted to understand the characteristics of men who sought sexual gratification essentially with strangers in such places as public restrooms in city parks. In the research, Humphreys stationed himself at public restrooms (tearooms) and served as a watch queen, the person who keeps watch and signals to the others when the police or strangers approach. In addition to his role as watch queen, Humphreys gathered personal information about these men in a number of ways. For some, he revealed his status as a researcher and asked them to disclose personal aspects of their lives; for others, he copied down their license plates, eventually obtained their home addresses through various agencies, and then followed up a year later in their homes. He disguised himself and posed as a social health interviewer (in point of fact, the data he collected in this portion of his research were a part of a study of the social health of men in the community). The information he gathered from the study was very useful in changing existing stereotypes of men involved in these acts. As Lee Rainwater, in the foreword to Humphreys's book (1970) states, "Humphreys demonstrates that tearooms represent neither the moral danger to unsuspecting youth nor the simple public nuisances of which they have been accused" (p. xv). At the same time, the extent of the deception and the manner in which Humphreys gathered the information resulted in an enormous public backlash.

Studies such as those by Milgram and Humphreys raise serious questions about the psychological impact of research on human subjects. Arguably IRB standards for approving research involving invasion of privacy, sensitive issues, covert observation of sensitive behavior, and deception have become more stringent. This swinging of the pendulum toward a more conservative approach to research with the potential to cause psychological and/or physical harm to the participant has been influenced by both public and professional (e.g., Baumrind, 1964) responses to research such as that of Milgram and Humphreys. IRB members reviewing research must ask themselves whether the potential benefits to be derived from a particular study outweigh the potential risks. In such **risk-benefit analyses**, IRB members are especially vigilant of research that involves sensitive topics, deception, and covert observation of behavior, considering the extent to which they think such studies may harm the participant. Our litigious society, where lawsuits are increasingly common, places additional pressure on IRB members to take a conservative stance with regard to research that has the potential to harm the individual.

Although we may think that the current federal regulations have eliminated questions of research abuse, the evidence, some of it involving research with children, suggests otherwise (Beh, 2002; Wadman, 1998). For interested readers, information about an important legal ruling dealing with research sponsored by Johns Hopkins can be viewed at: http://www.hopkinsmedicine.org/press/2001/september/010907.htm. In this research, some children were given the opportunity to live in homes that differed in the level of intervention undertaken to reduce lead paint levels in the dwelling. Two parents claimed that they were not informed in a timely manner of the lead paint dust levels in their homes. As a result of the lawsuits that were brought by the parents, a ruling was made by the Court of Appeals that "no parent or surrogate could consent to the participation of a child or disabled person in nontherapeutic research in which there is *any* risk of injury or damage to the person. The decision requires court approval before this research may take place" (http://www.hopkinsmedicine.org/press/2001/september/summary.htm).

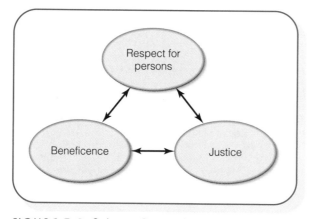

FIGURE 5.1 Belmont Report Principles

For these and a number of other important reasons, IRB review of undergraduate research is important (Kallgren & Tauber, 1996).

The Belmont Report. The work of the National Commission for the Protection of Human Subjects of Biomedical and Behavioral Research, established by the National Research Act in 1974, led to the drafting of what is known as The Belmont Report (Maloney, 1984). The Belmont Report [named after the conference center where the commission's meetings were held (OPRR, 1993)] was published in the Federal Register in 1979 and is "usually described as an *ethical* statement about research with human subjects" (Maloney, 1984, p. 21). The report emphasizes the assessment of risk-benefit criteria in reviewing human subjects research, the creation of guidelines for selecting human subjects, the characteristics of informed consent, steps to monitor and assess the work of Institutional Review Boards, and guidelines for informed consent involving children, prisoners, and those who are institutionalized with mental infirmities (Maloney, 1984).

Importantly, the report also identifies three ethical principles that guide such work: **Respect for Persons, Beneficence, and Justice.** Figure 5.1 illustrates these relationships.

Within the principle Respect for Persons, two aspects are emphasized: Individuals are autonomous agents, and those whose autonomy is diminished need protection. The principle of Beneficence stresses the obligation to safeguard people's well-being. Extensions of this category include "1) do not harm, and 2) maximize possible benefits and minimize possible harms" (Maloney, 1984, p. 34). The principle of Justice addresses the double-edged sword of research: Who should benefit? Who should encounter risk? What is the fair distribution of these aspects of research?

● ●

REFLECT AND REVIEW

What are IRBs trying to accomplish and why were they formed? What three ethical principles did the Belmont Report establish?

What Is Research? What Are Human Subjects? IRB Nuts and Bolts

IRBs evaluate research proposals, but what constitutes research? In the regulations, research is defined as "a systematic investigation, including research development, testing and evaluation, designed to develop or contribute to generalizable knowledge" [45 CFR 46.102(d)]. To me, the operational phrases here are systematic investigation and generalizable knowledge. If the food service coordinator wants to survey students on campus to find out whether to switch brands of coffee, he or she may send an institution-wide e-mail to students asking for their opinion. Although sending the institution-wide e-mail might be considered a systematic investigation, I don't think that this project qualifies as research because it is doubtful the intention is to contribute to generalizable knowledge. As another example of a project that would not qualify as research, you might administer the Vandenberg and Kuse Mental Rotations Test (MRT) (1978) to students in a cognitive psychology class. The Vandenberg and Kuse MRT is one of the instruments used to assess mental rotation, a type of spatial ability. In this scenario, students would not turn in their tests but instead might score their own tests at their seats. The purpose of this class exercise is a demonstration, not the collection of data to yield generalizable results.

If you wanted to use these data for research purposes, however, you would need to have the research project approved by your IRB, which might actually have some concerns about the implicit coercion involved in collecting data during class time. In fact, one ethical issue involving research with college students has been called "using a **captive population**" (Council, Smith, Kaster-Bundgaard, & Gladue, 1997). This is a situation in which research that is not related to the content of the class is conducted during class time. And some might argue that collecting any research during class time is inappropriate, given the pressure it places on students to consent.

And what are human subjects? The regulations state that human subjects are "living individual(s) about whom an investigator (whether professional or student) conducting research obtains (1) data through intervention or interaction with the individual, or (2) identifiable private information" [45 CFR 46.102 (f)]. Using this definition, anonymous archival data would not require IRB approval. For example, I might be interested in the relationship between residence hall vandalism, residence hall size, gender, and students' class year. From my college's Physical Plant Office, I can obtain residence hall vandalism charges for each hall in a given semester. I can also obtain the breakdown of students in each residence hall by class year and gender. These data will allow me to statistically analyze the relationships of interest, but the process involves no intervention or interaction with subjects and the data have no personal identifiers. However, if I wanted to also know the relationship between the residence hall environment and vandalism and sought to administer an instrument like the Moos (1988) University Residence Environment Scale to students in each residence hall for that purpose, the project would then require IRB review.

IRB membership. Federal regulations have established that an IRB must have a minimum of five members, with at least one person whose expertise is scientific and another whose expertise is nonscientific (45 CFR 46.107). Additionally, at least one of these members must come from the community (i.e., be unaffiliated with the institution in question). This unaffiliated person cannot be in the immediate family of anyone at the institution. Ideal characteristics for this person include such attributes as assertiveness and self-confidence (Porter, 1986). Those who serve in these roles (Porter, 1987) see themselves as representing the interests of the community, advocating for human subjects and "speaking up," being sensitive to ethical issues, and promoting the clarity of documents involved in the research.

It makes sense that the membership of the IRB includes people whose knowledge and interest reflect that of the majority of proposals the committee reviews. For example, on our college IRB, we had three members of the Psychology Department (two women and one man), a member of the Human Development Department (a woman), a member of the Philosophy Department (a man), and a member from the community who is a clergywoman. Approximately 65% of the proposals we review come from the Psychology Department. When the faculty member in Philosophy went on sabbatical, we replaced him with a faculty member in Anthropology to broaden our base of expertise. When proposals include approaches and/or populations that are beyond the scope of our expertise, we might include additional members to review that proposal.

Further, when vulnerable populations (e.g., children, prisoners) are involved, the regulations suggest that the IRB include a representative of the population or someone who has knowledge about and experience in working with the population. As was discussed in Chapter 4, vulnerable populations are those for whom we have concerns about their capacity to give informed consent. As an example, when a student conducted a project that involved administering surveys to incarcerated women about their social support systems, we asked a former prison counselor to join the IRB for that review.

The Levels of IRB Review

To address the fact that some proposals involve more sensitive issues than others, IRBs are permitted to have different levels of review (CFR 46.101): **exempt review, expedited review,** and **full review.** These categories are explained in the paragraphs that follow. For those seeking a visual representation of these categories, Pritchard (2001) provides a series of useful tree diagrams to help understand what kind of research falls into each category.

Exempt. (1) Research conducted in established or commonly accepted educational settings, involving normal educational practices (e.g., collection of course evaluation of instruction); (2) research involving the use of educational tests (cognitive, diagnostic, aptitude, achievement) (e.g., taking state mastery tests), survey procedures, interview procedures, or observation in public *unless* [italics added]: (i) information obtained is recorded in such a manner that human subjects can be identified, directly or through identifiers linked to the subjects; and (ii) any disclosure of the human subjects' responses outside the research could reasonably place the subjects at risk of criminal or civil liability or be damaging to the subjects' financial standing, employability, or reputation.

There are some other categories of exemption. Research is exempt if the research involving the use of educational tests, survey procedures, interview procedures, or observation of public behavior involves elected or appointed public officials or candidates for public office. Also, the research is exempt if it involves the collection or study of existing data, documents, records, pathological specimens, or diagnostic specimens, if these sources are publicly available or if the information is recorded by the investigator in such a manner that subjects cannot be identified, directly or through identifiers linked to the subjects. There are other exemptions, but the reader is directed to the entire policy for the details.

Expedited review. The federal guidelines also permit what is referred to as expedited review (CFR 46.110). Expedited reviews pose no significant ethical issues and involve no vulnerable populations; such reviews can be completed in a brief length of time.

The Secretary of Health and Human Services (HHS) has published a list of research in the *Federal Register* that qualifies as exempt. An IRB may use the expedited review procedure to review either or both of the following: (1) Some or all of the research appearing on the list of exempt research and found by the reviewer(s) to involve no more than **minimal risk** (see discussion later of minimal risk), (2) minor changes in previously approved research during the period (of one year or less) for which approval is authorized.

The list in the *Federal Register* includes 9 to 10 categories of research that qualify for expedited review (depending on how one segments them). Three of these categories, and in particular the third category, are of particular relevance to social scientists:

1. Research involving materials (data, documents, records, or specimens) that have been collected or will be collected solely for non-research purposes (such as medical treatment or diagnosis).

2. Collection of data from voice, video, digital, or image recordings made for research purposes.

3. Research on individual or group characteristics or behavior (including, but not limited to, research on perception, cognition, motivation, identity, language, communication, cultural beliefs or practices, and social behavior) or research employing survey, interview, oral history, focus group, program evaluation, human factors evaluation, or quality assurance methodologies.

The regulations permit expedited reviews to be conducted by the IRB chairperson or by his or her designee (someone with an appropriate level of experience). The only action an expedited reviewer cannot take is disapproval (this has to be done by the full IRB).

It is important to recognize that the decision to consider research as exempt or use the expedited review process is made by the local IRB. Some IRBs review all research, whether or not it qualifies for exempt status.

Minimal risk. A risk is minimal where the probability and magnitude of harm or discomfort anticipated in the proposed research are not greater, in and of themselves, than those ordinarily encountered in daily life or during the performance of routine physical or psychological examinations or tests [46.102(i)].

Full review. When the research project involves more than minimal risk or the use of a vulnerable population of subjects (e.g., children), a review by the full committee is required.

REFLECT AND REVIEW

Explain the difference in requirements for exempt, expedited, and full IRB review. Why is it important to have a nonscientist on the IRB?

Health Insurance Portability and Accountability Act (HIPAA)

In 2003, the privacy rule provisions of the Health Insurance Portability and Accountability Act (HIPAA) went into effect. These regulations affect researchers who use health information (e.g., medical records) from a health care provider, a health plan, or a health care clearinghouse that transmits the information electronically (e.g., to insurance providers). What this means for student researchers (as well as for faculty researchers) is that if you want to use information in medical records for which you have not previously obtained informed consent, you have to "de-identify the data." There are 18 categories of data (e.g., name, social security number, date of birth, geographical subdivision smaller than a state, e-mail address, and so on) that must be de-identified before the data meet the HIPAA requirements that protect the privacy of the individual. Although it is unlikely that student researchers doing a one-semester project would use medical records, it is important to know that this policy exists. The existence of this policy also reflects the fact that the regulations governing the IRB process change.

IRB Actions

Possible actions for the IRB are approval, approval contingent upon revision, tabling, and disapproval (Gillespie, 1999). In my experience, full IRB review almost always requires revisions, whereas straightforward approval is more likely to be the case for expedited IRB review.

Under these guidelines for review, a good deal of research that students conduct may qualify for exemption. This includes anonymous survey research projects about nonsensitive topics distributed through campus mail. An example of such research might be a survey that sought to compare the television viewing habits of first-year vs. fourth-year students in college. However, to demonstrate that there are always exceptions to the policy, Gillespie (1999) argues that IRB review may be required even for anonymous survey research distributed as a class exercise if the measures are sensitive (e.g., for depression, disordered eating, illegal substance use).

Some institutions review all research proposals (to make a determination about the kind of review, if any, the proposal requires). In this manner, they are not placing the responsibility for that decision on the researcher but are assuming it themselves. Through experience, IRB members have found that they do not always agree with a researcher's assessment that the research qualifies as exempt.

IRB review at other institutions. Some students assume that approval from their local institutional IRB covers the data they plan to collect from another institution. For example, students may plan to have friends at other institutions distribute questionnaires through that institution's campus mail system. This approach is legitimate only if the student has the IRB at the second institution review and approve the research proposal. Normally, this is a routine process, but it still involves preparing the necessary documentation, submitting it by a deadline, and so on. On occasion, students' requests to employ their peers at another institution may actually be refused. One student hoped to have crew teams at a number of large institutions complete a survey that he had developed, only to be told by the IRBs there that the student population was "off limits" to outside researchers. Words to the wise: plan ahead and be prepared with a possible contingency plan.

• •

APPLY YOUR KNOWLEDGE

Give an example of (1) a project that would not be considered research, (2) a project that would fall under the Exempt category, (3) a project that would involve Expedited Review, and (4) a project that would require Full Review.

Effective Communication in the Research Process

Before discussing the specific components of the research proposal, it is important to emphasize a value that should be central to the entire research endeavor: effective communication. As Sieber and others have indicated, it is important to communicate effectively with the subject. "Conducting research on human subjects is analogous to producing and directing a play" (Sieber, 1996, p. 73). Effective communication is the foundation for all aspects of the research process.

In a sense, the relationship between the researcher and the participant is not unlike that of the therapist and client, at least in terms of communication. In his book *The Psychiatric Interview* (1954/1970), the eminent therapist Harry Stack Sullivan outlines some principles for a therapeutic encounter that might well be adopted by the successful researcher. Sullivan describes the initial stages of the interview as the formal inception, and he makes it clear that the therapist (read researcher) should behave as if the person is expected and should treat the individual with "respectful seriousness" (p. 60).

As Sullivan says "respect for the other person, and awareness of the other person's feeling of security, is the first element of the expertness in interpersonal relations which any client will look for in an interviewer" (p. 31). You, the researcher, are trying to be professional—to act with confidence and, as Sullivan points out, "The chief handicap to communication is anxiety" (p. 217). That anxiety is as likely to be the researcher's as it is to be the subject's!

Sullivan talks about the kind of communication in which you ask questions to make sure you really understand what the person says, which was particularly important for the work he was doing with people diagnosed with schizophrenia. Language is also central in effective communication about research. An instructive study by Waggoner and Mayo (1995) highlighted just how many terms used in consent forms are often misunderstood by participants. As one example, only 41% of the respondents in their sample knew the meaning of the word "protocol," and only 22% understood the concept of being chosen randomly. In one of the more amusing examples, one respondent thought an occult blood test was a blood test that witches use, and overall only 15% understood this term.

Components of the IRB Proposal

If you plan to submit a research proposal to an IRB, what can you expect? The following list describes the components that would be requested in a typical IRB proposal. Increasingly, IRB forms at institutions are available to download from the institution's website.

What Each Proposal Should Address

- Purpose of the project: What is the point of the research?
- Description of the participants: Who will the participants be? How will they be recruited? Will they be compensated (either monetarily or through course credit)?
- Procedures: What are the instructions to participants? What will participants do in the study? Where? When?
- Apparatus/Measures: What apparatus or measures will be used? Attach all measures (e.g., questionnaires, surveys).

- Informed Consent: How will informed consent be obtained? How will participants' confidentiality and anonymity be protected? Attach the informed consent document.

- Deception: Will the study involve any deception? If so, include a justification of the necessity for deception.

- Debriefing: How will participants be debriefed? Attach the debriefing document.

At our institution, justification is required if the study involves any of the following: covert observation, studies of ethnic and group differences, intervention research, use of deception, invasion of privacy, aversive (noxious) stimulation, induction of mental or physical stress or deprivation (e.g., food, water, sensory, sleep), invasive procedures (e.g., drugs, blood samples, surgery), potentially embarrassing situations, or other ethical issues concerning the dignity and welfare of the participants.

Informed Consent

Some components of the proposal require the research to address specific points. The informed consent document is one of these and is a cornerstone of the research process. In fact, the first principle of the Nuremberg Code stresses that human participants must give voluntary consent. Informed consent implies the capacity to consent, freedom from coercion, and comprehension of the risks and benefits involved. Knowledge that they are free to withdraw from research at any time must also be part of informed consent. Participants must be free from threats, or coercion, as well as from undue inducements; for example, inappropriate financial payments or other benefits for participation. When vulnerable populations, such as children or prisoners, are involved in research, additional considerations may be in order. If your research involves vulnerable populations, you are advised to contact your IRB for assistance.

Components of informed consent: Overview. One of the essential components of research that receives an expedited or full review is the informed consent document, which is "an ongoing, two-way communication process between subjects and the investigator, as well as a specific agreement about the conditions of the research participation" (Sieber, 1992, p. 26). Participants must have sufficient information to make a truly informed decision to participate in the research study. If participants cannot give informed consent (and thus technically are called subjects), informed consent must be obtained from their legal representatives. For example, when those participating are minors or when they are mentally incapacitated, the consent of a legal representative (such as a child's parent or an adult's guardian) is required. Consent documents must be clearly written and understandable to participants. Translation into the participant's native language may be required. The consent form must include language that is nontechnical, comparable to the language in a newspaper. Scientific, technical, or medical terms must be plainly defined. The consent form may not include language that appears to waive participants' legal rights or appears to release the investigator from liability for negligence.

The informed consent agreement includes specific statements about the following aspects (see Appendix A for an example):

1. A statement that the project is research, its purpose, the length of time it will take, and what will be involved (the procedure).

2. A statement of whether there are any foreseeable risks or discomforts. These include not only physical injury, but also possible psychological, social, or economic harm, discomfort, or inconvenience. Often, in research where there are no known risks or discomforts, you can simply state that.

3. A statement of whether there are any benefits to participants that might result. Rather than claiming that the research will make a significant contribution, you can typically say that although the direct benefits of this research to society are not known, the individual may learn more about a particular ability or concern (e.g., spatial ability) that the research examines.

4. A statement of the extent to which **anonymity** and **confidentiality** will be protected. Anonymity and confidentiality are two aspects of informed consent that are often confused. Anonymity has to do with whether the identity or any identifying information about the participant is known. If you receive a campus survey by mail that does not request your name or any information that uniquely identifies you, then the data you provide are anonymous. When there are identifying data, confidentiality involves the extent to which that information about the individual will be safeguarded or protected. The informed consent document should outline the extent to which identifying information will be protected, and how that will be done (see Sieber, 1992, for a more complete discussion of these issues). Breaches of confidentiality can occur easily (Angoff, 1984), and it is important to safeguard against them.

5. If more than minimal risk is involved, the consent document needs to indicate whether compensation for any harm or injury that might occur is available. In the kind of social and behavioral research typically done by students in the social sciences, a particular topic

itself may be upsetting (e.g., acquaintance rape), and the research needs to provide a source to which the subject can turn if she or he is upset following the research (e.g., the student health center).

6. A statement that the research is voluntary, that the participant is under no obligation to answer any question(s) or take part in any procedure that he or she finds uncomfortable, that refusing to participate will result in no penalty or loss of benefits to which the participants would otherwise be entitled, and that the participant may discontinue participation at any time and ask that his or her data be withdrawn from the study.

7. A statement about whom to contact with questions or concerns about the research, and whom to contact if there is an adverse event. In addition to the researcher's name, address, and telephone number, a contact person not involved with the research also needs to be listed. This alternative contact person might be the IRB chairperson or another IRB member.

8. The researcher should give the participant a copy of the informed consent document and keep a copy for his or her files.

Comprehension is a cognitive process, and informed consent documents often contain so much information or so much technical information that they are hard to understand (McEvoy & Keefe, 1999). McEvoy and Keefe provide a number of helpful wording suggestions for each of the components of informed consent. They also include two approaches to calculating the readability of the informed consent documents (or any of the other research components). As explained in Chapter 4 (Dustin's tip number 8), word processing programs typically contain options for assessing the reading level of text you have composed. Brody (2001) discusses ways in which informed consent can be made more meaningful and is developing an instrument to measure the degree to which subjects correctly answer questions concerned with the fundamental features of the research.

● ●
REFLECT AND REVIEW

What is the difference between anonymity and confidentiality?

● ●
APPLY YOUR KNOWLEDGE

Draft your own informed consent document (Appendix A provides a template).

Other Sensitive Issues

IRBs are alert to issues of sensitive content, such as research dealing with clinical issues. If the topic of the research may be emotionally charged; for example, research on disordered eating, depression, or learning disabilities of the participant or his/her family members, the researcher needs to indicate how he or she will handle the reactions of individuals who may become upset. One approach to this problem is to offer information in the debriefing document about where participants can seek help if they are upset. Usually this approach involves listing the campus counseling center and its telephone number. An additional step might be to provide appropriate websites or citations where the participant could learn more about the issue in question.

In the case of research on depression in nonclinical populations, researchers may actually delete an item that would be problematic if answered positively. For example, in the Beck Depression Inventory (BDI) (Beck, Ward, Mendelson, Mock, & Erbaugh, 1961), one item states, "I would like to kill myself if I had the chance." Novice researchers may choose to delete the item (they can still calculate the measure's internal consistency) to avoid the situation of dealing with a positive response.

When researchers are dealing with populations in the community where the potential exists for discovering troubling issues such as child abuse or neglect, the informed consent document must include a statement about the degree to which the participant's identity will be protected. If I were doing research on single-parent families or dual-career couples, and child care arrangements, for example, I might include a statement like the following disclosure on the informed consent document: "Although all information will be identified with a code number and not your name, there are circumstances under which I would be compelled by law to communicate about your situation with the appropriate authorities. These circumstances involve instances of child abuse or neglect." As you might imagine, some researchers argue that an informed consent document with such a statement limits the participation of a critical subsample of the population and hampers important research. In my experience, researchers have often tailored their questions to avoid problem areas that would lead them to include this kind of disclosure statement on the informed consent document.

Although all states require mental health workers to report suspected child abuse or neglect, fewer require this action of researchers (Jensen, Fisher, & Hoagwood, 1999). From an ethical rather than a legal standpoint, some would argue that all suspected child abuse or neglect needs to be reported, whatever the legal standing of the person who is alerted to it.

Vulnerable Populations and Their Implications for Research

As was discussed in Chapter 4 dealing with recruiting participants, research involving vulnerable populations requires full IRB review. As full IRB review at many institutions occurs once a month, if that frequently, planning research with vulnerable individuals is unwise in a semester-length research project. Vulnerable participants or subjects include prisoners, pregnant women, children, and fetuses (45 CFR 46). Additionally, it is possible that any given IRB may expand that list to include a variety of other possibilities, such as welfare recipients, those newly immigrated, or nursing home patients. It is always prudent to consult your local IRB about this issue.

In my experience, student researchers are often interested in research involving children, that is, those under the age of majority. In Connecticut, the age of majority is 18. For children to participate in research, there must be what is called **active consent** from the parent or guardian. Active consent means the parent or guardian must sign an informed consent document that *specifically assents* (agrees) to the participation of the child in question. For example, in a research project planned for a school classroom, it is not sufficient simply to have a lack of dissent (that is, no consent form objecting to the research is returned to the school). Given the length of time involved in securing permission from a series of gatekeepers, beginning with a principal or superintendent, moving to the parent or guardian, and ending with the child (if age-appropriate), research with children is not recommended in projects involving a single semester. Chapter 4 contains a section dealing with advice and procedures to follow if such research is undertaken.

The Child's Assent (Agreement)

What about the assent of the child? Federal guidelines do not specify an age at which children must be asked to assent to research participation. IRBs are given wide latitude with regard to establishing the age and form of assent for a given project (Nelson, 2002). In the experience of many of those who work with children, the age of 8 to 9 marks a developmental period in which children more routinely can be asked to provide assent, using age-appropriate explanations of what they are being asked to do.

Nelson (2002) makes the point that the research should be considered from the child's point of view, including the physical environment in which the research takes place (e.g., its child-friendliness).

"The concepts of minimal risk, prospect for direct benefit, assent, and permission are the basis for the special protections for children. This basis rests on the moral foundation of respect for children, justice, and the scope of parental authority" (Nelson, 2002, p. 383). Federal regulations specify the conditions under which the permission of one parent vs. two parents (where possible) is sought [46.408(b)]. The federal regulations also specify that the assent of the child should be solicited when the child is capable [46.408(a)]. Although the determination of whether the child is capable of such assent is made by the local IRB, "the objection of a child of any age is binding, unless the research holds out the prospect of direct benefit that is important to the child and achievable only through the experimental procedures" (Jensen, Fisher, & Hoagwood, 1999, p. 165).

Lifespan, a comprehensive health system in Rhode Island that includes the Hasbro Children's Hospital, offers useful IRB forms to use as models for those interested in research with children, especially involving pediatrics. The forms provide language about assent for children and adolescents. If you are interested in these templates (called Lifespan Child, and Adolescent Assent, Examples 1 and 2), they can be accessed at the following website: www.lifespan.org/research/irb/irbformslist.asp. The templates point out that when a child is 8 years of age or older, he or she must assent before becoming a participant in the research project.

REFLECT AND REVIEW

Explain when active consent is required and why.

The Question of Deception and Its Alternatives

One issue that always merits particular care in the IRB review process is research that involves deception. A significant amount of research in social psychology involves some kind of deception (Fisher & Fyrberg, 1994). Obviously, there may be a tension between the goals of informed consent and the realities of research involving deception. In her chapter on deception research, Sieber (1992) states, *"If it is to be acceptable at all, deception research should not involve people in ways that members of the subject population would find unacceptable"* (pp. 64–65). Out of the ethical and procedural difficulties involved with deception, alternatives have emerged; these include simulations, approaches to studying real behavior including ethnography and participant observation, and consent to concealment (Sieber, 1992). In research involving **consent to concealment**, participants are told that some information about the study will be withheld until the study's completion. Sieber (1992) argues that some of the more extreme forms of deception (**consent and false informing** and **no informing and no consent**) are unnecessary. In consent and false informing, although participants consent to participate, they are given false information about focus of the research. When subjects are neither informed nor consenting, they are essentially unaware that the research is happening (e.g., there may be a spy in an otherwise natural setting). Sieber (1992) raises a number of questions she hopes researchers will ask before engaging in research involving deception. Of these, the most important from my perspective is the following: "Is the study of such overriding importance and so well designed that deception is justified?" (p. 70). IRBs themselves want to learn more about research involving deception to evaluate research proposals fairly (Sieber & Baluyot, 1992).

Deception: Contribution of the American Psychological Association

Although the regulations surrounding IRBs start with the federal government, the profession of psychology, in the form of the ethical principles established by the American Psychological Association (APA), also addresses the treatment of human subjects in the research process. The American Psychological Association has its own set of ethical principles, first published by the APA in 1953 (American Psychological Association, 1953) and most recently revised in 2002. The most recent code, Ethical Principles of Psychologists and Code of Conduct (American Psychological Association, 2002), parallels the principles contained in the Belmont Report, with additional principles related to publication credit (8.12), plagiarism (8.11), and the duties of those who review the research of others who submit their work for publication (8.15). There are sections dealing with Informed Consent (8.02), Client/Patient, Student, and Subordinate Research Participants (8.04), Offering Inducements for Research Participation (8.06), Deception in Research (8.07), and Debriefing (8.08). Every student should have a copy of this document, which can be read in *The American Psychologist* (2002), pages 1060–1073, or by requesting a copy through the American Psychological Association.

Principle 8.07 of the APA's Ethical Principles (2002, p. 1070) is devoted to the topic of deception. It reads:

(a) Psychologists do not conduct a study involving deception unless they have determined that the use of deceptive techniques is justified by the study's significant prospective scientific, educational, or applied value and that effective nondeceptive alternative procedures are not feasible. (b) Psychologists do not deceive prospective participants about research that is reasonably expected to cause physical pain or severe emotional stress. (c) Psychologists explain any deception that is an integral feature of the design and conduct of an experiment to participants as early as is feasible, preferably at the conclusion of their participation, but not later than at the conclusion of the data collection, and permit participants to withdraw their data.

As we can see from the personal example that introduced this chapter, the effects of deception can be long-lasting and are not necessarily benign. In terms of the assessment of costs vs. benefits, the study that involves deception needs to be worth doing; that is, it needs to contribute substantially to the literature *and* the IRB must be persuaded that alternatives using deception would not adequately examine the hypotheses.

Other reasons for carefully considering whether deception is justified include the effect of deception on participants' attitudes when they participate in subsequent research. For example, they may grow more suspicious (Orne, 1962; Smith & Richardson, 1983), although some studies report no such reactions (e.g., Holmes, 1976 a & b). In research by Fisher and Fyrberg (1994) about students' evaluations of research involving deception, students judged the contributions to society of these studies involving deception to be higher than the costs to the participants in those studies. They also thought that forewarning participants (telling them in advance that the research might involve deception) would restrict the participant pool. At the same time, half the participants thought that the debriefing might cause some embarrassment in those who had participated. From 40% to 70% of the individuals (across the three studies they evaluated) responded that they thought the participants in those studies would be bothered to learn that they had undergone deception. Also, there was no indication that exposure to a class discussion about ethical issues in research involving deception would help to reduce these feelings of annoyance. Although students saw value in research that involved deception, it was not without cost. Therefore, a prudent researcher continues to pursue all other approaches to the research before proposing a study that involves deception.

REFLECT AND REVIEW

Under what conditions can the use of deception in research be justified?

APPLY YOUR KNOWLEDGE

Go to the recent journals section of your library and locate an article that involves deception. Try to think of a way in which the research could have been accomplished without deception.

Debriefing/Explanation of Research

At the conclusion of a research project, participants need to be more fully informed about the study. The reasons for such explanations in a study involving deception are obvious, but other fundamental reasons relate to the point made by Harry Stack Sullivan (1954/1970) and raised earlier. This is the point regarding respect for the client (read research participant). Sharing more fully the study's hypotheses communicates a respect for the individual and also encourages continued interest in research.

Principle 8.08 of the APA's ethical guide (2002, p. 1070) specifically addresses debriefing, or the process of giving the participants information about the research in which they were involved.

> (a) Psychologists provide a prompt opportunity for participants to obtain appropriate information about the nature, results, and conclusions of the research, and they take reasonable steps to correct any misconceptions that participants may have of which the psychologists are aware. (b) If scientific or humane values justify delaying or withholding this information, psychologists take reasonable measures to reduce the risk of harm. (c) When psychologists become aware that research procedures have harmed a participant, they take reasonable steps to minimize the harm. (p. 1070)

Although it is not required, I think it is a useful educational step to include one or two references to the relevant literature on the debriefing document for participants to take away from their experience (see Appendix B for an example). This step underscores the idea that participation in research can be meaningful, which is one of the reasons that subject pools exist. Through participation, students learn more about the process of doing research and see models of behavior that they can emulate.

Alternatives to Participation for Students in a Subject Pool

Principle 8.04(b) of the APA Ethical Principles of Psychologists and Code of Conduct (2002, p. 1069) stipulates that alternatives be provided to students in courses where research participation is required. In other words, participation in research cannot be required. In a study of undergraduate departments, Landrum and Chastain (1999) report the following alternatives to research participation: reviewing a journal article, writing a short paper based on the observation of an experimental session or a case study in which the student is the participant in some kind of simulation, participating in a discussion led by a lab assistant after viewing a videotape related to psychology, hearing a colloquium or other research presentation (even those of students in upper-level psychology courses), and creating an individualized research project approved by the instructor.

Guidelines from the APA even urge that the course catalogue contain subject pool requirements (Sieber, 1999). Very few departments (fewer than 8% in a study by Sieber, 1999) had subject pools that were technically voluntary; that is, no penalties of any kind for nonparticipation, and no benefits (other than the educational ones) to participation. Sieber argues that "alternatives to subject pool participation should be nonpunitive, educationally valuable, equitable, and attractive" (1999, p. 63).

With regard to the federal guidelines, "the central controversy about college student participation involves whether participation for course credit is considered coercive" (Tickle & Heatherton, 2002, p. 399). Pressure to participate is likely to be reduced if students are able to sign up for studies advertised on a research bulletin board, rather than being solicited in classes. If college students have not reached the age of majority, steps need to be taken to obtain parental/guardian consent. On informed consent documents, students may be asked to indicate that they are at least the age of majority in that state in order to qualify for the research.

As Gillespie (1999) points out, actually requiring participation (or its alternatives) from all students in a course may remove the possibility of coercion, although it is certainly the case that individual researchers might still be guilty of undue lobbying for a particular project.

Does Social and Behavioral Research Need IRB Review?

A good many social scientists chafe under the requirement of IRB review, arguing that the procedures are inappropriate for the kinds of research done in the social and behavioral sciences. Oakes (2002) identifies two problems that help to explain the growing frustration of social and behavioral scientists with the IRBs: 1) that regulations were developed for biomedical research, and 2) that the interpretations of the regulations have become stricter. There is some sense that the IRBs overestimate the possible risks involved in research in the social sciences (Pattullo, 1984). Among the risks posed by research in social science, Oakes (2002) lists: "invasion of privacy, loss of confidentiality, psychological trauma, indirect physical harm, embarrassment, stigma, and group stereotyping" (p. 449). Oakes (2002) argues that education is essential to help researchers understand the "legal, ethically sound, and scientifically legitimate" roles that IRBs play (pp. 453–454).

Also, because the federal regulations give local IRBs the ability to interpret the regulations and to add requirements reflective of community standards (Sieber, 1992), IRBs in different parts of the country may reach different conclusions about the same proposal. This inconsistency is obviously troublesome (Kass & Sugarman, 1996). The image if not the reality of injustice may result as ". . . different standards are being applied to research at different institutions and in different parts of the country" (Rosnow, Rotheram-Borus, Ceci, Blanck, & Koocher, 1993, p. 824). Researchers complain about obstacles erected by IRBs; IRB committee members complain about researchers' lack of appreciation for ethical safeguards (Council, Smith, Kaster-Bundgaard, & Gladue, 1997). But one of Rosnow et al.'s concerns (1993) is the cost of not doing (i.e., not permitting) the research. "In general, we believe that a mirror must also be held up to the review process, so that its existence, fairness, and effectiveness can be examined and justified" (p. 825).

What are some of the complaints about IRBs? Faculty members seem to be more dissatisfied with the work of IRBs (e.g., proposal turnaround time) than are their graduate students (Ferraro, Szigeti, Dawes, & Pan, 1999). The slowness of the proposal turnaround time was also a common complaint in the research of Liddle and Brazelton (1996) involving 10 public research institutions. Some respondents in this research did not comply with regulations—8% did their research without obtaining IRB approval. Who is likely to comply? "Faculty satisfaction with IRB functioning appears to be an important factor in compliance with IRB procedures" (Liddle & Brazelton, 1996, p. 6).

In criticizing the current regulatory environment, Kapp (2002, p. 39) states, "Typically, IRBs have essentially taken a 'hands-off' approach to review of the scientific merits of research protocols, ignoring the logical link between the quality of the science and the justification for allowing any risk to volunteers." It has even been suggested that something like a research intermediary (RI) could provide closer continuing review of research projects once subjects had consented to research projects (Reiser & Knudson, 1993). The RI would work to update the IRB and community about new legislation and ethical debates and would specifically report to the IRB about the condition of research sites.

Tropp (1982) examines the argument that federal regulations place an unnecessary burden on social scientists and states that we can identify "classes of nonrisky social science research that need not be regulated" (p. 395). Of primary interest to us may be his argument that mail, telephone, or interviewer-delivered surveys that do not involve questions of a sensitive nature (e.g., substance abuse, sexual behavior, violence, suicidal ideation) need no regulation. To this list he also adds oral histories, journalism, linguistics, and a number of other approaches. When the studies in question involve normal adults whose participation has not been coerced, and whose answers cannot be linked to their identity, regulation, he argues, is unnecessary and a waste of IRB energy. With IRBs often overwhelmed by the need to review larger numbers of proposals, Tropp argues that IRB review should be focused on risky research.

Some recent decisions by the federal government reflect a reconsideration of whether all social science projects qualify for IRB review. In 2003, the Office for Human Research Protections stated that oral history interviews, in general, do not qualify as research and thus are not subject to IRB review. The argument put forth was that these oral history projects (in general) are not designed to facilitate "generalizable knowledge" presumably because such interviews are tailored to the individual. For that reason, oral history interviews (in general) do not meet the government's definition of research.

● ●

APPLY YOUR KNOWLEDGE

With a peer, argue the pros and cons of IRB research for the social sciences.

Advice for Preparing Your IRB Proposal

Despite some reinterpretations of the concept of research, most projects undertaken by social scientists will continue to require IRB review. To that end, here is some advice regarding preparing your research proposal for IRB review:

1. Plan ahead. IRBs do not meet at the drop of a hat. Most have a schedule of meetings (e.g., once a month) and only come together for proposals requiring a full committee review. If your proposal requires full review, there will be a deadline for submission of the proposal. You may have to wait another month (or more) if you miss the deadline.

2. Be clear about the timetable for submission, who receives your proposal, and whether you are expected to provide a specific number of copies of the proposal.

3. Understand the levels of IRB review. It makes a difference in how quickly your proposal can be evaluated whether it falls under the exempt, expedited, or full review category.

4. Most institutions have a form you must complete that includes all of the information the IRB will need to evaluate your research project. Make sure that you have carefully completed all of the sections of this submission form. Pay particular attention to your informed consent document and your debriefing statement. Researchers often fail to follow the guidelines for submission (Brinthaupt, 2002).

5. Include all measures and descriptions of apparatus. It is not sufficient to vaguely refer to a measure or piece of equipment that you plan to use but have not yet obtained. The IRB needs to review exactly what the participants will be asked to complete or experience.

6. Make sure that your faculty adviser has signed the form you submit (most IRBs require this) and has carefully reviewed your proposal.

7. If your proposal requires a review by the full IRB, you will probably be asked to attend that meeting with your faculty adviser. Never fear; this can be an excellent experience. Students who meet with the full IRB for a proposal review generally find the meeting to be extremely helpful. The feedback from this meeting invariably results in a better research project.

8. Often the reason for full IRB review involves research with a vulnerable population, typically children. Make sure that you have all of the necessary permissions to do the research. Often such research involves children in a school setting, and written approval from gatekeepers, typically the principal or school superintendent, is usually required. The IRB will not approve a proposal without such documentation.

9. If your research involves deception, be sure that you justify its use in your proposal and explain why alternatives are not feasible.

Oakes (2002, p. 469) also provides a list that is very helpful in preparing your proposal. One of his recommendations has special appeal: "Ask yourself if you would honestly want someone you love to participate in your study."

The IRB As an Educational Experience: Training Modules

Most of the students are positive about their experience with IRB review, especially those who have undergone a full review. But researchers are more likely to appreciate their IRB experience if they fully understand the need for such review. To help researchers better understand the IRB, and its history and procedures, the federal government has developed a number of useful training modules. At the website http://cme.nci.nih.gov, the Continuing Cancer Education Curriculum for Health Professionals, there is a module entitled Human Participant Education for Research Teams. This educational module provides a good overview of the issues with which researchers need to be familiar. More extensive training for researchers is a goal of the federal government (Kapp, 2002).

SUMMARY

You are now fairly knowledgeable about the inner workings of the IRB, and its purpose and procedures. With this information, you should know which level of IRB review applies to your project (exempt, expedited, or full). You have the knowledge you need to prepare the beginning and ending documents of an IRB proposal: Informed Consent and Debriefing. You can also complete the federal government training module recommended at the end of this chapter to further your understanding of IRBs.

APPLY YOUR KNOWLEDGE QUESTIONS

In the event that you did not have time to do them earlier, here is the list of APPLY YOUR KNOWLEDGE questions in this chapter. Try them now:

1. Give an example of (1) a project that would not be considered research, (2) a project that would fall under the Exempt category, (3) a project that would involve Expedited Review, and (4) a project that would require Full Review.

2. Draft your own informed consent document (Appendix A provides a template).

3. Go to the recent journals section of your library and locate an article that involves deception. Try to think of a way in which the research could have been accomplished without deception.

4. With a peer, argue the pros and cons of IRB research for the social sciences.

WEB RESOURCES

There are a number of research methods workshops on the web that may enhance your knowledge of the topics in this chapter. Here is a list of these workshops and their web address:

Ethical Issues

Effective Debriefing

www.wadsworth.com/psychology_d/templates/
student_resources/workshops/resch_wrk.html

Managing Your Data

6

A Penny Saved . . .

Introduction and Chapter Overview

Managing your data is a critical part of successful research projects. Although the term *data* is usually linked to the quantitative or qualitative outcomes of your research project, I think it is also appropriate to discuss the word processing documents you create under this heading. How many times have you failed to save a file before Word suddenly quits? How many times have you actually deleted new text you have created when going from one computer to another and/or from a floppy disk to hard drive (or vice versa)? These problems have happened to all of us.

This chapter will provide useful suggestions and tips for managing your data and word processing files. These suggestions and tips take time, energy, and patience, but are well worth the effort. You will learn the value of completely dating and labeling your files and naming your variables. Types of **coding schemes** (how to determine how your data should be entered) will be described as will the benefits of entering every item rather than just recording a scale total. Strategies for dealing with missing data and out-of-range mistakes will be explained. The sequence of doing data analyses, from checking for data entry mistakes and preliminary analyses, to final analyses, will be described. The chapter will also cover the finer points of content analysis.

As you read this chapter, keep one larger point in mind. Data and analyses of these data are tools; they do not speak for themselves. You, the researcher, must communicate their meaning when you present your findings (see later sections of this chapter and Chapter 7).

Data Entry

Organizational skills are paramount in successful data entry and data management. Time spent up front in labeling and numbering questionnaires, interviews, or any kind of behavioral output is well spent. Dating and labeling begins with the questionnaires or recording sheets themselves and extends to the opportunities for labeling variables in statistical packages. Unlike the familiar refrain, "Less is more," in this context, *more is actually more*. There is no substitute for thorough and complete labeling and dating. Although putting your data aside and returning to it six months or a year later is not going to happen in a one-semester research project, it often does in researchers' careers. Establishing good research habits now will serve you well in the future.

What to Label

You certainly want to number every questionnaire or behavioral reporting sheet from 1 to N. I recommend writing the number on the questionnaire itself, typically in the upper right-hand corner. If the questionnaires look identical, but there was an experimental design and the conditions under which the questionnaires were filled out (or behavioral measures recorded) were different, you certainly want to identify that difference in your label. For example, if you examined the effect of nature on problem solving by having live plants in the data collection room in the experimental condition and no plants in the room in the control condition, you need to label that fact. If the first 10 participants were in the control group, you might label them 1C, 2C, and so on. If the next 10 participants were in the Experimental condition, you might label them 11E, 12E, and so on. When you actually enter the data in your computer for statistical analysis, you will be able to code whether the participant was in the control or experimental group as one variable with two levels or choices (more on that later).

If there is any chance that you would *ever* separate the pages of the questionnaire (for example, if you had a number of open-ended responses that produced qualitative data that you might look at later or if another person might be coding those data), then it is advisable to label *each* page of the questionnaire with the participant number and condition (if relevant). The time it takes to label thoroughly is well spent.

I also recommend that you record the date of data collection on your questionnaires. This step is particularly important if you are going to collect the data and then put them away for a while, but I also recommend it as a routine step for every researcher. Even with the passage of a week, you may not remember how many participants you ran in a given session. Dating the questionnaires or response sheets answers that question. If you collect data at more than one session on a single day, your "dating" will also include the time of day.

Use of Spreadsheets

Rather than moving directly to a statistical package like SPSS, some instructors have their students start with a spreadsheet program. Such a program, like Excel, is widely available, whereas some schools either do not have SPSS or a comparable program or have a site license. A site license is a purchased permission to simultaneously use a certain number of copies of the program; often a school will have a license for just a few copies of a particular statistical software program. A program like Excel is accessible, easy to use, and has great utility for creating derived measures (like score totals), graphs, and so on. Most statistical packages such as SPSS allow you to directly import Excel files for further data analyses. By using both Excel and SPSS, you limit the time you need to spend on SPSS, which may be important if your school has few copies of the program available for simultaneous use.

Labeling in a Statistical Package

A statistical package such as SPSS gives you the opportunity to name the variables in your analyses and to provide names for the values or levels of those variables (if appropriate). My advice is to provide labels wherever there is the opportunity to provide labels. Remember, more is more. For example, for the variable Sex, you may simply use that variable name, but the numerical values of 1 and 2 can be labeled as (1) men, and (2) women (or vice versa, depending on what you select). In addition to helping you remember what the numerical values represent (and it is easy to forget, even in the span of a week), those value labels are then typically included on your statistical printout, which makes the analysis easier to interpret.

Remember to Label

- participant numbers
- experimental conditions
- date of data collection
- variable names
- value names

Deciding on a Coding System

Before entering your data into a computer program such as SPSS, you need to develop your coding scheme. The coding scheme is the organizational approach you will use to enter your data. Each horizontal line of data represents one participant. Each vertical column of data represents the value of a particular variable for each participant.

What seems to present a small challenge to students is figuring out what should go in a given column. In particular, students have trouble understanding the idea of variables and values. To understand the difference between variables and values, it helps to think in terms of experimental design. Let's take our example of looking at problem solving in rooms that have no evidence of nature (control) or have live plants (experimental condition). In this example, the independent variable (IV), which is the presence of nature or not, is represented by a single column. The levels or values of the variable (experimental condition or control) are represented by two different numbers (usually 1 and 2, respectively). The output measure might be the number of word problems that a person solves in his or her condition. Let's imagine that there were 10 word problems, and the person's score on those problems could vary from 0 (none correct) to 10 (all 10 correct). In this experiment you may also have asked for

Participant #	Sex	Condition	Age	Score
1	1	1	19	7
2	2	2	19	5

FIGURE 6.1 Sample Data Coding Scheme

demographics such as sex and age. Sex is a single variable (one column) that is usually represented as having two levels, men and women, represented by 1 and 2, respectively. If you have asked for age in an open-ended manner (i.e., Age _____), then the individual's age (e.g., 19) is represented in a single column. That number communicates the information of age directly, whereas a categorical variable like Sex is represented by numbers that stand for values (e.g., 1 could stand for men and 2 for women).

The box above (Figure 6.1) represents the data scheme for your first two hypothetical participants from our example. Participant 1 was a man (1), who was in the experimental condition (1), who was 19, who answered seven problems correctly. The second line represents participant 2, a woman (2), in the control condition (2), who was also 19, who answered five problems correctly.

Specificity Is Flexibility

But in our age example, if you asked the question of age in terms of age brackets (e.g., 16–20, 21–25, 26–30), each of those brackets would need to be represented by a number (1, 2, and 3, respectively). The participant who is 19 would have checked the 16–20 bracket, which you would then have entered as a 1 under the column that represents Age. You can always take a variable that has been represented with specificity (such as exact age in years), and collapse the ages to create categories (if there is some reason to do this in your study such as using age as a quasi-independent variable).

You can also collapse categories themselves to create categories with more power; that is, to create categories with more participants. For example, consider a study that looked at satisfaction with college and class year. You asked people their class year: first, second, third, or fourth. But you may not have many participants in their junior year (year 3) for some reason. Many juniors participate in study abroad programs, which often lowers their numbers in research studies relative to the other class years and makes analyses with sufficient power a problem. You could decide to collapse class year into underclassmen (1s and 2s) and upperclassmen (3s and 4s), or you might be interested in the contrast between first-year students (1s) and everyone else (2s, 3s, and 4s) on your outcome measure of satisfaction with the college experience.

Thus, through recoding, you can always create new variables by collapsing. You can also create new variables through particular functions in statistical packages. Most statistical programs have the capability of creating new variables (like creating a scale total from the addition of the separate items in the scale). Most statistical programs will permit you to do analyses for part of the sample using the "Select cases" function (or its equivalent). Such functions allow you to restrict the analysis to one level or value of a variable, or to part of a sample. For example, if you wanted to look at some research questions separately for women in a study where you had Sex as a variable entered as separate values for men and for women, there are ways to restrict the analysis to women using the "Select cases" function (these functions are described in more detail later in the chapter).

All of these data reduction choices are possible—*if* you start out with specificity.

However, what you cannot do is to make data more specific than its initial form allows. When in doubt, ask demographic questions in the most specific form possible (like an open-ended age question) so that you have the ability to collapse categories if desired or necessary.

The width of a variable. Sometimes students have difficulty understanding that a given column, which holds one variable, can be as numerically "wide" as needed. Students have been well-versed in basic arithmetic, remembering the idea of a 1s column, a 10s column, a 100s column, and so forth. However, in statistical packages such as SPSS, a given column, representing one variable, can be as numerically "wide" as necessary; a number of any size can be represented in a single column. Columns hold *variables*; a single variable can be represented by a number of any size. In a sense, SPSS is a spreadsheet with statistical functions.

● ●

REFLECT AND REVIEW

With regard to coding data, explain the difference between a variable and a value.

APPLY YOUR KNOWLEDGE

Develop your own coding scheme for the following variables: class year, age, and college major.

A Word About Keeping Data Backed Up

A number of general principles are involved with "saving" files. Two basic principles or rules involve the frequent saving of files as you work on them during a session, and the saving of files in some distinctive fashion at the end of a given session.

When you learned word processing techniques and the use of a computer, someone probably told you to save the file you are working on frequently, and to work on the hard drive and save your file to a disk as a backup. Most of you have probably experienced the loss of material you just added to a file when your word processing program quit unexpectedly. That loss of information is a vivid reminder of why it is important to save your data frequently. There are different rules of thumb—every 10 minutes, every paragraph. Select a rule of thumb that works for you and *follow it.*

With the portability and availability of computers, people may be working on multiple computers (their own, those in the library or student union) and transporting disks from computer to computer. To make sure that you do not copy over files that you need, or that you do not replace newer files with older files, rather than the other way around (as all of us have done), you need a labeling system, and you need to stick to that system. Perhaps every time you work on a file and quit for the day, you need to update the file name and save it as MethodReport6.doc instead of MethodReport5.doc.

Finally, I noticed recently that our library staff posted the following sign at the entrance to the library where you have to walk through an electronic security gate: "Warning! The library's security system may affect any computer floppy disks you bring through the gates. Remove them from your bags and pass them around the gates when entering or exiting." What this warning suggests is the need to prepare for the unexpected—have backups of your backups; make sure that important information is available in more than one place.

How to Enter Scales: Scale Total vs. Individual Items

Many scales have a Scale Total, the sum of the respondent's answers to each of the scale's items. Typically it is the scale total that is used in analyses in your research. For example, the scale total for the Rosenberg

Self-Esteem Scale (1965) might be used in a correlation between self-esteem and Grade Point Average. The Rosenberg scale has 10 items. Why, then, should you enter the value for each item (in a separate column) for each person? For the Rosenberg scale, the difference in effort required would be having one column (the scale total) where you enter the *total* for each participant vs. having 10 columns, where each item on the Rosenberg has its own column, and you enter each person's score for each item separately. Why should you expend the extra effort to record each participant's score for each item?

There are a number of good reasons for expending the extra effort to enter each item on the scale for each person. First, this method enables you to address the problem of missing data. A second reason is that individual items are easier to check for out-of-range values as well as missing data. Third, you can run a reliability analysis (i.e., Cronbach's alpha) for that scale for your *own* data if you have entered individual items. You cannot run a reliability analysis on score totals.

Dealing with Missing Data

Frequently, participants do not answer every item on a questionnaire. Sometimes this is a purposeful omission on their part. Sometimes people skip an item because they simply miss it, especially when items are printed too close together on a page, for example, or are not numbered consecutively or at all.

Each participant is valuable, and particularly important when the number of participants is small. So, up to a point (see following comments), you can fill a missing data point with the numerical mean on that item for any item that is a continuous variable. You calculate the numerical mean from the rest of the sample. But at some point, people have omitted or skipped so many items that their data are questionable. There is no hard and fast rule for this cutoff point, but generally I feel confident using the approach of replacing missing data if people omit or skip no more than a third of the items in a scale. Thus, using this rule of thumb, if a scale has 15 items, people need to have completed 10 of those items for their data to be maintained in the sample.

Replacement of missing data works when the variables in question are *continuous*, such as the items on the Rosenberg scale, but it does not work for categorical variables such as Sex or any other kind of grouping variable (a variable that you would use as an independent variable in an analysis). Think about it—if a person has omitted his or her race, there is no "average race" that you can use as a replacement in the same way that a numerical mean from continuous data can be used and not change the outcome of your study.

It is also important to mention that some researchers do not endorse the practice of replacing missing values with means. Some researchers think that it is inappropriate to fill in missing data, even if it does not change the sample mean. These researchers argue that the participant may have purposely left the item blank, and that substituting a replacement value violates the participant's intention. With regard to replacing missing data, you will need to discuss with your instructor whether he or she endorses this practice.

Reliability Analysis

The other good reason to enter every item for every person is that it provides you with the capability of doing a reliability analysis (see also Chapter 3). The reliability analysis allows you to calculate the internal consistency of a given measure for *your* sample. We often use the published internal consistency (e.g., Cronbach's alpha) for a given measure to select an instrument for use in our study. We look for measures that have high internal consistency, which means that each item on the scale correlates highly with every other item on that scale. High internal consistency means that the items are all measuring the same construct or idea. But sometimes the published internal consistency of a given measure and the internal consistency of that measure for *your* sample are quite different, and usually not in a desirable direction (your alpha may be noticeably lower). The internal consistency of the measure in your sample may be very important to know as it will relate to the chance that you will have significant results.

I remember demonstrating to a Research Methods class how to calculate a reliability analysis on some data I had collected but had not yet analyzed. Much to my dismay, the Cronbach's alpha for my sample for a particular measure (which will go unnamed) was .30, whereas the reported alpha in the literature for this measure was much higher. Fortunately, I had other measures of importance in this study, so that all was not lost. I could have tried to raise the alpha of the measure with low reliability by eliminating items that were dragging down its reliability. However, being able to raise the reliability from .30 to nearer .70, an acceptable level, is highly unlikely.

After Data Entry

Data Entry Mistakes

One of the first things you want to do after entering your data is to check for entry mistakes and for missing data. To check for entry mistakes, do a Frequencies analysis for *each* variable (each column) in your data file. What this Frequencies analysis will show you is, for each variable, how many participants have a given numerical value. Let's say that you look at the variable Sex in your hypothetical study of 60 participants. The Frequencies analysis for Sex shows the following:

Men	Value 1	24
Women	Value 2	29
	Value 3	5
Missing data		2

Frequencies Analysis

What this frequency distribution tells you is that for five people, you have made a mistake because you entered the value 3 instead of the **within-range values**, in this case defined as either a 1 or a 2. Within-range values are the values that fall within the legitimate range for a given variable; they are the values that are permissible for that variable. In the example of the variable Sex, there are only two choices on your questionnaire (Male or Female) and two corresponding numerical labels, 1 and 2.

As another example, if you have a Likert scale for a number of items with the values 1–5, strongly disagree to strongly agree, and your Frequencies analysis for that item reveals some 6s or 7s, you have out-of-range values, which represent data entry mistakes. You then need to look down the column for the problem variable and identify which participants have 6s or 7s for any of the Likert scale items. Then you need to go back to your original data (from your questionnaires or behavioral recording sheets), get the correct information for that participant, and correct the entry in the data file.

In our first example, the Frequencies analysis for Sex also revealed two participants with missing data. Although you can't use a substitute mean value for this demographic variable because it is categorical, you will at least be alerted to the problem that your data analysis will not include these two people in any analysis that requires the use of the variable Sex. But for all continuous variables such as those represented in our Likert scale example, the Frequencies analysis will reveal which variables have missing data. Then you can calculate the mean for that item from those participants who completed it. Finally, you can then replace the missing data cell for a given participant with the appropriate sample mean you have calculated from all those who completed the item.

Adding New Data to the Original Data File

Some statistical software programs like SPSS do not update as they go along. For SPSS, new data have to be added to your original data file, and analyses must be rerun if they are affected by the addition of new data (e.g., if you add data from additional participants).

Reverse Scored Items

Some scales such as the Rosenberg Self-Esteem Scale (Rosenberg, 1965) contain items that must be reverse scored. Items need to be reverse scored when they ask about a construct in a manner that is the opposite of the way the majority of the items are phrased. For example, if the items are phrased in a positive manner (e.g., I am a cheerful person), an item that is stated negatively (e.g., I am not a happy person), would need to be reverse scored so that all of the numerical values are consistent with the idea that higher scores represent a more positive outlook.

There are two general ways of handling **reverse scored items.** Reverse scored items can be done as you actually enter the data, once you get the hang of it. For example, on a reverse scored item with five values, 1 becomes 5, and 5 becomes 1, 2 becomes 4, and 4 becomes 2; 3 remains 3. Alternatively, reverse scored items can be dealt with after the data are entered. After the data are entered you can reverse the values for any given item by using a Recode command (or its equivalent, depending on the statistical software). The advantage of entering raw data values and then reversing using a Recode or similar function is that entering raw values gives you another opportunity to check the accuracy of the data you have entered. It is critical to check and double-check the accuracy of the data you have entered before analyses are run.

• •

REFLECT AND REVIEW

Explain the merit of doing a reliability analysis and how you need to enter the data to calculate one. Can missing data be replaced for a categorical variable? Why or why not?

Preliminary Analyses

You know your data best. You may have an intuitive sense for whatever your formal analyses will ultimately reveal simply from looking through your data and entering it. In talking to students, I often hear comments like "I don't think the group differences will be significant because . . . everyone seemed to have pretty high (or low) scores."

It is often useful to run some preliminary analyses such as descriptive statistics (means and standard deviations) on your continuous variables. These analyses will give you a sense of "what is going on" with your data. Also, whenever you do any kind of analyses of group differences involving continuous dependent variables (such as a t-test, one-way ANOVA, factorial ANOVA, MANOVA, etc.), *always* look at your means to see if they make sense in terms of the statistical outcome of the analysis. For example, if you have a statistically significant finding, when you look at the means, you should see some numerical spread or gap between them. If you don't have statistically significant group differences but the means are spread (perhaps a 3- to 4-point gap), look at the standard deviations, which may be too large to have yielded statistically significant group differences based on the sample size.

Significance Levels and p Values

Significance levels indicate the degree to which a particular group difference or relationship may have happened by chance. The convention in the field of behavioral science is to set the alpha or significance level at .05. What that level means is that to call a particular finding significant, it must be at that .05 level or better. That is, the finding needs to be of such strength that there is only a 5 in 100 possibility that it occurred by chance, or, better yet, an even smaller chance (e.g., 1 in 100). Hypothetically, if you had a large enough sample, you could obtain a significant p value for any given analysis. However, if your study has sufficient power, it is inappropriate to add more participants just until a p value becomes significant.

Computer programs now give precise p or probability values. The researcher must then decide whether to report his or her findings in terms of the conventional format ($p < .05, p < .01, p < .00, p > .05$) or to use exact p values. There are advantages to each. The conventional approach may be easier to immediately understand. There is less numerical variability to keep track of, and so on. On the other hand, exact p values provide the reader with more precision. If a finding approaches significance, reporting the exact p value (e.g., $p = .068$) gives an indication of how close the finding was to the cutoff point. Remember, however, that when a print-out gives you a p value of .000, it does not mean that the probability is zero. Rather, it means that the probability is very small, less than 1 chance in 1,000, and the computer program stops with this level of precision. One rule is clear: Whichever method you adopt (conventional or exact), be consistent throughout your paper.

A note about significance levels. A particular finding is not more significant than another finding. Students often say that a finding at the .01 level is more significant than a finding at the .05 level. No, but what you can say about a finding at the .01 level is that it is less likely to have occurred by chance than a finding at the .05 level.

A Few Comments About SPSS

It is beyond the scope of this book to cover all aspects of SPSS. For that reason, I recommend that you refer to your notes from the course in which you were introduced to SPSS (presumably statistics) or use a handy guide like Kirkpatrick and Feeney's (2005) *A Simple Guide to SPSS® for Windows® for Version 12.0.* The comments I make will direct you to the sections of Kirkpatrick and Feeney that highlight some useful aspects of SPSS with which you may not be familiar. One important section is Appendix B, Data Transformations (pp. 106–115). This section covers three important functions: Computing a New Variable, Recoding Values of an Existing Variable, and Selecting Cases for Analysis. Let me mention the reasons for using each of these, and you can then consult Kirkpatrick and Feeney for the step-by-step descriptions for each of these functions.

The Compute Function

The Compute function is very useful because it allows you to create new variables out of existing variables. The most common use of the Compute function in my experience is to create a scale total after you have entered the items for a scale individually in order to run a reliability analysis. For example, what if you had a marital satisfaction scale that consists of three items (MS1, MS2, and MS3)? You probably entered these items as individual variables in order to run a reliability analysis. Using the Compute function, you would be able to have SPSS calculate a scale total for the sum of these three items for each participant.

The Recode Function

The Recode function also receives a good deal of use by students and allows you to do a number of things. One way to use this function is to create a new variable in which you replace the old values of a given item with new values. Although it is possible to put these new values into the "existing" variable, Kirkpatrick and Feeney recommend that you create a new variable, with its own name, to store the results of the recoding. In this way, you leave the original variable untouched in case you need to use it in the future. Imagine that you needed to reverse score an item with four values: 1, 2, 3, and 4. Using the Recode function, the values in the new variable are as follows: 1 becomes 4; 4 becomes 1; 2 becomes 3; and 3 becomes 2.

Another use of the Recode function is to collapse categories. Although Kirkpatrick and Feeney do not discuss this in their section on Recoding, it is pretty straightforward. Let's imagine that for a Class Year variable, you initially coded your data: 1 = freshmen, 2 = sophomores, 3 = juniors, and 4 = seniors. However, perhaps you had very few juniors participate in your research because many juniors were studying abroad, and you therefore decided to have just two class year groupings: freshmen and upperclassmen. Following the instructions that Kirkpatrick and Feeney give for the Recoding into Different Variables function, your 3s become 2s and your 4s also become 2s. You also need to say that 1s stay 1s and 2s stay 2s to make sure that your original participants who were 1s and 2s are included as values in the new variable. You will now have just two categories: 1s (freshmen) and 2s (upperclassmen: sophomores, juniors, and seniors).

The Select Cases function

The final function discussed in the section on Data Transformations is Selecting Cases for Analysis. Using this option allows you to restrict your analysis to just a part of your data set. For example, what if you wanted to see if a correlation between two different variables differed for freshmen and seniors? You could first restrict your analysis to freshmen, and run the correlation. Then you could do a second analysis by restricting your subsample to seniors, and run a second correlation. The Select Cases function allows you to do this.

The Analyze function

Most of the researcher's time is spent using the Analyze function, which lists many choices in its drop-down menu. In my experience, the most commonly used analyses are Descriptive Statistics (especially Frequencies, Descriptives, and Crosstabs), Compare Means (especially Independent Samples *t*-Test; Paired Samples *t*-Test, and One-Way ANOVA), General Linear Model (especially Univariate and Multivariate), Correlate (especially Bivariate), Regression (especially Linear), and Scale (especially Reliability Analysis). Let me briefly mention the reasons for using each of these, and you can consult the pages referenced in Kirkpatrick and Feeney for the step-by-step instructions in SPSS.

Descriptive Statistics: frequencies, Descriptives, and Crosstabs

The Frequencies function under the Descriptive Statistics category is helpful for a number of reasons. First, as discussed previously, it is one of the best ways to check the accuracy of the data you have entered. Under Frequencies, an option that also may be of interest to you is Charts, where you have the choices None, Bar, Pie, and Histogram. If you want to illustrate a particular finding you may want to select one of these Chart functions (refer to pages 18–24).

● ●

APPLY YOUR KNOWLEDGE

Take one variable with multiple values (e.g., sex, class year) from your own data set or from the sample data sets that SPSS provides, and create a bar chart, a pie chart, and a histogram for that variable.

When you use the Descriptives function, you can obtain the means and standard deviations for all of your interval scale items. Usually students have created interval scale items for such demographic characteristics as age in years. Most of the rating scales that students select to use or create themselves are also based on an interval scale, such as a rating scale from 1 to 5. You can use the Descriptives function to obtain information about central tendency and dispersion, such as the mean, standard deviation, minimum, and maximum scores. The minimum and maximum again give you the ability to check to make sure that the values for a given variable are within the permitted range (refer to pages 18–24).

Crosstabs is a function under Descriptive Statistics. Crosstabs is actually the function that permits you to do chi-square analyses. Chi-square is appropriate when each dimension of interest is categorical. For example, if you wanted to determine whether the proportion of men owning cars on campus was different from the proportion of women owning cars on campus, chi-square is the appropriate test (pp. 97–102).

Compare Means

Under the Compare Means heading, you will be likely to use the Independent Samples *t*-Test, the Paired-Samples *t*-Test, and the One-Way ANOVA. The Independent Samples *t*-Test (pp. 29–33) is used for the situation where you have one independent variable with just two levels (such as Sex: men and women), and one outcome or dependent variable, such as GPA. Commonly, the Paired Samples *t*-Test (pp. 34–37) is used in the situation where the same individuals have taken a measure, such as an intelligence test, at two different times, and you want to compare their performance. The One-Way ANOVA (pp. 38–48) is appropriate when you have just one dependent variable, but your independent variable has at least three levels or values. If you have a significant finding, you will need to do a Post Hoc test because with at least three levels of your independent variable, you do not know where the significant comparisons lie. With more than two levels, you can't tell where the significant differences lie (that is, between which groups) without doing a follow-up test.

General Linear Model

Under the category of General Linear Model, you will be most likely to use the Univariate function, which Kirkpatrick and Feeney cover, and perhaps the Multivariate function, which they do not cover. Under the Univariate function, in a between-groups design, you have the situation where you have more than one independent variable, but just one dependent variable (pp. 49–57). Kirkpatrick and Feeney cover this as the Two-Way Between-Groups (Independent Groups) ANOVA. The Multivariate function is appropriate if you have more than one related dependent variable (such as seven subscales of a scale). MANOVA does not require more than one independent variable; the critical issue is the number of dependent variables. There must be at least two.

Correlation and Regression

Correlation (pp. 75–79) is the statistical function that answers the question whether two variables are related across the sample. Regression (pp. 80–86) gives you somewhat more precision, because you are asking whether a given variable significantly predicts a particular outcome variable of interest. You might ask whether high school GPA is a significant predictor of college GPA. Regression gives you the answer. Multiple regression (pp. 87–96) asks whether more than one predictor variable significantly predicts the outcome variable of interest. If we asked which of two predictor variables, high school GPA and number of AP courses, better predicts the outcome variable college GPA, we would use multiple regression.

Scale

Although not covered by Kirkpatrick and Feeney, the Scale function has a common use. That function is to determine the internal consistency of a measure by using the Reliability analysis. Basically, if you select the Reliability Analysis, a window will open where you can move over all of the items from a particular scale (listed in your box of variables) to the box labeled "Items." Then, you make sure that "Alpha" is checked under the visible "Model" option. You will also want to click on the Statistics option, where you will then check "Item," "Scale," and "Scale if item deleted" under the Descriptives category. The print-out will give you the Cronbach's alpha, and it will also tell you what the alpha would be were any given item deleted. This information will enable you to determine whether deleting a particular item will raise the alpha. If so, you can go back to your Item box, delete the item that is holding down the alpha level, and then rerun the analysis. You repeat this process until you have deleted all of the items that are lowering the Cronbach's alpha.

Where to Begin Your Data Analyses

In conducting your data analyses, go back to your hypotheses and do the statistical tests that answer those hypotheses. As a refresher, you may want to look back at Chapter 2 where we discussed which kinds of hypotheses and research questions are best addressed by which statistical test. When you do your analyses, start with your major hypotheses and answer those questions before moving to the less important hypotheses.

Some researchers advocate going fishing (Bem, 2000) with your data and not writing up your paper until you know what your data show (even when you uncover findings for which you had not generated any hypotheses). I generally recommend a more straightforward approach. Your study posed certain research questions; your research design was developed to test these questions; your data analyses should be approached as a means to answer those questions.

Also, when you begin to go fishing, you increase the possibility of committing **Type I error.** Type I error is the likelihood that a significant finding will emerge that is due to chance. For that reason, you want to approach data analysis with the idea that you want to accomplish as much as possible in as few analyses as possible. If you are interested in the possibility of interaction effects, your data analysis typically will involve factorial ANOVA instead of one-way ANOVA. If you have multiple dependent variables with some degree of relationship (like scales of self-esteem, self-efficacy, and locus of control), you will want to do a multivariate analysis of variance (MANOVA) instead of separate ANOVAs, to control for Type I error.

On occasion you may have to do separate analyses with the same dependent variables (DVs) because you don't have enough participants filling each cell of your independent variables (IVs). For example, what if you were interested in the relationship of sex, class year, and campus residence hall location (north, central, south) to an outcome variable such as satisfaction with college? Perhaps your sample didn't include any men who were juniors, who also lived on north campus. So, instead of doing a 2 (sex) by 4 (class year) by 3 (location) factorial ANOVA, you need to potentially do three separate analyses: sex by class year, sex by location, and class year by location. Although this is not ideal, you might have to approach the analyses in this way to fill your data cells. If so, you can adjust for the possibility of Type I error by using a **Bonferroni correction.** In the Bonferroni correction, you divide the number of analyses you did with the same dependent variables (three in this case) by your level of significance (typically an alpha of .05) to produce a new, more stringent alpha of .017 (.05/3). This new more stringent alpha reduces the possibility that you will accept a finding as significant that was, in fact, a result of chance.

Going Fishing

Perhaps your formal hypotheses were not supported, but upon further exploration of your data you did discover some significant findings. As an example, in the research on offensive humor mentioned in Chapter 3, the major hypothesis was that being in the experimental condition, which involved participants who had been told that they would have to read sexist jokes aloud, would lead to lower ratings of humor and higher ratings of offensiveness of these jokes than for participants who were not told they would have to read the jokes out loud. This hypothesis was not supported, but the researchers did find a gender difference: women found the sexist jokes significantly less funny than did men. Although no hypotheses about gender differences had been stated, it is permissible to report this finding and even go on to suggest future research that might involve or build on this result. Sometimes findings emerge that, although unanticipated, lead to exciting new directions in research. As mentioned earlier, Bem (2000) is an advocate of going fishing. Bem (2000) suggests that you "go on a fishing expedition for something— anything—interesting" (p. 5). He talks about this fishing expedition in terms of "exploratory data analyses" (p. 5). Also, because these kinds of exploratory analyses may change what you had planned to write about, Bem recommends that you actually wait to write your article, any part of your article, until you have analyzed your data! As I stated earlier, I generally advocate a more straightforward approach based on your plan of research (answering the research questions you had posed). At the same time, I think it is fine to report unexpected findings and to suggest where they might lead you (or others) in the future.

An interesting ethical question is the extent to which a researcher is obligated to mention his or her insight about the best "next steps" in a particular line of research. Unexpected findings often lead to new ideas about how to develop a particular line of inquiry, and it seems reasonable to mention these ideas when you discuss your findings. My own view is that there are always more than enough ideas for future projects, and sharing them with the intellectual community is the hallmark of a researcher with integrity.

"Cleaning Up Your Act"

When you write about your data, you will need to tell the reader "what you did to 'clean up your act'" (Grigorenko, 2000, p. 106), or how you handled data that presented problems (e.g., missing data, out-of-range values, etc.). Every study has some participant response problems, which in turn lead to data analysis problems. As we saw in the section on Dealing with Missing Data, not all participants answer all questions, for any number of reasons. In addition to dealing with missing data in your analyses, you need to tell your reader how you addressed the problem, and why you chose a particular solution. If you eliminate participants' data for any reason (such as being an **outlier**), you have to tell the reader, and also mention what criterion or criteria you used to reach that conclusion. An outlier is a data point at some numerical distance from the other data point values in a particular data set. In research involving a touch screen computer that was used to record participants' responses to a way-finding task (Devlin & Bernstein, 1997), the software was designed so that it would "time out" if a participant did not record a response within 99 seconds, the computer default value. For a number of participants, there was a software problem and latencies of longer than 99 seconds were recorded. These participants were dropped from the analyses, with an appropriate explanation to the reader about these adjustments.

With regard to your set of data, Grigorenko (p. 107) argues that you need to make your sample size clear. You can accomplish this goal, she says, by presenting your degrees of freedom in every analysis. This step is important because your sample size may actually vary slightly from analysis to analysis. For example, if two of your participants failed to indicate their gender, an analysis that included gender would involve a different sample size than an analysis that did not include gender.

● ●

REFLECT AND REVIEW

When would you need to use a Bonferroni correction?

Content Analyses

Before turning our attention to the finer points involved with getting ready to write about your results, it is important to review and expand on some of the challenges of content analysis that were discussed in Chapter 2 dealing with qualitative research design and how to analyze open-ended questions. A content analysis is a reductive systematic analysis of written responses that leads to some thematic categorization.

Two general categories of data are quantitative and qualitative. Students are generally familiar with analysis involving quantitative data, which involves some form of statistical approach (e.g., *t*-test, one-way analysis of variance, chi-square). Qualitative data, such as those that might lead to the need for a content analysis, typically involve participants' written answers to one or more questions, in narrative style.

Developing content categories. As was discussed in Chapter 2, qualitative analyses present their own kind of challenges. A particular kind of qualitative analysis that research methods students may encounter is the open-ended question. Even in a study that is primarily quantitative, such as one where participants fill out a series of scales that are used as dependent variables in analyses, there may be open-ended questions. An example would be a study on student satisfaction among college students in their first year. As a final question the researcher asked, "What was your most memorable experience during the first year of college?" Imagine that this question was placed by itself, on the last page of the study, so that participants were staring at an entire page thinking of their response. In this situation, there is a demand characteristic inherent in the formatting of the question (think of the points made by Schwarz, 1999, that were discussed in Chapter 3). Contrast this with the situation where this last question about the memorable experience was placed as the last question, but with only half a page of space available for a written response, or a quarter page. At the extreme, imagine that you, the researcher, have left space for just a couple of lines for a written response. Clearly, the amount of space that is provided for an answer will influence what the respondent writes.

And the extent of the response has an impact on the challenge you face in making sense of this response, and performing a content analysis. Eventually in a content analysis, you may do descriptive analyses (think percentages) or even non-parametric analyses (think chi-squares) using these new categories, but first you have to figure out what to do with the responses.

To digest these written responses and do a content analysis, I recommend a series of steps. First, read through all of the responses, and do this a number of times. Remember the question, "What was your most memorable experience during the first year of college?" Make some mental notes about the kinds of memorable experiences people mention—did these experiences involve classroom achievements, interpersonal relationships, or sports triumphs? In addition to the specific experience, you might also think about other aspects of the experience that you might want to code, such as emotional tone. Did the experience involve positive or negative emotions?

Next, if each person has only written two or three lines, it isn't too hard to create a condensed list of responses on separate sheets of paper or in a computer file. That is, you can create a separate document (something like a spreadsheet) with the individual's participant number and then his or her response to the question next to it. It is much easier to think about themes and categories when the responses are more immediately available (that is, you don't have to flip through one response page per participant), and you don't have to carry around all of your questionnaires if you want to work on analyzing the data linked to this question. If the responses involve entire pages of handwriting, many researchers will photocopy the entire page (carefully labeled with the individual's participant number), and then work from these photocopies instead of from the complete questionnaire. Having fewer sheets of paper to handle will make it easier to perform content analyses.

After you have read through these condensed sheets a number of times (three to four), see if you can create a list of categories that reflect the major topics that came up in students' responses. You want a balance between categories that are too general ("interpersonal event") and those that are too specific ("met someone from Petoskey, Michigan"). How many categories you develop will to some extent reflect the number of participants you have, but I would be surprised if you had more than 10 meaningful categories. Even 10 might be too many to achieve the generality–specificity balance mentioned before. I would recommend a maximum of 6 to 7. For those very specific events mentioned only by one person that don't seem to fit in any of your categories, you can always use the faithful "Other" category.

Once you have developed your list of categories, try to come up with a brief operational definition of the category. Why? Because if you are going to reach some conclusions based on these categories, you will need to convince other people of the validity of these categories. You do this through the process of having other people read and categorize the written statements. This process is called developing

inter-rater reliability. The judgments about categories need to be independent of the judge; that is, any reasonable person who reads the operational definitions of the categories should reach the same conclusion about which statement belongs in which category. If the categories are too general and a given statement might belong in more than one category, reaching high inter-rater reliability will be a problem. Inter-rater reliability should reach at least 90%. An example of an operational definition for "sports-related memorable event" might be: "any mention of an athletic or sports activity (recreational, intramural, JV, or Varsity) in which the person participated." What if the participant's most memorable event of the first year of college was the following: "Went to the NCAA Women's Basketball Final and watched my team win." Although this is a sports-related event, the individual in question did not actually *participate* in the athletic event. Hence, with the operational definition we have developed, this particular memorable event would not fit into the sports-related category. This disconnection demonstrates the kind of fine-tuning that needs to be done to develop workable categories.

Summary of Steps in a Content Analysis

1. Read through all of the written responses

2. Create a condensed list of the responses

3. Create a list of categories (no more than six to seven)

4. Develop an operational definition for each category

5. Conduct inter-rater reliability analyses on a sample of each category

Content categories and statistics. Once you have developed your categories, each category can be represented as an individual data column. If a given participant mentioned an event in that category, he or she might have a "yes," represented as a "2" for data entry. A lack of a response for a particular category would be represented as a "no" and probably as a "1" for data entry. Once the categories are represented as data columns, it is possible to use the categories in statistical analyses. For example, you might ask the question whether men and women differ in some category of memorable events, such as sports. You could then do a chi-square analysis (remember, both dimensions in this analysis are categorical variables—men vs. women, yes vs. no) to determine whether the proportions of men and women differ with regard to this category.

In the most basic form, you could do a frequency analysis to see the percentages of "mentions" for each category, to determine which category of memorable event for the first year of college was most popular in the sense of being mentioned with the greatest frequency.

REFLECT AND REVIEW

What are the advantages and disadvantages to doing a content analysis?

Writing About Results

Before you even get to the step of writing about your results, keep in mind some of the advice that Salovey (2000) gives. In his chapter "Results that get results: Telling a good story," he describes important steps you can take to make your results compelling. Some of these tips should be considered at the time that you are *running* your analyses, in addition to the point at which you begin to tell the story of your data. Among Salovey's major points are to "begin with what is most important" (p. 122), to "keep the order of presentation parallel to other sections of the article" (p. 123), and to "provide top-down structure" (p. 123). He further argues that "thorough reporting is good form" (p. 128). Let's consider these points as they relate to actually running your analyses.

What Is Important?

When you start your analyses, make sure you know what *is* important. Go back to your original hypotheses and review the steps you planned to take to evaluate these hypotheses (see Chapter 2). As was discussed in Chapter 2, you should know the kinds of statistical tests you are going to run *before* you collect any data. Especially when you are working against a deadline, as you often are in a one-semester course, it is important to start your formal analyses with your major hypotheses. You do these formal analyses after running all of your checks for out-of-range values and missing data, and generating descriptives; that is, means and standard deviations, and frequencies, or counts, for your variables.

Parallel Order

Related to the idea of what is important is a parallel order of presentation throughout the article. Salovey argues that you should have a parallel structure in the Introduction, Method, and Results so that the reader knows what to expect. Imagine that the primary focus of your article is gender differences in spatial ability and a secondary focus is the role of different approaches to testing (e.g., timed vs. untimed tests) that can affect results. Given this order of priority, you would start the introduction with a review of the relevant gender differences in spatial ability. Then you would move to examples of different approaches to testing for gender differences (e.g., untimed vs. timed tests) to show their effects. Similarly, in the Method section you would talk first about the tests of gender differences in spatial ability that you used, for example the Vandenberg and Kuse Mental Rotations Test (Vandenberg & Kuse, 1978), and then about the different testing conditions you implemented (timed vs. untimed). Your major analysis in the Results section would look at gender differences in the context of the different testing condition.

Top-Down Structure

When Salovey talks about the importance of providing top-down structure, he explains that you need to set a context for the results, rather than simply spitting them out: ". . . remind the reader why those data are proffered and . . . reflect on the relationship between the reported data and the original hypotheses described, one hopes, in the introduction" (p. 124).

Thorough Reporting

One of the final points he makes in his chapter is the importance of thorough reporting. Salovey gives examples of the kinds of thoroughness he has in mind, for example, giving measures of dispersion or spread, if the kind of analysis you are doing is sensitive to dispersion. With regard to running your analyses prior to writing about your analyses, you need to think about what "extra" aspects of the analysis you will want to report and the most effective way of communicating this information. I recommend that you read Salovey's entire chapter to benefit from all of the good advice he provides. Figure 6.2 illustrates the components that are evident in results that readers will find compelling.

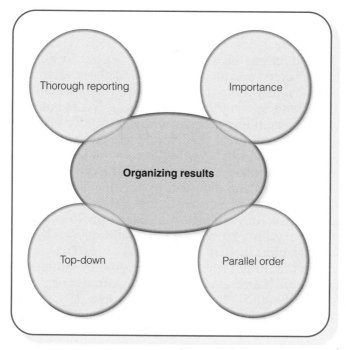

FIGURE 6.2 Components of Results

Writing Up Analyses: Explanations First!

Students often find reading the Results sections of articles a challenge, especially when they have taken only a semester of statistics. It isn't getting any easier to understand Results sections with the increased use of advanced statistical techniques. Even seasoned researchers sometimes have difficulty understanding the nuances of path analysis and causal modeling.

So, how is the more novice researcher to write up his or her own Results section? As was mentioned in Chapter 1, journals differ quite dramatically in the sophistication of the research designs reported in their articles and subsequently in the data analysis techniques used by authors who publish in these journals. I would recommend looking at such journals as *Psychological Reports, Perceptual and Motor Skills, Journal of Applied Social Psychology,* and *Journal of Social Psychology* for projects that may be limited in scope and straightforward, with results sections that you will understand.

Straightforward

Straightforward is the operative word in Results sections. This word does not mean dull; it means laying out what you did in a clear and logical fashion. As noted previously, Salovey (2000) recommends that you follow the same pattern (parallel order of presentation) throughout the paper; and that you discuss the results in the order in which the particular research questions were discussed in the literature review and in the statement of the hypotheses. This clear order will help the reader anticipate what is going to come next.

When you begin your results section, restate your hypotheses and spell out the kind of analyses you did. Identify the independent and dependent variables or whatever you are using (categorical dimensions for chi-squares, etc.). For example, in a study done to examine the relationship between sailing experience and spatial ability (Devlin, 2004), I began by indicating whether there was full or partial support for the hypotheses, and for which ones, by restating the hypotheses in the context of the results: "Results indicated full or partial support for four of the hypotheses. Results supported both Hypothesis 1, that men would have higher Mental Rotations Test scores than would women, and Hypothesis 2, that sailing team members would have higher Mental Rotations Test scores than would students in the other categories" (p. 1415). I then went on to explain the specific analyses that were used to produce those results.

Here is another example from a study on whether men and women differ in the kinds of directions they give to people who need help finding their way.

> The main purpose of this study was to examine whether men and women differed in the kinds of information they provide in giving directions. To evaluate whether written directions differed by gender in terms of the six primary assessments (use of cardinality, relational terms, landmarks, mileage, errors of omission, and errors of commission), a MANOVA was conducted. This analysis included only those people who provided written descriptions with a map supplement. Those who drew maps without written descriptions were excluded because of the lack of comparability of information. (Devlin, 2003, p. 1536)

What you see in this example is that there is a good deal of explanation about what the study tried to accomplish before ever mentioning a specific numerical result. There is even a comment about somehow "cleaning up your act" was accomplished (who was excluded and why)! You are setting the stage for the reader at the beginning of the Results section.

Summary of How to Write Results

- Tell a story

- Be straightforward

- Restate your hypotheses near the beginning

- State whether your hypotheses were supported

- Explain your selection of statistics

- Tell the reader how you "cleaned up your act"

REFLECT AND REVIEW

Explain what it means to say that results should tell a story.

APPLY YOUR KNOWLEDGE

Write the first sentences of your Results section. To do this, restate your major hypothesis(es) in everyday language and explain what you were trying to accomplish in this study. State what your IV(s) and DV(s) are and how they relate to your hypothesis(es).

SUMMARY

By this point, you should know what to do with your data after collecting them. Specifically, you know the importance of taking care of your data—labeling them carefully and completely. As Smith (2000) commented about the importance of accuracy in citation and reference scholarship, "If you have any obsessive-compulsive tendencies at all, let them take over . . ." (p. 156). I would extend this recommendation to your work with your data. You have seen how critical it is to date and label your questionnaires in their raw form, and to approach the labeling of your data in a data file with the same zeal. You have a good understanding of what a coding scheme is, and how to transform raw data into computer variables with values. You have seen how to handle "glitches" in your data, from missing data and data entry mistakes, to outliers. You have seen the value in starting with data specificity, so that you can collapse and transform your data if you desire. You have a working knowledge of content analysis, and you understand its relationship to inter-rater reliability. You also understand the importance of organization in writing up your results, starting with your major hypotheses.

APPLY YOUR KNOWLEDGE QUESTIONS

In the event that you did not have time to do them earlier, here is the list of APPLY YOUR KNOWLEDGE questions in this chapter. Try them now:

1. Develop your own coding scheme for the following variables: class year, age, and college major.

2. Take one variable with multiple values (e.g., sex, class year) from your own data set or from the sample data sets that SPSS provides, and create a bar chart, a pie chart, and a histogram for that variable.

3. Write the first sentences of your Results section. To do this, restate your major hypothesis(es) in everyday language and explain what you were trying to accomplish in this study. State what your IV(s) and DV(s) are and how they relate to your hypothesis(es).

WEB RESOURCES

There are a number of research methods workshops on the web that may enhance your knowledge of the topics in this chapter. Here is one of these workshops and its web address:

Common Mistakes in Student Research

www.wadsworth.com/psychology_d/templates/
student_resources/workshops/resch_wrk.html

The Light at the End of the Tunnel

Report Writing and Presentations

Introduction and Chapter Overview

In a one-semester research project, you generally have very little time to write, let alone rewrite, the paper. Each section—the Abstract, the Introduction, the Method, the Results, the Discussion, and the References— has its own challenges. You can make the write-up a more manageable process by following the timeline that was offered in Chapter 1. You will note that during week 4, when you are generating your IRB proposal, you are encouraged to begin a draft of the Introduction. Similarly, during week 8, you can write the Method section. There is no reason to wait to begin writing the paper until the end of the semester. Start earlier with the information you have available.

This chapter will talk about the unique challenges in each section of the research paper. In addition to offering some suggestions for writing each section of the paper, some basics of APA style will be reviewed. There will also be a section on grammatical pitfalls that commonly appear in research papers. The chapter will end with some skills that may be useful in poster presentations and oral presentations, and some suggestions for conferences where you might think about presenting your work.

The Title

Before describing what people consider to be the basic components of the paper, starting with the Abstract, let's talk about titles. Consider the following three titles of papers by students:

1. Athletics and Mindfulness: Furthering the Positive Psychological Influences on Youth through Athletics with the Application of Mindfulness
2. Ratings of Intelligence: Judging a Face by Its Glasses
3. The Effects of Different Types of Glasses on Perceived Level of Intelligence

Which of these titles, in your view, does the best job of communicating content *and* interesting the reader in reading more? Although the second and third titles describe the same research project, the student author of the second title has generated interest as well as knowledge with her title. Therefore, I would pick "Ratings of Intelligence: Judging a Face by Its Glasses" as the title that best communicates information and interest. What would you expect to read about in this paper? Presumably the paper would involve ratings of intelligence in terms of whether people wore glasses or perhaps in terms of the kinds of glasses they wore. In fact, the student researchers in this project performed an experiment with one independent variable (glasses), with three levels: whether the participants rated pictures of people who wore (1) no glasses, (2) normal glasses, or (3) "fashion" glasses. In this between-subjects design, the participants rated the stimulus figure (a photograph of a person displayed on a computer screen) on intelligence. They also rated a few other variables related to confidence. Although the second title is good, it might be even better if it indicated that variables in addition to intelligence were rated, as in the revision "Ratings Of Intelligence and Confidence: Judging a Face by Its Glasses."

In his chapter entitled "Titles and abstracts: They only sound unimportant" Sternberg (2000b) argues that the title and abstract play the most important roles in whether your article is read by others. The *Publication Manual of the American Psychological Association* (2001) suggests that the length of a title should be 10–12 words. Our first example is 17 words long; the second is 9 words; the third is 12 words.

APPLY YOUR KNOWLEDGE

See if you can rewrite the first title so that it communicates the information within 10–12 words.

The Abstract

If students find the Abstract one of the most difficult sections of the paper to write, they are not alone. Many professionals feel that way as well. The major difficulty in writing the Abstract comes with trying to fit a lot of information into a limited number of words. Many people may read only your Abstract. If that limited exposure is the case, it is even more important that this paragraph contain useful and complete (as complete as you can be in 120 words) information about your study. *The Publication Manual of the American Psychological Association* (2001) states that the Abstract should be no more than 120 words and should contain the following elements for an empirical article (p. 14):

- What you are investigating
- The number of participants, and their primary identifying characteristics, such as sex and age
- The procedure you used to gather data, including any test names, equipment employed, and so on

- The outcome of the study, with associated statistical information
- The meaning and relevance of the findings

Here is a sample abstract from a recent article (Devlin, 2004, p. 1409). Does it meet the APA criteria? How might it be improved?

> The relationship between sailing experience and men's and women's spatial ability was examined by assessing the sailing history and Mental Rotations Test scores of 230 participants. The 102 men and 128 women came from three groups: college sailors ($n = 65$), members of the general student body ($n = 110$), and college crew team members ($n = 55$). Participants completed the Vandenberg and Kuse Mental Rotations Test and Lawton's Way-finding Strategy Scale and Spatial Anxiety Scale. Demographic variables and sailing experience were also assessed. Men scored significantly higher on the Mental Rotations Test than did women, and sailing team members scored significantly higher on that test than did student body members and crew team members. Results are discussed in terms of current explanations for sex differences in spatial ability.

Note, with regard to the representation of numbers in the Abstract, that all numbers, with the exception of those that begin a sentence, are expressed as numerals. See the Method section in this chapter for more information about the stylistic presentation of numbers in research papers.

The Introduction

Although the entire research paper may be shaped like an hourglass (Bem, 2000), the Introduction should be shaped like a funnel (picture the top half of the hourglass). Figure 7.1 graphically presents this organization. The Introduction should start with an overview of the literature on a given topic or topics, which reflects the empirical threads that are being woven together in the research. Gradually, the Introduction should taper to the point where specific hypotheses are being proposed, often in the form of a list of statements, one hypothesis listed and numbered after another.

What goes between the beginning topic sentence and the statement of hypotheses? Look back at the sections toward the end of Chapter 1 entitled The Literature Review; Conflicts and Gaps; Seminal Studies and Becoming an Expert; Limitations and Future Directions; and Critique, Critique, Critique. These sections outline the kinds of issues you were considering as you prepared to select a topic and design a study. Now what you need to do is to write about that literature you considered in designing your study. And you need to do the writing in such a way that you avoid simply writing article summaries.

It is easy to fall into the trap of simply writing article summaries; that is, writing about each article you read, one after the other, giving

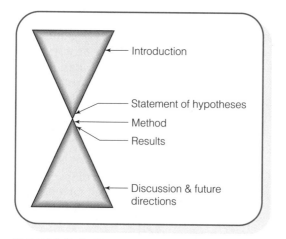

FIGURE 7.1 **The Research Paper Hourglass (after Bem, 2000)**

each the same weight and emphasis. What I mean by this is that it is easy to write about the articles in a formulaic way, talking about the hypotheses, aspects of the method, and whether the hypotheses were supported for each article. Kendall, Silk, and Chu (2000) refer to something like this when they talk about avoiding laundry lists and stacking abstracts (p. 49). Often in research methods classes students are asked to actually *create* article summaries as a way to help keep the students on track toward the goal of completing a project in one semester. That is a perfectly reasonable and useful approach. But the problem is that with all of these article summaries in hand, it is tempting to simply write about one study after another, note cards falling gently to the floor. . . .

Avoid the temptation to write your Introduction as a compilation of article summaries. Instead, consider the following kinds of questions and issues as you prepare to write:

1. What are the primary theories you considered?
2. What are the seminal or foundational studies that most researchers in this area cite?
3. What are the major findings?
4. Are there any anomalous findings?
5. Have there been methodological problems in the past; that is, issues of internal validity?
6. Has the research been limited to a narrow population; that is, issues of external validity?
7. Are some studies "better" than others in terms of their quality (design and sophistication, strength of findings)?

Once you have considered these questions, make an outline of your Introduction that reflects these issues (and others you may generate). What you are trying to do is create clusters or chunks of articles that belong together rather than simply stringing together the basic components of one article after another. For example, you might have a paragraph devoted to a common finding, such as the fact that men typically score higher on tests of mental rotation than do women. To communicate that information, you might have a sentence something like the following:

> Men are consistently reported to have higher scores on tests of spatial ability than do women, particularly on tests of mental rotation (e.g., Collins & Kimura, 1997; Dabbs, Chang, Strong, & Milun, 1998; Devlin, 2004; Halpern, 1986; Harris, 1978, 1981; Hyde, 1981, 1990; Malinowski, 2001; Masters & Sanders, 1993; Nordvik & Amponsah, 1998; Voyer, Nolan, & Voyer, 2000).

What you see in this sentence is the idea of chunking or grouping material that makes a similar point. You might not even mention any of these articles again in your paper.

Which research papers *do* deserve more attention in *your* paper? The articles that deserve more attention are those that have the greatest bearing on your study. The criterion of the greatest bearing may be in terms of findings from a particular study that you question or want to replicate for some reason; a design that you are following and expanding in some fashion (e.g., adding another level of the independent variable; using a more diverse population), and so on. Because some of the previous research papers you discuss will be summarized and others will be discussed in more detail, you will create an Introduction that varies in depth or weight—some articles are discussed briefly and with little detail; others are described in depth, down to the number of participants and the apparatus or particular instruments that were used. Greater specificity is usually devoted to the articles that are about research that is closest to your proposed study.

The First Sentence(s) in the Paper

The first few sentences in the paper deserve some mention because they generally set the stage for the reader. Although the rules of writing have loosened somewhat over the last few decades in terms of what used to be called "The Topic Sentence," it is still important to do a number of things in your introductory paragraph. You have to capture the attention of your readers and introduce the focus of the paper.

Consider the following introduction to a paper written by a research methods student:

> Education is an important factor when deciding how to raise a child, and for those with money, the "right" school is often the first step. In competitive social circles it is plausible for a child to be enrolled in a preschool before it has even left the womb. But with all the advantages and connections that these private schools may be giving their children, these parents may be forgetting an essential part of the child's education, his/her interracial interaction and racial awareness.

I thought this student did a good job of capturing the reader's attention and introducing the focus of the paper, interracial interaction and racial awareness, revealed at the end of the last sentence.

Now consider the following introductory sentences to another paper from a student in the same research group (in my research methods class, students often worked in groups, but each was responsible for writing his or her own version of the group research paper):

> Children learn misconceptions, stereotypes and create perceptions at young ages. Incorporating multiculturalism in the educational system is essential so students can truly integrate and develop within a diverse society. The acknowledgment and understanding of diversity is essential for children and adults of today's world. Misconceptions of different people fuel anger and mistrust.

In your view, what are the strengths and weaknesses of this beginning in contrast to the version we read earlier?

● ●

REFLECT AND REVIEW

Explain how to avoid writing an Introduction that is a series of article summaries.

● ●

APPLY YOUR KNOWLEDGE

Write the first paragraph of your paper, with special attention to the topic sentence and the goal of interesting your reader.

The Method Section

In many respects, students find the Method section the easiest to write because it has a built-in structure: Participants, Apparatus/Materials, and Procedure.

The *Publication Manual of the American Psychological Association* (APA, 2001) indicates what each of these sections should include, and the reader is directed to pages 17–20 for thorough coverage. You can also look at the sample papers in section 5.29 of the manual (pages 305–320). Basically, you want to provide enough detail in the Method section that a reader could replicate your research. The basic elements of each component of the Method are described in the sections that follow.

Participants

Provide the number of participants in each condition, by gender if appropriate. Tell the reader about any problems with attrition or other aspects of the sample (e.g., participants that dropped out or were excluded for some reason). Also, note that the entire sample is referred to with a capital N, whereas subsamples, such as participants in distinct conditions, are referred to with a lowercase n. Also note that all statistical copy, of which the sample size(s) (N, n) are an example, is presented in *italics*. Also, a little-known fact from the *APA Manual* is that the term "participants" is used when humans have given informed consent; if not, they are called "subjects" (see page 65 of the *APA Manual*). Animals, of course, are always referred to as subjects!

The *APA Manual* directs you to indicate how participants were selected and how they were assigned to condition. You also need to state whether there were any inducements (such as research credit or monetary payment). Indicate that the participants or subjects were treated according to ethical guidelines.

Apparatus/Materials

In this section, you basically describe the materials used in the study—equipment, surveys, or the nature of an intervention (e.g., if one group of students tried to solve problems in a 10' × 10' room and a second group tried to solve the same problems in a 20' × 20' room). You need to be specific about the equipment used if it is not common. Although it is not necessary to give the catalogue or item number for a stopwatch, it would be necessary for a computer on which students responded to some reaction time task. Similarly, you need to give as much detail as possible about any measures or surveys. Be sure to include reliability and validity information, particularly Cronbach's alpha for internal consistency, both in terms of the published literature and in terms of your own sample.

Procedure

The Procedure section outlines the steps you took in collecting your data. This is the section where you describe the lengths to which you went to ensure the study's internal validity—how participants/subjects were assigned to condition, whether randomization was employed, counterbalancing, and so on. Did you automate any instructions? Describe the instructions you gave to the participants and the nature of the debriefing they were given.

Statement of Research Design

Beyond the basic components of the Method section, Reis (2000) recommends that you include a clear and direct statement about your research design either at the beginning of the Method section or possibly at the end of the Introduction. When students hear this, they ask why such a section is needed when you already have a mandated procedure section. About this distinction, Reis answers: "The Design section differs from the Procedure section in that the latter is concerned with procedural details of what was done; the former describes the conceptual layout of constructs into conditions and variables" (pp. 82–83).

The Method section is also a place where you should pay close attention to the way you present numbers so that they conform to APA style. Here are some of the basic principles that come up in almost every Method section.

1. In general, numbers are expressed as symbols (numerals) at the cutoff point of 10 and above, and written out (e.g., "eight") below 10. However (and it seems that there are always such exceptions), if the same paragraph contains numbers both below and above 10 that are *grouped for comparison*, then all those numbers are expressed in numeral form. This exception does not apply when different categories of items are involved. The *APA Manual* (2001) gives the example "15 traits on each of four checklists" (p. 123) to illustrate when the exception does not apply. This example is correct because traits and checklists do not come from the same category and hence are not being compared.

2. Numbers are written as words whenever they begin a sentence; this stipulation even applies to the Abstract.

The Results Section

There are two general areas of difficulty for students writing Results sections. The first is that the statistical printouts of the data are hard to read and interpret for many students, and they don't know "what to report." The second challenge is that it is hard to talk about Results in a way that is reader-friendly, rather than in what you might call statisticalese.

Solving some of the problems related to knowing where to look on a printout for the important information and then knowing what you have to report comes with practice. You do get better at it. There are some general suggestions I can make about what is important in any given analysis, but this may be one of those times when you need to meet with your professor or TA for some help as well. I have also created a summary table to illustrate some common analyses with their typical format (see Appendix C).

Analyses of Group Differences

For analyses involving group differences, you will always want to report the means and standard deviations for each group involved. The means and standard deviations usually come first in a printout for approaches like analysis of variance. In any of these situations, you will also always want to report the degrees of freedom, which appear in different places depending on the analyses. Life becomes a bit harder when you have more complicated analyses like a between-subjects MANOVA, where you have the multivariate effect and then the between-subjects effects. The multivariate effect we usually report is Wilks's lambda, which is followed by an F value with its own hypothesis degrees of freedom and error degrees of freedom, and finally its significance level. The next level is generally the between-subjects effects, and for each effect of an independent variable you will have an F value, degrees of freedom, and a significance level.

Measures of Relationship

For measures of relationship, such as correlation, you give the statistical symbol for the test, for example, r, the number of participants, the value of the correlation, and the p value.

Nonparametric Statistics

In student papers, the most commonly used measure for categorical variables is the chi-square, an example of a nonparametric statistic (see also Chapter 2). A nonparametric statistic is one in which no assumptions are made about the distribution of scores in the sample.

To report the chi-square, you give degrees of freedom, the number of participants, the chi-square value, and the p value. Appendix C has an example of the way this information is presented. It is also important to give the percentages in each of the cells. For example, in a 2×2 chi-square, there are four cells. Imagine you had asked whether men and women differ in the percentages of each group owning a car on campus. Let's imagine that the chi-square was significant. You might report the following (hypothetical) values: "The analysis indicated that significantly more men (69%) than women (44%) reported having cars on campus; 31% of the men and 56% of the women reported not having cars on campus."

A Word About "Reading" Significance Levels

Although students have learned what an alpha level is and that by convention the disciplines in behavioral science generally set the alpha level at .05, recognizing that fact on the printout takes some practice. In a statistical software package like SPSS, the significance value for a particular analysis is usually found in the far right side of the printout under the column headed Significance. You scan across the row for the analysis of interest and read this number (which will be less than 1.0) on the right side of the printout. If the null hypothesis can be rejected, the number in the significance column will be *smaller* than .05! If you have not requested analyses for power and effect size, the significance column should be the last column on the right.

But so many times I see students look at this significance column, find a number like .965, and exclaim, "It's significant!" In our "bigger is better" culture, you have to pause and remember that "smaller is better" when it comes to significance levels. You hope to find numbers *smaller* than .05, such as .034, .022, and so on. Training yourself to understand the meaning of the values that are communicated just takes some time.

Reader-Friendly Results

The key to a successful results section is to provide a context for your results instead of just presenting numbers. As Salovey (2000) tells us, a successful results section involves "telling a good story" (p. 121). Although the *APA Manual* states that you should not discuss "the implications of the results" (p. 20) in this section, it is appropriate to state whether the hypotheses are supported.

Some authors advise you to start with simpler analyses such as descriptive statistics before presenting the more complicated analyses such as multivariate statistics (Grigorenko, 2000). Starting "simpler" would be considered a reader-friendly approach. To briefly reiterate the points made in Chapter 6, points from Salovey (2000) that I consider to be reader-friendly, "begin with what is most important" (p. 122), "keep the order of presentation parallel to other sections of the article"

(p. 123), and "provide top-down structure" (p. 123). One of the other points that Salovey (2000) makes is to not let "the structure of the statistical test determine the structure of your prose" (p. 125). Salovey tells us to talk about the findings using language that the reader can understand, before reviewing the statistical tests.

REFLECT AND REVIEW

How does a statement of research design differ from the procedure section? Why is the statement of research design needed?

APPLY YOUR KNOWLEDGE

Do some browsing through the articles you have found for your literature review to select one or two that have reader-friendly results. In your view, what are the characteristics you see that create reader-friendly results?

The Discussion

It is tempting to write a Discussion section that sounds like an expanded Results section, but the Discussion section needs to do more than simply talk about the results. You may begin by summarizing the findings, but you do not restate the numerical results in this summary. Instead of simply restating that one group performed better or worse or faster or slower, you want to talk about the implications of such findings. For example, instead of saying "People who wore glasses were judged to be more intelligent than people who did not wear glasses," you might say, "The fact that people who wore glasses were judged to be more intelligent than people who did not suggests that we use physical clues to make judgments about behavioral characteristics."

Salovey's (2000) suggestion that the order of presenting the results should follow the order in which the issues are presented in the Introduction and Method sections applies to the Discussion as well. Your major hypotheses, whether supported or not, need to be addressed first; then move on to a discussion of the findings that are less central to your study. I also think that Salovey's mandate for the results "to tell a good story" (p. 121) applies to the Discussion, too.

Another helpful way to look at the Discussion comes from Calfee (2000), who views the Discussion as a form of argumentation, with a claim (hypothesis), evidence (data), and a warrant; Calfee calls the warrant "connective tissue" (p. 135). "Warrants . . . aim to convince readers that the evidence supports the claim, and that no other interpretation is plausible" (p. 135). To create a successful argument, says Calfee, you have to switch shoes, and attack the claim you are trying to make from an opposing standpoint. For example, if I am trying to make the claim that experience such as sailing is causally related to performance on the Vandenberg and Kuse (1978) Mental Rotations Test, I have to address criticisms about lack of random assignment to condition, or possible genetic or hormonal influences. That is a tall order, but an effective Discussion about such data needs to address what I call the "What abouts . . . ?" and "Did you take account ofs . . . ?" An effective Discussion must address the other plausible explanations for your findings.

Nonsignificant Findings

Although I haven't collected formal statistics on the percentage of research methods projects in any given year that yield "significant" findings, my guess is that the percentage is below 50. Lots of papers have negative results to discuss, and there is always a temptation to bring up every possible post hoc explanation for the lack of significant findings. Almost every research methods paper I read talks about the problems with sample size (too small) and the lack of power. Another common theme is the limited ecological or external validity because of the lack of diversity in the sample. Where I teach, the student body is overwhelmingly European-American, and in addition, the percentage of women majoring in such disciplines as psychology, education, and human development is considerably higher than the percentage of men in those disciplines. Limited sample size and limited diversity of the sample are obvious drawbacks to most undergraduate research projects. Although it's tempting, avoid building an *entire* Discussion section around these drawbacks to your study when your findings are not significant. Instead, follow Calfee's (2000, pp. 141–142) advice: ". . . pick those matters that, on reflection, you view as significant insights that you gained from the experience."

REFLECT AND REVIEW

Explain Calfee's idea of a warrant and why you need to switch shoes (take the view of a critic) to write a good Discussion.

APPLY YOUR KNOWLEDGE

Make a list of issues *other* than sample size and the homogeneity of the sample that threaten the internal and external validity of your research.

Statistical vs. Practical Significance

Even when you have significant findings, the practical significance of your data may be less than impressive. A correlation of .30 may be significant in a given study, but it explains only 9% of the variance about a particular result. Reporting effect sizes is becoming more common in undergraduate research because the statistical packages make that easy, and effect sizes are also a way to help tease apart findings that are not simply significant, but are sufficiently large to have practical significance. For example, in the study I did comparing college sailors, student body members, and crew team members on a test of spatial ability (Devlin, 2004), the largest effect size ($\eta^2 = .11$) was for the sex difference (men had higher scores), a common finding in the literature, whereas the effect size for the differences between the scores of sailors, crew team members, and student body members, with sailors having higher scores than the other two groups, while significant, was quite small ($\eta^2 = .03$). A portion of your Discussion should address this issue of statistical vs. practical significance so that you don't claim more for your findings than they merit.

References

Don't laugh. The care with which the references are done reflects significantly on you (Smith, 2000). There are a number of basic rules about References that students seem to have difficulty following. A number of such rules are discussed in the following list.

1. Citations and References must match. Although you may consult more references than you actually *cite* in your paper, if you are using APA style, only those articles that you cite in your paper belong in your references.

2. Secondary sources. There are some special rules for the category of secondary sources. A **secondary source** is a source that you did not read in its original form and only read about as mentioned in a derivative, or secondary source. An example might be an unpublished manuscript that a faculty member talked about in a published paper, but which is not readily available to you. Another example is the discussion of studies in textbooks.

In general, it is to your advantage to avoid secondary sources. You need to read material in its original form. When you read about a study in someone else's paper or in a textbook, you are relying on the rendition of the facts and the interpretation of the information provided by that other person, not the original author. Although there might be bona fide reasons for using a secondary source, for example, the manuscript is unpublished or written in a foreign language, avoid the practice of using secondary sources. When the original is readily available, there is no excuse for using a secondary source, such as a textbook or someone else's discussion of an article. What usually happens to students is that they have not allowed sufficient time to obtain the original source and are backed into using a secondary source. Don't be one of those students! Plan ahead!

If you must use a secondary source to obtain information, the reference section lists only the secondary source, and not the original. For example, if you mention Smith's research, as cited in Jones (1988), only the complete reference for Jones (1988) appears in the References. The reason for that rule is that the reader needs to be able to verify the information that *you* provided, and Jones was the source of the information about Smith's work, not Smith him or herself.

Appendixes

Most published papers do not include appendixes because of the amount of space they take up. However, your professor may require that your research methods paper include your informed consent document, each of your scales, and your debriefing statement. If you need to include these, they will come after the References. Each appendix will be labeled alphabetically and separately (e.g., Appendix A), with the title of the appendix listed after the identifying letter:

Appendix A

Informed Consent Document

Tables and Figures

If you have them, where you put your tables and figures depends on how you view the status of the manuscript. If you consider it a "finished product" for your research methods class, you can incorporate the tables and figures into the body of the paper. A table will appear on a separate page, usually inserted as the next page after the table is first mentioned. If you say "See Table 1" somewhere on page 16, then Table 1 will be on page 17. However, if you consider your research methods paper something like a manuscript to be submitted for publication, then the tables and then figures will come after the References. I recommend that you consult the sample papers in the *Publication Manual of the American Psychological Association* (2001) on pages 305–320 for visual examples of how tables are laid out. To me, these sample papers present the clearest way to see what tables should look like. Sections 3.62 to 3.74 of the *APA Manual* provide detailed information about tables.

Similarly, figures have their own rules. In submitted papers (rather than "completed" projects that will not be published), the order is References, tables, and then figures. The caption of the figure goes on a separate page that precedes the figure itself (also on a separate page). Again, consult the sample papers in the *APA Manual* (pp. 305–320) for examples of figures. Sections 3.75 to 3.86 of the *APA Manual* (2001) provide detailed advice about preparing figures.

If the paper is to be a finished product in the form of an unpublished manuscript, as is the case with most research methods papers, the figure, with its caption, will appear on a separate page following the page on which it is first mentioned. However, it is wise to check with your instructor to see which approach he or she wants you to follow.

The *APA Manual* Behemoth

Multiple times a semester, students will complain to me that they are being asked to master the *Publication Manual of the American Psychological Association* (2001) in too much detail. My usual reply is that APA style is the backbone of writing in psychology. But remember that the *Publication Manual* is a reference book. You need to consult it as you write, and mastering the nuances of APA style will communicate to other people that you know what you are doing. A similar point is made by Smith (2000), who discusses the importance of citations and references. Smith stresses the importance of citing appropriately and of having a sufficient number of recent references to convince your reader that you know the literature.

You should also recognize that not all journals in behavioral science follow APA style. One that does not is *Perceptual and Motor Skills (P&MS)*. When citations are presented in parentheses in the text as they are in *P&MS*, they are ordered chronologically, rather than alphabetically. This practice does not conform to APA style, which uses alphabetical ordering of citations in text that are in parentheses. Although I heartily recommend using existing publications as a model or template for format, make sure you know whether the journal is following APA style before you use it as a model.

Most instructors recognize that the entire *APA Manual* is hard to digest and master, and I must admit that I do not know all of the details of APA style. But I do know enough to consult the manual at every point where there is any doubt about a given form of citation or presentation of numerical information. When in doubt, consult the manual!

If you are a visual learner and/or are overwhelmed by the level of detail in the manual, I strongly suggest that you become familiar with pages 305–320, the section that provides sample papers. At a quick glance, you can check the form of the title page and the abstract, what section headings look like, and so many other details of the typical paper. In my view, the sample papers are an excellent starting point for trying to answer some of the common questions that arise.

List of Common Questions

Here are some common questions students have about APA style and the page numbers that provide the answers:

1. What about the use of secondary sources? (See our earlier discussion of this issue and p. 247 in the *APA Manual*.)

2. How do I reference electronic databases? (See p. 231.) Make sure that the URLs are correct and working (pp. 268–281).

3. What is the order of references if the same author published more than one article in the same year, and how is that indicated in the text and references? (See p. 221.)

4. How do you present a reference to a chapter from an edited book? (See p. 229.)

5. When should I use a table? (See p. 137.) Students often ask when they should use a table as opposed to presenting numerical information, such as means and standard deviations, in text. The general rule (*APA Manual*) seems to be that you move to a table when you reach four numbers; with fewer, you can communicate effectively in a sentence. So, with this criterion, if you are presenting the means and standard deviations for both men and women on some task (hence you have four numbers), you should present them in a table.

6. What should be capitalized? (See pp. 94–100.)

7. When do I use italics? (See pp. 100–103.)

8. What kind of special treatment do statistical symbols get? (See pp. 138–144.) See especially Table 3.9, Statistical Abbreviations and Symbols.

9. When do I use the large N, when the small n? (See p. 139.)

10. What kind of typeface is appropriate? (See p. 285.) Yes, the *Manual* even gives us some guidance about typefaces. For readability of text, the *Manual* recommends serif styles like Times New Roman and Courier. Also, professors generally know when students are trying to fill space by using large typefaces like **Chicago** or Monaco or fonts over 12 points.

11. How should I indicate p values? State the alpha level and report the exact probability (see p. 25).

12. How many decimal places should I use? Use of two decimal digits is recommended (see pp. 128–129). A little-known but useful rule is that you do not use "a zero before a decimal fraction when the number cannot be greater than 1" (APA, 2001, p. 128). This stipulation means that you do not use a zero in front of an alpha level, such as .05, nor in front of correlations. However, you *would* use a zero in front of any statistical value (such as a *t* value, *F* value, χ^2, etc.) that happened to be smaller than 1 (e.g., 0.35).

13. What should I do with my data after the semester is over? In the event that you may publish your research project, your data should be maintained a minimum of five years (see p. 342), in case there is any question about aspects of your project. If you have no intention of publishing the paper, I would at least save the data until the following semester in case the professor has a question. Also, you may decide to present your paper at a conference and you will need your data to do that.

Other Useful Sections of the *APA Manual*

In addition to the extensive list of rules governing citations, references, the use of numbers and symbols, and so on, the *APA Manual* contains some sections dealing with basic writing issues such as grammar and punctuation. These sections can help you to improve writing assignments in all of your courses.

1. Grammar (pp. 40–61); really spend some time on these pages. You will learn a lot that will improve your writing in every course.
2. Active voice (p. 41).
3. Punctuation (pp. 78–88); commas, semicolons, and so on.
4. Spelling (pp. 89–94); see especially the list on page 89 (datum, which is singular, vs. data, which is plural).
5. Language bias. The *APA Manual* has an entire section entitled Guidelines to Reduce Bias in Language (pp. 61–76), including a very good table, Table 2.1, Guidelines for Unbiased Language, that is worth your attention. Also, try to use the words "men" and "women" instead of "males" and "females" when you are talking about human participants. Humans are men and women; infrahuman species may be males and females.

● ●

APPLY YOUR KNOWLEDGE

Go through the *APA Manual* and find the answers to one or two questions you have that were not addressed in the previous section.

Some Things Are Worth Memorizing

There are some aspects of the *APA Manual* that I think are worth memorizing—that is, knowing so well that you don't have to check every time. The following list describes the particular aspects of the *APA Publication Manual* that I think are worth committing to memory.

1. Block quotations (p. 118). Note that quotations longer than 40 words should be indented in block form. Further, there is a special citation form if the citation for the quotation is included at the end of the quotation, rather than in the sentence leading into the quotation. If the citation comes at the end of the block quotation, the last sentence in the quote ends with a period, and then the quotation source looks like this example, which appeared in Devlin (2001, p. 25):

> In summary, a model of the acquisition and representation of spatial knowledge must adequately account for (1) acquisition and representation based on episodic experience and subsequent generalization, (2) different types of knowledge and forms of representation, (3) systematic inaccuracies and distortions in the cognitive representation, and (4) behavioral errors associated with inaccurate and hierarchically organized knowledge. (Golledge et al., 1985, p. 132)

Note that there is no period following this citation.

2. Direct quotations: A direct quotation must always be accompanied by the author, year, and page number from your source. What this requirement means in practice is that you have to either take very good notes, or you need to photocopy the pages from which you are going to take a direct quotation. It is so easy to change "the" to "this" or to make any number of small wording choices that ultimately lead to incorrect quotations. Here is an example of a direct quotation within a sentence (from Devlin, 2004, p. 1417):

> This outcome is consistent with the notion that sailing emphasizes what the orientation strategy measures—"monitoring position of self relative to points of reference in the environment" (Lawton, 1994, p. 769).

3. Sparing use of quotations: Now that you have seen how to use block quotations and direct quotations in sentences, use them sparingly! A general practice is that quotations should be used relatively infrequently. To get a sense of how often they are used, you might consult some published papers. Many published papers have no block quotations and few if any direct quotations in sentences. Try to paraphrase and put the ideas you are citing in your own words.

4. Issue numbers in references. Try to determine whether you need issue numbers for your references. The APA rule is that you only need issue numbers if each issue begins pagination (page numbering) with the number 1 (that is, starting over with a new page 1 in each issue). APA journals (those published by the American Psychological Association) number continuously throughout the year; therefore, if you are citing an APA journal, you will not need issue numbers. I suggest that you go to the APA website (www.apa.org) where you will find a list of the journals the organization publishes, and then make a copy of this list as a reference for yourself.

With regard to non-APA journals, some number continuously; others don't. Sometimes it is possible to make a very good guess by noticing that the page numbers of an article you want to reference are high, for example, 565–586. Such page numbers are unlikely to be contained in a single issue, and you can make a pretty good guess that the journal in question numbers continuously. Other times, you can't use this method to make an intelligent guess because the page numbers are low. When in doubt, you can check current issues of the particular journal in your library (or electronically) and see what page numbering convention the journal uses.

5. Use of "et al." for a work cited in text. Use of "et al." occurs the first time you cite an article if it has more than five authors (pp. 240–241). If there are fewer than six authors, mention *all* last names in text the first time you cite the reference. After that, the use of "et al." is permitted for that particular citation. Also, in the References, if there are more than six authors for a given reference, you give the surnames and initials of the first six; those beyond the six are represented with "et al." (see p. 209 of the *APA Manual*).

6. Numbers (pp. 122–130). There are a lot of rules surrounding the expression of numbers. However, some of the simple and widely used rules are worth memorizing. Among these I would list:

a. All numbers 10 and above are expressed in numerical form. "There were 11 separate tests in this study."

b. All numbers below 10 but that are grouped for comparison with numbers 10 and above in the same paragraph are expressed in numerical form. "There were 3 participants who were dropped from the original 105 students who completed the surveys."

c. All numbers in the Abstract (except at the beginning of a sentence) are expressed in numerical form (p. 125). "One hundred participants participated in 3 separate conditions."

Some Stylistic Conventions

What follows is a list of conventions that I have come to adopt over the years. I think they are widely employed in the literature and their use will help convince your reader that you know what you are talking about.

1. Try to avoid saying "as mentioned above/below" in your paper because when a published paper comes out, the page breaks may be different than in the submitted manuscript. Instead, talk about whether a particular issue was mentioned earlier or will be discussed later in the paper.

2. Typically, we do not give the first name of an author when talking about an article (for some reason, I have found that students like to include the first names). We say "These findings were supported by other research done by Smith and Jones (1999)," not "by Grace Smith and Tom Jones (1999)."

3. Generally speaking, we do not "prove" anything in the behavioral sciences. Our research may show or illustrate or demonstrate and so on. Our research supports hypotheses; it does not prove them.

4. Be precise in your use of cause-and-effect language. As was discussed in Chapter 2, be very careful about your use of cause-and-effect language, particularly stating that a certain variable affected, or influenced, or had an effect on another variable. More often than not, students (and professionals as well) use this language in studies where the grouping variable is a quasi-independent variable (like sex, or class year, or religious affiliation, or any other variable that is not randomly assigned). In studies using such quasi-independent variables, you cannot make any claims about causation. The best that you can do is talk about the relationship between variables. In an article I wrote (Devlin, 2004), the title used in the published paper was "Sailing Experience and Sex as Correlates of Spatial Ability." I think that in one of the early versions I had entitled it "The Influence of Sailing Experience and Sex on Spatial Ability." You can see that I had fallen into the trap of suggesting more than the paper could deliver because both sex and sailing experience are aspects of the individual that are not assigned by the researcher.

5. Avoid passive sentence beginnings. Calfee (2000) suggests only somewhat in jest that you impose a financial punishment for long sentences. I would add that you fine yourself for any sentence that begins "It was found that . . ." or "Another study determined that . . .". Another poor practice is to start your sentence with the author or authors' names; for example; "Devlin (2004) found that sailors had

higher mental rotation scores than did non-sailors." What you want to do is to identify the *important* findings of the study or the important point you are trying to make, and start the sentence with that point. You might transform the earlier example, and restate the sentence: "The mental rotation scores of sailors were higher than those of non-sailors (Devlin, 2004)."

Common Grammatical Pitfalls

Over the years, I see the same grammatical mistakes committed by students, and I have compiled a list of these common mistakes, which I provide following this paragraph. You should also know that the *APA Manual* contains a very useful section on grammatical issues (pp. 40–61), which I highly recommend. There are also helpful sections on punctuation (pp. 78–88). Before launching into the specific grammatical errors, let me make a comment about spell checking functions in word processing programs. Spell checkers may catch the majority of spelling errors, but they do not identify words that are used incorrectly. For example, when students write "principle idea," what they really mean is "principal idea," indicating that the student is talking about the main or primary idea. Have someone whose writing you admire proofread your work. Some schools have writing centers where students can go to have a peer tutor read over their work. Now, on to grammar.

1. The missing referent. Watch the use of words like "It," "This," and "They" without a modifier or clear referent. Specify to what each refers. Consider the choice between a) "This is a problem" and b) "This finding is a problem." Which of these is correct? **B.** My question in response to the statement "This is a problem" is "**What** is a problem????" To what does the "This" in the sentence refer? Many students complain that specifying the referent in every situation seems like overkill. On the contrary, specifying the referent communicates clearly.

2. The "Which" hunt (relative pronouns). Knowing whether to use "that" or "which" proves to be something of a challenge to many of us. Much of the time, we select *which* when we should use *that* (hence the concept of a Which hunt). Consider the following sentence: Many theories have emerged _____ indicate a bias favoring masculine characteristics. What goes in the blank—that or which? *That.* Why? A clause that includes *that* is considered restrictive in the sense that you need the clause to complete the meaning of the sentence. Although clauses involving *which* can be either restrictive or unrestrictive, they are typically nonrestrictive and just add additional information. Also, *which* clauses are commonly set off with a comma.

3. Affect vs. effect. Learn the difference between *affect* as a verb and as a noun and *effect* as a verb and a noun.

As a verb, *affect* means to influence. As a noun, *affect* means one's mood or emotional demeanor. As a verb, *effect* means to bring about or accomplish; as a noun, *effect* means the outcome or result of an event.

Nine times out of 10, you want the verb *affect* and the noun *effect*. Consider these two examples, both of which are correct: a) What was the effect (i.e., outcome) of the new policy? b) How did the new policy affect (i.e., influence) the employees?

4. Number vs. amount; fewer vs. less. Many writers have difficulty deciding which of the following sentences is correct: a) The individual's health can affect the number of sick days he or she takes or b) The individual's health can affect the amount of sick days he or she takes. **A is correct.** You could say, "The individual's health can affect the number of sick days he or she takes, but not the amount of insurance reimbursement he or she collects." A similar challenge is the decision between the following: a) There were fewer people in attendance at the Sunday matinee or b) There were less people in attendance at the Sunday matinee. **A is correct.** The general rule is that if the entity you are talking about is discrete (can be divided into individual elements), you want to use number, not amount; similarly, if your entity is discrete, you want to use fewer, not less. If the entity you are talking about is a conglomerate, use amount or less (whichever is appropriate for the sentence). So, one would say, "Although the amount of money collected at the Sunday matinee was greater, fewer people paid with 50-dollar bills."

5. Subject–pronoun agreement. A common grammatical mistake is the use of a singular noun and a plural pronoun. Does this sentence look familiar? "The participant completed the questionnaire, and then they received the Debriefing form." Usually the mistake is using a singular subject (in the grammatical sense) and a plural pronoun. The correct form of this sentence is "The participant completed the questionnaire, and then he/she received the Debriefing form." I usually recommend to students that they write their sentences using plural subjects, so that they avoid the he/she problem. Thus, our sample sentence becomes "The participants completed the questionnaire, and then they received the Debriefing form."

6. Subject–verb agreement. A related problem is subject–verb agreement—learning to use plural subjects with plural verbs and singular subjects with singular verbs. In writing empirical papers, students are often unaware that the word data is the plural form of datum. So if you are writing about your data, you need a plural form

of the verb, such as in the sentence "The data were impressive." The *APA Manual* has a list of these troublesome plurals on page 89.

7. Possessives. Another source of difficulty is the correct use of the apostrophe to indicate possession. Usually the problems center around "its" (the possessive form of the personal pronoun) and "it's" (the contraction of it is). Just remember that it's (the contraction) translates into "it is," as in the sentence "It's a beautiful day." *Its*, the possessive of the personal pronoun it, is possessive as it stands. When referring to grammar, one might say, "Its power comes from proper use!"

8. Lengthy sentences. Calfee (2000) tells writers to "Charge yourself by the word. And double the charge for sentences longer than 20 words" (p. 141).

9. Latin abbreviations. For example (e.g.) vs. that is (i.e.). The abbreviation *e.g.* (always followed by a comma) means "for example." The abbreviation *i.e.* (also always followed by a comma) indicates "that is" (what follows its use provides further clarification).

10. While vs. whereas (subordinate conjunctions). Think of the saying "Nero fiddled while Rome burned" or "People often activate such schemas while walking alone." In these examples, the use of *while* communicates simultaneous activity, and that is the way in which *while* is commonly used. *Whereas*, on the other hand, is commonly used to indicate a contrast: Men were more likely to use cardinal directions, whereas women were more likely to rely on landmarks.

● ●

REFLECT AND REVIEW

In the following example, select the correct choice:

a. "Men scored higher on the activity variable while women scored higher on the social variable."

b. "Men scored higher on the activity variable, whereas women scored higher on the social variable."

   B is correct.

Your Manuscript Checklist

At the end of the paper, ask yourself the following questions about the paper you have written. I also recommend that you read over the 50 tips that Sternberg (2000a) gives in his chapter entitled "Article writing 101: A crib sheet of 50 tips for the final exam" (pp. 199–206).

- Is my title no more than 12 words and does it attract the reader's interest?
- Does the Abstract contain all the necessary information within 120 words?
- Is my literature review the shape of a funnel (wide to narrow)? (Remember that you are introducing a broader area of study in the first paragraph, but you have concluded the literature review with a statement of your hypotheses.)
- What do I think of the paper's topic sentence or thesis statement?
- Does each paragraph have a key or lead sentence that describes what the paragraph is about or contains?
- Have I identified any seminal (i.e., foundational) studies or theories?
- Have I placed my study within a coherent theoretical and/or methodological context?
- Have I identified any gaps or inconsistencies in the literature?
- Is my literature review more than a series of article summaries? (Remember that it is better to be selective than to merely compile a laundry list.)
- Which references seem most appropriate for my paper, especially when reflecting upon the Results?
- What about threats to internal validity, like the number of participants, the kind of participants, the quality of the measures, inconsistent treatment of participants, demand characteristics, lack of counterbalancing?
- What about threats to external validity—to what extent do the findings generalize to other populations?
- Do I understand my results? Would someone else?
- Have I provided enough detail for someone to replicate my research?
- Did I clearly link the results to the hypotheses I claimed to test?
- Did I do any data exploration or fishing (Bem, 2000)?
- Have I written the Discussion anticipating the criticism of a reviewer—and have I addressed those likely criticisms? (It is much better to address the limitations of your research upfront than to have to respond to the limitations later when they are identified by a reviewer.)

- Have I defended my results in the face of plausible alternative hypotheses?
- In what way does the study contribute to the field?
- How would I describe the contribution(s)?
- Do I think the study was worth doing?
- Does the Discussion actually discuss, or merely restate, the results? (Some instructors have their students pause and reflect on each sentence the student writes, asking such questions as "Is this part of the Method? If so, which part? Participants? Instruments? Procedure? Where should the sentence go within the appropriate section? Is this a Result? If so, where should it be introduced within the Results section?")
- Are the limitations of the study identified (but not to the point that they become the focus of the Discussion)?
- Are directions for future projects identified?

Presentations at Local and Regional Conferences

Chapter 1 mentions that proceedings of conferences are places to look for research ideas. Conferences are also places for you to present your research, and, increasingly, students who graduate from college have conference presentations or poster sessions to their credit. If we take psychology as an example, there are local (NEPA; New England Psychological Association), regional (EPA; Eastern Psychological Association) and national (APA; American Psychological Association) conventions. NEPA is in the fall, EPA is in the spring, and APA is in the late summer. Some departments even sponsor their own research conferences, as is the case with the psychology department at my institution. The conference is sponsored by the department chapter of Psi Chi, the national honor society in psychology. At our 2004 conference, 49% of the 37 presentations were made by students from the research methods class. You can ask your professors about the disciplinary conferences in your field where you could go to do a poster or presentation of your research.

In my experience, most students who have done research methods projects usually select the poster presentation format to present their work. Doing a formal presentation in a paper session at a regional conference can be somewhat intimidating for a first experience. Imagine that you completed your research methods project in the spring of your sophomore year. During the fall of your junior year, you could submit a proposal for a poster presentation at a local conference in your discipline. Usually a submission of this sort can be done online and involves an abstract and a two- to three-page summary of the sections of your project (Introduction, Method, Results, and Discussion).

Creating a Conference Poster

Although each conference may have guidelines that vary from those listed next, the following parameters give you some idea of what to expect. These guidelines are modified from the instructions to presenters for the 2004 Environmental Design Research Association (EDRA) Conference.

1. Overall size: Posters are generally mounted on moveable bulletin boards and are allotted a particular space, generally no larger than 4' × 8'.

2. Material: Posters can be printed out on regular sheets of paper and pinned to the bulletin board. An alternative method is to create a large document (e.g., 42" × 48") on one sheet of paper (more on that later).

3. Type size: Titles and author names and affiliations should be about 1 inch high (~150 points, depending on the font); the text of the paper needs to be 3/8 inches high (~38 points, depending on the font).

4. Content: My advice is to make "bullets" of the major points in each of the sections: Introduction, Method, Results, and Discussion. It is not necessary to use complete sentences.

5. Make your findings available: Bring "small versions" of your paper to hand out to interested attendees. You can also have a sign-up sheet next to your poster for people who would like the paper sent to them.

6. Staffing your poster: Each poster session is usually allotted a given period of time (e.g., 1–3 p.m.) on a particular day of the conference. Different subdisciplines (e.g., social psychology, neuroscience) usually have separate poster sessions. You are expected to put up your poster before the session starts and be available at the poster to talk to attendees who wander by and ask questions. Remove your poster at the end of the session.

7. Guidelines for a successful poster: EDRA provided the following description of a successful poster. Successful posters:

   a. Attract attention, provide a brief focused overview, and initiate discussion

   b. Limit the use of text (you do not need full sentences; consider the use of bullet points and key phrases)

c. Use good graphics (simple, clear, drawings, photos, or charts, or tables—imagine making a picture of your work)

d. Are self-explanatory, with graphics labeled as needed and text providing your major "take home" message

e. Have content visible from six feet away

The Large Poster

Some colleges and universities have large-scale printers that can be used to generate posters printed out on one large sheet of paper (~42" × 48"). Our institution has an HP DesignJet 800[PS] printer with a paper width of 42". Although the text and graphics for such posters can be generated in PhotoShop, it is also possible to do a fine job in PowerPoint, with which most students are quite familiar. You can create an effective poster with graphics using the Power Point approach. Full size posters are in the range of 42" × 48". It is possible to copy and insert such images as your college seal and photographs that may illustrate your research (e.g., a photograph of a rat swimming in a Morris Water Maze). Posters that are visually pleasing and that include graphics attract far more attention than those composed solely of text! Investigate whether your institution has the capability to produce these large-scale posters. Specialty printing shops are also places where you may be able to have a large poster printed from a computer file, although it can be expensive.

Oral Presentations

Students are doing a form of public speaking when they make oral presentations. Although making such presentations can provoke anxiety, there are some steps that you can take to reduce this anxiety and polish your presentation.

- First, to create a good presentation, tell a story. Stories have a beginning, a middle, and an end; stories engage people (Shaw, Brown, & Bromiley, 1998). Tell people why and how you become interested in the topic (the beginning), what you did to investigate it (the middle), and how it turned out (the end).

- Remember that you are the expert about your own study. You know more about it than anyone in the audience. Remembering that you are the expert should help reduce the anxiety you may feel about speaking in front of people.

- Know your presentation well enough that you can "tell" your story; never read your paper.

- Practice your talk! In particular, practice your first couple of sentences. I often find that the first few sentences are the most difficult to utter. Practice out loud. Get used to hearing yourself utter the words.

- Manage your level of detail; not everything is important and people listening to an oral presentation become overloaded very quickly. If you are using PowerPoint or overhead transparencies, have no more than three lines of information on each transparency or screen. You can use these as prompts to yourself.

- Be selective about the literature you cite (only the studies most critical to the development of your own study) and state your hypotheses clearly.

- Be selective in the Method. Give the numbers of participants and briefly describe the conditions; give the names of the measures/instruments.

- Be selective in the Results; give the essentials of your main findings: means, standard deviations, and p values. There is no need to give the statistical equation as you would write it in a paper.

- Be selective in your Discussion; state whether the findings support earlier research; one or two implications; one or two future directions; and one or two limitations.

- If possible, use "visuals" such as diagrams, charts, graphs, or histograms to display your findings. This "visualization" will stay with your audience longer than will a sentence about the findings.

The Ideal Paper

- Captivating title
- 120-word Abstract
- Funnel-shaped literature review
- Statement of hypotheses
- Statement of research design
- Method: Participants, measures, procedure
- Results tell a story
- Discussion written with skeptics in minds
- References are complete and accurate

Other Opportunities for Presentation

The National Conferences for Undergraduate Research (www.ncur.org) holds an annual conference in the spring to highlight undergraduate student research. If you use an Internet search engine such as Google with the terms "undergraduate research conference," you will find 10 or more pages of listings of undergraduate conferences, from an annual Western Anthropology/Sociology Undergraduate Research Conference to conferences in mathematics and psychology. If you want to present your research, there are multiple venues; you just have to look.

● ●

APPLY YOUR KNOWLEDGE

Using an Internet search engine such as Google, do a search with the terms "undergraduate research conference" and locate at least one conference where you could potentially present your work.

● ●

SUMMARY

Writing is never easy, and that is why I sometimes get started on a writing project by doing the References first! At least I know I have accomplished something. This chapter has given you a closer look at the typical sections that go into a research paper. Just as you looked at articles to help generate your research ideas, you can also look at these articles now to see how they are written up. The *APA Manual*, used widely in the behavioral sciences, should be your constant companion during the writing process.

You now know the key points in each of the different sections. You need an interesting and informative title, and an abstract of no more than 120 words with its particular requirements for content. You need a literature review that starts broadly and narrows to the hypothesis(es). The Method section should have a statement of your research design and three fully described sections: Participants, Apparatus/Materials, and Procedure. Your Results section should start simply and with full sentences, not simply a string of numbers. The Discussion section needs to be written with skeptics and opponents in mind, and your References section needs to be complete and accurate.

APPLY YOUR KNOWLEDGE QUESTIONS

In the event that you did not have time to do them earlier, here is the list of APPLY YOUR KNOWLEDGE questions in this chapter. Try them now:

1. See if you can rewrite the first title so that it communicates the information within 10–12 words (p. 206).

2. Write the first paragraph of your paper, with special attention to the topic sentence and the goal of interesting your reader.

3. Do some browsing through the articles you have found for your literature review to select one or two that have reader-friendly results. In your view, what are the characteristics you see that create reader-friendly results?

4. Make a list of issues *other* than sample size and the homogeneity of the sample that threaten the internal and external validity of your research.

5. Go through the *APA Manual* and find the answers to one or two questions you have that were not addressed in the previous section (pp. 220–222).

6. Using an Internet search engine such as Google, do a search with the terms "undergraduate research conference" and locate at least one conference where you could potentially present your work.

WEB RESOURCES

There are a number of research methods workshops on the web that may enhance your knowledge of the topics in this chapter. Here is one of these workshops and the associated web address:

APA Style

www.wadsworth.com/psychology_d/templates/
student_resources/workshops/resch_wrk.html

Good researching!

APPENDIX

Sample Informed Consent Document

I hereby consent to participate in Professor Smith's research[1] about spatial ability and wayfinding.[2]

I understand that this research will involve taking a timed test of spatial ability and completing a series of questionnaires.[3]

Although I understand that the direct benefits of this research to society are not known, I have been told that I may learn more about my spatial abilities and concerns.[4]

I understand that this research will take about 30 minutes.[5]

I have been told that there are no known risks or discomforts related to participating in this research.[6]

I have been told that Professor Smith can be contacted at (860) 439-2330.[7]

I understand that I may decline to answer any questions as I see fit, and that I may withdraw from the study without penalty at any time.[8]

I understand that all information will be identified with a code number and *not* my name.[9]

I have been advised that I may contact the researcher, who will answer any questions that I may have about the purposes and procedures of this study.[10]

I understand that this study is not meant to gather information about specific individuals and that my responses will be combined with other participants' data for the purpose of statistical analyses.[11]

I consent to publication of the study results as long as the identity of all participants is protected.[12]

I understand that this research has been approved by the Connecticut College Human Subjects Institutional Review Board (IRB).[13]

Concerns about any aspect of this study may be addressed to Professor Ann Devlin, Chairperson of the Connecticut College IRB (439-2333).[14]

I am at least 18 years of age, and I have read these explanations and assurances and voluntarily consent to participate in this research about spatial ability.[15]

Name (printed) _____

Signature _____

Date _____

Explanation of Items

1. Informed consent requires a statement that the activity is research.

2. Provide a brief statement of the focus of the research.

3. You need to provide a description of what participants will be asked to do.

4. You need to state whether the research will produce any benefits to society or the individual.

5. You need to state the length of time that will be involved.

6. You need to state that there are no known risks or discomforts to participating in the research (assuming there are none). If there are risks, you have to spell them out.

7. Give a telephone number where the researcher can be contacted.

8. Provide a statement that people may decline to answer questions and may withdraw from the study without penalty at any time.

9. State that the information will be identified with a code number and not the individual's name. If it is appropriate, indicate the extent to which confidentiality will be protected (i.e., under what circumstances it would be broken).

10. State that the researcher will be available to answer any questions about the study.

11. State that responses are to be combined with other partici-pants' data and are not meant to gather information about specific individuals.

12. Provide a statement that the participant consents to the pub-lication of the study results as long as the identity of partici-pants is protected (otherwise, you don't have permission to use the data for publication).

13. State that the research has been approved by your institu-tion's Human Subjects Institutional Review Board (IRB).

14. State that concerns may be directed to the Chairperson of your institution's Human Subjects IRB, and provide the Chairperson's name and telephone number.

15. Provide a copy of the document for the participant and keep one for yourself.

Sample Debriefing/Explanation of Research Form

First of all, thank you for participating in this research dealing with spatial cognition. In this research, I am comparing the spatial abilities of people who vary in their experience with sailing. In addition to Introductory Psychology students at Connecticut College, members of the sailing teams at Connecticut College and other schools are filling out these questionnaires. One of the issues in the literature on spatial cognition is the role that experience may play in developing better spatial abilities. Typically researchers have asked about childhood toy play (e.g., Lincoln logs, building blocks) to estimate exposure to toys that may stress spatial ability. To my knowledge, no research has actually focused on experience with a spatial activity like sailing, and that is the purpose of this research.

In addition to sailing experience, this research also assessed the impact of gender (typically males do better on the mental rotation task, the first questionnaire you completed), and handedness (left-handed individuals have been reported to possess better spatial abilities).

If you are interested in this topic and want to read the literature in this area, please contact me (Professor Smith) at (860) 439–2330.

The following list gives two sources you may want to consult to learn more about this topic:

Hyde, J. S. (1990). Meta-analysis and the psychology of gender differences. *Signs, 16*, 55–73.

Tracy, D. M. (1987). Toys, spatial ability, and science and mathematics achievement: Are they related? *Sex Roles, 17*, 115–138.

Common Statistical Measures: What and How to Report

Statistical Test	What to Report	How It Looks
t-test	*M*s and *SD*s for each group *t* value, *df*, *p* value (equal variances assumed or not assumed, according to outcome of Levene's Test for Equality of Variances)	$t\,(120) = 0.50$, $p = .62$
ANOVAs	*M*s and *SD*s and *n*s for each group *F* value, *df*, *p* value for each IV and interaction(s) for the outcome measure (DV) If Tukeys or Simple Effects tests are needed, give the *p* value for each significant contrast	$F\,(4, 117) = 0.74$, $p = .57$
MANOVAs	*M*s and *SD*s and *n*s for each group for each Dependent Variable Wilks's lambda, *F*, *df*, and *p* and effect size/eta squared for each multivariate effect	Wilks's lambda $= .87$, $F\,(6, 436) = 5.36$, $p = .01$; $\eta^2 = .07$

Statistical Test	What to Report	How It Looks
MANOVAs	For each IV that was significant from the multivariate level, indicate the F, df, and p and effect size/eta squared for the univariate tests where there were group differences on each Dependent variable If Tukeys or Simple Effects tests are needed, give the p value for each significant contrast	$F (2, 220) = 6.26$, $p = .01; \eta^2 = .05$
Correlation	r value, N, and p value	$r (43) = .87, p = .01$
Chi-square	Chi-square value, df, N, and p value Percentages in each of the cells	$\chi^2 (1, N = 90) = 6.73$, $p = .01$
Regression	F, df, p, Beta	Example of vocational maturity predicting vocational indecision: $F (15, 99) = 4.63$, $p = .000$, $Beta = -.378$, $p = .000$ (Mikulinsky, 2002, p. 42)
Multiple Regression	R-square, F, df, p, Beta, t, p and names of variables. Note that some researchers prefer β, the standardized regression coefficient, instead of $Beta$	Example where career-oriented variables are used as a block in a hierarchical regression to predict vocational indecision: R-square $= .24$, $F(3, 135) = 14.16, p = .000$ Beta t p VMS $-.375$ -4.72 .000 VDE .011 015 .000 CES $-.234$ -3.00 .884 (Mikulinsky, 2002, pp. 42–43)

Active consent: consent given for a potential research participant by a parent, guardian, or person with legal authority who signs a document that specifically assents (agrees) to the participation of the minor, or individual unable to consent for him or herself, in the research (Chapter 5).

Actual criterion: a concrete measure we use to assess a conceptual construct (Chapter 3).

Anchoring: initially obtaining as much information as possible about a research participant's usual whereabouts, or the identity of those who would know about the person's whereabouts (Chapter 4).

Anonymity: lack of knowledge of the identity or any identifying information about the research participant (Chapter 5).

Archival data: pre-existing data such as statistics found in newspapers, the U.S. Census, and so on (Chapter 1).

Attrition bias: participants who drop out of a study have characteristics that are not representative of the original sample (Chapter 4).

Belmont Report: a 1978 report from the federal government that describes principles to follow in the ethical treatment of human subjects (Chapter 5).

Bonferroni correction: a correction to address the problem of Type I error by dividing the alpha level by the number of analyses (Chapters 2 and 6).

Captive population: conducting research on a population that is not the focus of their typical activity (such as research in a class that is not part of the class curriculum) (Chapter 5).

Categorical or nominal data: data categories with no inherent order, such as men and women (Chapter 2).

Ceiling effect: a clustering at the upper end of the scale, so that the true distribution is obscured (Chapter 3).

Coding schemes: the organizational approach you use to enter your data (Chapter 6).

Cohen's kappa: a method for calculating the degree of agreement between raters that corrects for chance agreement (Chapter 2).

Common Rule: Federal policy for the protection of human subjects adopted in 1991 (Chapter 5).

Conceptual criterion: abstract standard or ideal we want to assess; can never be measured completely (Chapter 3).

Confidentiality: the extent to which the identity or identifying information about the research participant is safeguarded or protected (Chapter 5).

Consent and false informing: consent given by participants who are given false information about the focus of the study (Chapter 5).

Consent to concealment: consent given by participants who are told that some information about the study will be withheld until the study is finished (Chapter 5).

Content analysis: generally qualitative data in narrative form that are placed into categories based on similarity of theme (Chapters 1 and 6).

Continuous or interval data: data in which the distance between numerical values (e.g., 1 to 2) is the same across all values (Chapter 2).

Convenience sample: a sample that you obtain through the availability of the population, such as students who are passing through the student union (Chapters 1 and 4).

Cover story: an explanation given to participants about why they are being asked to fill out measures or be exposed to some intervention that provides a mask for the actual purpose of the research (Chapter 2).

Criterion contamination: the part of the actual criterion that your measure includes but should not (Chapter 3).

Criterion deficiency: the part of the actual criterion that your measure misses (Chapter 3).

Criterion relevance: the overlap between the conceptual criterion and the actual criterion (Chapter 3).

Cronbach's alpha: a measure of internal consistency, which varies between 0 and 1. It is an index of the extent to which each item on a scale correlates with every other item on the scale (Chapter 3).

Debriefing: a statement, usually written, provided to participants upon completion of their involvement in a particular study. The debriefing statement explains the hypotheses and purpose of the study in some depth (Chapter 5).

Demand characteristics: aspects of the research process, including the behavior of the researcher, that unintentionally influence the participant's responses (Chapters 2 and 3).

Demographics: background information about participants, such as sex, race, and so on (Chapters 1, 2, and 3).

Double-blind experiment: an experiment in which both the participants and researcher are blind to which participants are receiving the treatment and which are receiving a placebo (the control) (Chapter 2).

Effect size: the degree to which your intervention affects the numerical value of the dependent variable of interest, expressed in terms of the standard deviation of the parent population (Chapter 2).

Exempt review: research that does not require Institutional Review Board (IRB) review (Chapter 5).

Expedited review: IRB review of research that poses no significant ethical issues, and involves no vulnerable populations (Chapter 5).

External validity: the extent to which our findings may generalize to other populations and to the real world (Chapter 2).

Floor effect: A clustering of responses at the lower end of the scale, so that the true distribution of responses is obscured (Chapter 3).

Full review: IRB review that involves the full committee; research with more than minimal risk and/or the use of vulnerable populations such as children (Chapter 5).

GIS: Geographical Information Systems (GIS) databases are archival sources of information that provide geographical information, such as the locations of hospitals and railroad lines within a city (Chapter 1).

Informed consent: a document describing the research study in question and the particular rights of the participants. The participant signs and dates the form if he/she chooses to participate (Chapter 5).

Internal consistency: the extent to which each item in a scale is measuring the same construct or idea (Chapter 3).

Internal validity: the extent to which the research process actually evaluates the proposed hypotheses (Chapters 2 and 3).

Inter-rater reliability: the degree to which two or more people agree on the coding of data (Chapter 6).

JSTOR: a collection of online academic journals containing older issues (with a moving wall of five years) (Chapter 1).

Manipulation checks: questions or assessments of the participant to determine whether the manipulation of the independent variable was convincing to the participant (i.e., that the manipulation had the intended effect) (Chapter 2).

Mediating variables: variables that impact or affect the relationship between the variables of interest (Chapter 2).

Minimal risk: risk level for research that you don't expect to involve greater risks than those you would encounter in everyday life or when you are doing routine physical or psychological activities (Chapter 5).

Narrative interview: a qualitative interviewing approach that asks participants about their history with a particular issue (Chapter 2).

No informing and no consent: neither consent nor informing occurs in the project so that subjects may be unaware that research is occurring (Chapter 5).

Nonparametric statistic: a statistic, such as chi-square, in which no assumptions are made about the distribution of scores in the sample (Chapters 2 and 7).

Nuremberg Code: emanating from the Nuremberg Trials that judged war criminals, the Nuremberg Code consists of 10 major points that describe principles in the ethical treatment of human subjects (Chapter 5).

Operational definition: a variable of interest that is defined by the operations used to measure it (Chapter 3).

Outlier: a data point that is at some numerical distance from the other values of a variable (Chapter 6).

Paradigm: a particular way of looking at or examining a topic that is used consistently (Chapter 1).

Peer review: evaluation by a group of the researcher's peers of the quality of research or work submitted for publication, usually with its identifying information removed (Chapter 1).

Pilot study: a test of effectiveness of your manipulation(s) on a small group of participants before launching the full study (Chapters 2 and 3).

Positivism: an approach to science in which only those events that can be observed and tested are thought to reflect the truth of experience (Chapter 2).

Power: the probability of rejecting Ho (the null hypothesis), assuming Ho is false (Chapter 2).

Project Muse: an electronic resource for current journals (over 220 scholarly journals) (Chapter 1).

PsycINFO: a database of citations and summaries that covers journals, books, technical reports, and dissertations in psychology and psychology-related disciplines such as psychiatry, medicine, nursing, education, sociology, anthropology, and linguistics (Chapter 1).

Reliability: the extent to which a measure produces the same results over multiple administrations (e.g., test–retest reliability) (Chapter 3).

Reliability analysis: a way of calculating the internal consistency of your measure (Chapters 3 and 6).

Remailing software: software, used in electronic research, that transmits but does not store information and can remove the identifying information of the sender (Chapter 4).

Respect for Persons, Beneficence, and Justice: the three ethical principles from the Belmont Report that guide the work of IRBs (Chapter 5).

Reverse scored items: items whose numerical values need to be switched to keep the total consistent (e.g., that higher scores mean more positive responses) (Chapter 6).

Risk-benefit analyses: analyses made by Human Subjects IRBs' weighing of the potential harm versus the potential benefits to be gained from proposed research projects (Chapter 5).

Schema: a mental representation of a category, such as Marxists (Chapter 2).

Secondary source: a source that you did not read in its original form and only read about in a derivative source. A journal article summarized in a textbook is an example (Chapter 7).

Seminal studies: foundational and important studies in a given area of research (Chapter 1).

Significance levels: levels set by the researcher (conventionally at .05) to determine the likelihood that a result did not happen by chance (Chapter 6).

Single-blind experiment: an experiment in which the participant does not know whether he or she is receiving the treatment (e.g., drug) or not (e.g., placebo) (Chapter 2).

Snowball sample: sample obtained by a participant recommending another participant for the study, who in turn recommends a third participant, and so on (Chapter 1).

Social desirability: modification of their answers by participants to present themselves in a more favorable light (Chapter 3).

Subject mortality: typically in longitudinal designs, the rate at which participants drop out of a study (Chapter 2).

Tailored design method: a method for distributing surveys developed by Dillman in which the approach varies (is tailored) depending on the population, content, and survey sponsorship (Chapter 4).

Title 45 Part 46 of the Code of Federal Regulations: (45 CFR 46); the section that describes the ethical treatment of human subjects (Chapter 5).

Type I error: rejecting the null hypothesis by chance (Chapters 2 and 6).

Type II error: failing to reject the null hypothesis when an effect exists (Chapter 2).

Validity: characteristic of a measure or protocol that assesses what it actually claims to measure (e.g., leadership) (Chapter 3).

Vulnerable populations: populations for whom we might have concerns about their capacity to give informed consent. Examples include children, prisoners, and fetuses (Chapters 4 and 5).

Within-range values: values that fall within a legitimate range for a given variable (Chapter 6).

Ackerman, T. F. (1989). An ethical framework for the practice of paying research subjects. *IRB: A Review of Human Subjects Research, 11,* 1–4.

Adair, J. G. (1973). *The human subject: The social psychology of the psychological experiment.* Boston: Little, Brown and Company.

Adams, P. L., & Bleiberg, E. (Eds.). (1998). *Handbook of child and adolescent psychiatry: Advances and new directions* (Vol. 7). New York: John Wiley and Sons, Inc.

Alkin, M. C. (1992). *Encyclopedia of educational research* (6th ed.). New York: Macmillan.

American Educational Research Association. (1999). *Standards for educational and psychological testing.* Washington, DC: Author.

American Psychiatric Association. (2000). *Handbook of psychiatric measures.* Washington, DC: Author.

American Psychological Association. (1953). *Ethical standards of psychologists.* Washington, DC: Author.

American Psychological Association. (2001). *Publication manual of the American Psychological Association* (5th ed.). Washington, DC: Author.

American Psychological Association. (2002). Ethical principles of psychologists and code of conduct. *American Psychologist, 57,* 1060–1073.

American Sociological Association. (1997). *ASA style guide* (2nd ed.). Washington, DC: Author.

Anderson, J. C., Funk, J. B., Elliot, R., & Smith, P. H. (2003). Parental support and pressure and children's extracurricular activities: Relationships with amount of involvement and affective experience of participation. *Journal of Applied Developmental Psychology, 24,* 241–257.

Angoff, N. R. (1984). An inadvertent breach of confidentiality. *IRB: A Review of Human Subjects Research, 6*(3), 5–6.

Antony, M. M., Orsillo, S. M., & Roemer, L. (2001). *Practitioner's guide to empirically based measures of anxiety.* Norwell, MA: Kluwer.

Arneill, A. B., & Devlin, A. S. (2002). Perceived quality of care: The influence of the waiting room environment. *Journal of Environmental Psychology, 22,* 345–360.

Ashworth, P. (2003). The origins of qualitative psychology. In J. A. Smith (Ed.), *Qualitative psychology: A practical guide to research methods* (pp. 4–24). Thousand Oaks, CA: Sage Publications.

Averbach, C. F., & Silverstein, L. B. (2003). *Qualitative data: An introduction to coding and analysis.* New York: New York University Press.

Banaji, M. R., & Crowder, R. G. (1989). The bankruptcy of everyday memory. *American Psychologist, 44,* 1185–1193.

Bankston, C. L., III. (1999). *Encyclopedia of family life* (Vols. 1–5). Hackensack, NJ: Salem Press, Inc.

Bari, J. R. (1991). Parental authority questionnaire. *Journal of Personality Assessment, 57,* 110–119.

Baum, A., Revenson, T. A., & Singer, J. E. (Eds.). (2001). *Handbook of health psychology.* Mahwah, NJ: Lawrence Erlbaum Associates.

Baumrind, D. (1964). Some thoughts on ethics research: After reading Milgram's "Behavioral Study of Obedience." *American Psychologist, 19,* 421–423.

Bebko, J. M., Perry, A., & Bryson, S. (1996). Multiple method validation study of facilitated communication: II. Individual differences and subgroup results. *Journal of Autism and Developmental Disorders, 26,* 19–42.

Bechtel, R. B., & Churchman, A. (Eds.). (2002). *Handbook of environmental psychology.* New York: John Wiley and Sons, Inc.

Beck, A. T. (1978). *Depression inventory.* Philadelphia: Center for Cognitive Therapy.

Beck, A. T., Steer, R. A., & Brown, G. K. (1996). *Beck Depression Inventory manual* (2nd ed.). San Antonio, TX: Psychological Corporation.

Beck, A. T., Ward, C. H., Mendelson, M., Mock, J. E., & Erbaugh, J. (1961). An inventory for measuring depression. *Archives of General Psychiatry, 4,* 561–571.

Beh, H. G. (2002). The role of institutional review boards in protecting human subjects: Are we really ready to fix a broken system? *Law & Psychology Review, 26,* 1–47.

Bem, D. (2000). Writing an empirical article. In R. J. Sternberg (Ed.), *Guide to publishing in psychology journals* (pp. 3–16). New York: Cambridge University Press.

Bem, S. (1974). The measurement of psychological androgyny. *Journal of Consulting and Clinical Psychology, 92,* 155–162.

Berlyne, D. E. (1963). Complexity and incongruity variables as determinants of exploratory choice and evaluative ratings. *Canadian Journal of Psychology, 17,* 274–290.

Bersoff, D. N. (2003). *Ethical conflicts in psychology* (3rd ed.). Washington, DC: American Psychological Association.

Birnbaum, M. H. (2000). *Psychological experiments on the Internet.* San Diego, CA: Academic Press.

Booth, B. (1986). *Thesaurus of sociological indexing terms.* San Diego, CA: Sociological Abstracts, Inc.

Bordens, K. S., & Abbott, B. B. (2002). *Research design and methods: A process approach* (5th ed.). New York: McGraw-Hill.

Borgatta, E. F., & Borgatta, M. L. (1992). *Encyclopedia of sociology* (Vols. 1–4). New York: Macmillan Publishing Company.

Bradley, C. M. (2001). *Athletic identity, self-complexity, self-defining memories, and vulnerability to depression in Division I basketball players.* Unpublished honors thesis. New London, CT: Connecticut College.

Brewer, B. W., Van Raalte, J. L., & Linder, D. E. (1993). Athletic identity: Hercules' muscle or Achilles heel? *International Journal of Sport Psychology, 24,* 237–254.

Bridges, K. R. (2001). Using attributional style to predict academic performance: How does it compare to traditional methods? *Personality and Individual Differences, 31,* 723–730.

Brigham, D. (2002). *Color, laterality, and spatial task performance.* Unpublished honors thesis. New London, CT: Connecticut College.

Brinthaupt, T. M. (2002). Teaching research ethics: Illustrating the nature of the researcher–IRB relationship. *Teaching of Psychology, 29,* 243–245.

Brody, B. A. (2001). Making informed consent meaningful. *IRB: Ethics and Human Research, 23*(5), 1–5.

Brooks, J. L., & Greenhut, R. (Producers), & Marshall, P. (Director). (1999). *Big* [videorecording]. Beverly Hills, CA: Twentieth Century Fox.

Brooks-Gunn, J., & Ruble, D. (1980). The Menstrual Attitude Questionnaire. *Psychosomatic Medicine, 42,* 503–512.

Brown, G., & Devlin, A. S. (2003). Vandalism: Environmental and social factors. *Journal of College Student Development, 44,* 502–516.

Brown, R., & Kulik, J. (1977). Flashbulb memories. *Cognition, 5,* 73–99.

Bruno, F. J. (1986). *Dictionary of key words in psychology.* Boston: Routledge and Kegan Paul.

Bryant, C. D. (Ed.). (2001). *Encyclopedia of criminology and deviant behavior.* New York: Brunner-Routledge.

Butler, D. L. (1999). Why do students miss psychology experiments and what can be done about it? In G. Chastain & R. E. Landrum (Eds.), *Protecting human subjects: Departmental subject pools and institutional review boards* (pp. 109–125). Washington, DC: American Psychological Association.

Calfee, R. (2000). What does it all mean? The discussion. In R. J. Sternberg (Ed.), *Guide to publishing in psychology journals* (pp. 133–145). New York: Cambridge University Press.

Calhoun, C. (2002). *Dictionary of the social sciences*. New York: Oxford University Press.

Carson-Dewitt, R. (Ed.). (2001). *Encyclopedia of drugs, alcohol, and addictive behavior* (2nd ed.). New York: Macmillan Reference USA.

Cattell, R. B., Eber, H. W., & Tatsuoka, M. M. (1970). *Handbook for the 16PF.* Champaign, IL: Institute for Personality and Ability Testing.

Charmaz, K. (2003). Grounded theory. In J. A. Smith (Ed.), *Qualitative psychology: A practical guide to research methods* (pp. 81–110). Thousand Oaks, CA: Sage Publications.

Chicago manual of style (15th ed.). (2003). Chicago: University of Chicago Press.

Church, A. (1993). Estimating the effect of incentives on mail survey response rates: A meta-analysis. *Public Opinion Quarterly, 57*(1), 62–79.

Ciminero, A. R., Calhoun, K. S., & Adams, H. G. (1986). *Handbook of behavioral assessment* (2nd ed.). New York: John Wiley & Sons, Inc.

Code of Federal Regulations. Title 45 CFR Part 46. (1981, 1983, 1991). Washington, DC: Department of Health and Human Services, National Institutes of Health, Office for Protection from Research Risks.

Coen, A. S., Patrick, D. C., & Shern, D. L. (1996). Minimizing attrition in longitudinal studies of special populations: An integrated management approach. *Education and Program Planning, 19,* 309–319.

Cohen, J. (1960). A coefficient of agreement for nominal scales. *Educational and Psychological Measurement, 10,* 37–46.

Cohen, J. (1988). *Statistical power analyses for the behavioral sciences* (2nd ed.). New York: Academic Press.

Colman, A. M. (Ed.). (1994). *Companion encyclopedia of psychology* (Vols. 1 & 2). London: Routledge.

Cooper, M. L., Wood, K. M., Orcutt, H. K., & Albino, A. (2003). Personality and the predisposition to engage in risky problem behaviors during adolescence. *Journal of Personality and Social Psychology, 84,* 390–410.

Cooper, P. J., Taylor, M. J., Cooper, Z., & Fairburn, C. G. (1987). The development and validation of the Body Shape Questionnaire. *International Journal of Eating Disorders, 6,* 485–494.

Corcoran, K. J., & Fischer, J. (2000). *Measures for clinical practice: A sourcebook* (3rd ed.). New York: The Free Press.

Corsini, R. J. (1999). *The dictionary of psychology.* Philadelphia: Brunner/Mazel.

Costa, P. T., & McCrae, R. R. (1991). *NEO Five Factor Inventory*. Odessa, FL: Psychological Assessment Resources, Inc.

Costa, P. T., & McCrae, R. R. (1992). *NEO PI-R professional manual*. Odessa, FL: Psychological Assessment Resources, Inc.

Council, J. R., Smith, E. J. H., Kaster-Bundgaard, J., & Gladue, B. A. (1997). Ethical evaluation of hypnosis research: A survey of investigators and their institutional review boards. *American Journal of Clinical Hypnosis, 39*, 258–265.

Cronk, B. C., & West, J. L. (2002). Personality research on the Internet: A comparison of web-based and traditional instruments in take-home and in-class settings. *Behavior Research Methods, Instruments, & Computers, 34*, 177–180.

Crowne, D. P., & Marlowe, D. (1960). A new scale of social desirability independent of psychopathology. *Journal of Consulting Psychology, 24*, 349–354.

Damon, W. (1998). *Handbook of child psychology* (5th ed.). (Vols. 1–4). New York: John Wiley and Sons, Inc.

Davis, C. M., Yarber, W. L., Bauserman, R., Schreer, G., & Davis, S. L. (1998). *Handbook of sexuality-related measures*. Thousand Oaks, CA: Sage Publications.

Dawson, D. P. (1997). *Women's issues* (Vols. 1–3). Englewood Cliffs, NJ: Salem Press, Inc.

Delaney, J., Lupton, M. J., & Toth, E. (1987). *The curse: A cultural history of menstruation*. Urbana, IL: University of Illinois Press.

DePauli, C., Kelker, M. E., Slotterback, C. S., & Oakes, M. E. (2000). What's in a name? A comparison of attitudes toward food names and their nutrient descriptions. [Abstract]. *Proceedings and Abstracts of the Annual Meeting of the Eastern Psychological Association, 71*, p. 61.

Devlin, A. S. (1992). Psychiatric ward renovation: Staff perception and patient behavior. *Environment and Behavior, 24*, 66–84.

Devlin, A. S. (1996). Survival skills training during freshman orientation: Its role in college adjustment. *Journal of College Student Development, 37*, 324–334.

Devlin, A. S. (2000). City behavior and precautionary measures. *Journal of Applied Social Psychology, 30*, 2158–2172.

Devlin, A. S. (2001). *Mind and maze: Spatial cognition and environmental behavior*. Westport, CT: Praeger.

Devlin, A. S. (2003). Giving directions: Gender and perceived quality. *Journal of Applied Social Psychology, 33*, 1530–1551.

Devlin, A. S. (2004). Sailing experience and sex as correlates of spatial ability. *Perceptual and Motor Skills, 98*, 1409–1421.

Devlin, A. S., & Bernstein, J. (1997). Interactive way-finding: Map style and effectiveness. *Journal of Environmental Psychology, 17*, 99–110.

Dickert, N., & Grady, C. (1999, July 15). What's the price of a research subject? Approaches to payment for research participation. *The New England Journal of Medicine, 341*(3), 198–203.

Dillman, D. A. (2000). *Mail and internet surveys: The tailored design method* (2nd ed.). New York: John Wiley & Sons, Inc.

Doctor, R. M., & Kahn, A. P. (2000). *The encyclopedia of phobias, fears, and anxieties* (2nd ed.). New York: Facts on File, Inc.

Drink to that. (2003, September 19). *The Chronicle of Higher Education*, p. A20.

Dutton, S., Singer, J. A., & Devlin, A. S. (1998). Racial identity of children in integrated, predominantly white, and black schools. *The Journal of Social Psychology, 138*, 41–53.

EdITS. (2000). *EdITS 2000 Catalog of tests, books, guidance & instructional materials*. San Diego, CA: Author.

Educational Testing Service. (1991). *ETS test collection catalog* (Vols. 1–5). Phoenix, AZ: Oryx Press.

Erchull, M. J. (1998). *Fact or fiction: A content analysis of educational materials about menstruation*. Unpublished honors thesis. New London, CT: Connecticut College.

Erwin, E. (Ed.) (2002). *The Freud encyclopedia: Theory, therapy, and culture*. New York: Routledge.

Eyde, L. D., Moreland, K. L., & Robertson, G. J. (1988). *Test user qualifications: A data-based approach to promoting good test use*. Washington, DC: American Psychological Association.

Eyde, L. D., & Primoff, E. (1992). Responsible test use. In M. Zeidner & R. Most (Eds.), *Psychological testing: An inside view* (pp. 441–459). Palo Alto, CA: Consulting Psychologists Press.

Eyde, L. D., Robertson, G. J., Krug, S. E., Moreland, K. L., Robertson A. G., et al. (1994). *Responsible test use: Case studies for assessing human behavior*. Washington, DC: American Psychological Association.

Eysenck, H. J. (Ed.). (1973). *Handbook of abnormal psychology*. New York: Pitman Publishing Group.

Eysenck, H. J., & Eysenck, S. B. G. (1968). *EdITS manual for the Eysenck personality inventory*. San Diego, CA: EdITS/Educational and Industrial Testing Service.

Fernandez-Ballesteros, R. (2003). *Encyclopedia of psychological assessment* (Vols. 1 & 2). Thousand Oaks, CA: Sage Publications.

Ferraro, R. R., Szigeti, E., Dawes, K. J., & Pan, S. (1999). A survey regarding the University of North Dakota institutional review board: Data, attitudes, and perceptions. *The Journal of Psychology, 133*, 272–280.

Fisher, C. B., & Fyrberg, D. (1994). Participant partners: College students weigh the costs and benefits of deceptive research. *American Psychologist, 49*, 417–427.

Francoeur, R. T. (Ed.). (1999). *The international encyclopedia of sexuality* (Vols. 1–4). New York: Continuum.

Fung, M. S. C., & Yuen, M. (2003). Body image and eating attitudes among adolescent Chinese girls in Hong Kong. *Perceptual and Motor Skills, 96,* 57–66.

Furnham, A., & Baguma, P. (1994). Cross-cultural differences in the evaluation of male and female body shapes. *International Journal of Eating Disorders, 15,* 81–89.

Gallup, G., Jr. (2003). *Gallup poll. Public opinion 2002.* Wilmington, DE: Scholarly Resources, Inc.

Garner, D. M., & Garfinkel, P. E. (1979). The Eating Attitudes Test: An index of symptoms of anorexia nervosa. *Psychological Medicine, 9,* 273–279.

Garner, D. M., Olmsted, M. P., Bohr, I., & Garfinkel, P. E. (1982). The Eating Attitudes Test: Psychometric features and clinical correlates. *Psychological Medicine, 12,* 871–878.

Garner, D. M., Olmsted, M. P., & Polivy, J. (1983). Development and validation of a multidimensional eating disorder inventory for anorexia nervosa and bulimia. *International Journal of Eating Disorders, 2,* 15–34.

George, L. (1995). *Alternative realities: The paranormal, the mystic, and the transcendent in human experience.* New York: Facts on File, Inc.

Gerst, M. S., & Moos, R. H. (1972). Social ecology of university student residences. *Journal of Educational Psychology, 63,* 513–525.

Gilbaldi, J. (2003). *MLA handbook for writers of research papers* (6th ed.). New York: Modern Language Association.

Gill, D. L., Gross, J. B., & Huddleston, S. (1983). Participation motivation in youth sports. *International Journal of Sport Psychology, 14,* 1–14.

Gillespie, J. F. (1999). The why, what, how, and when of effective faculty use of institutional review boards. In G. Chastain & R. E. Landrum (Eds.), *Protecting human subjects: Departmental subject pools and institutional review boards* (pp. 157–177). Washington, DC: American Psychological Association.

Gilliss, C. L., Lee, K. A., Gutierrez, Y., Taylor, D., Beyene, Y., Neuhaus, J., et al. (2001). Recruitment and retention of healthy minority women into community-based longitudinal research. *Journal of Women's Health & Gender-Based Medicine, 10,* 77–85.

Goldman, B. A., & Mitchell, D. F. (1996). *Directory of unpublished experimental mental measures* (Vols. 1–3). Washington, DC: American Psychological Association.

Goodman, J. S., & Blum, T. C. (1996). Assessing the non-random sampling effects of subject attrition in longitudinal research. *Journal of Management, 22,* 627–652.

Grady, J. (2001). Becoming a visual sociologist. *Sociological Imagination: The Quarterly Journal of the Wisconsin Sociological Association, 38*, No. 1/2, 83–119.

Grant, C. A., & Ladson-Billings, G. (1997). *Dictionary of multicultural education.* Phoenix, AZ: Oryx Press.

Greenwald, A. G., McGhee, D. E., & Schwartz, J. L. K. (1998). Measuring individual differences in implicit cognition: The implicit association test. *Journal of Personality and Social Psychology, 74,* 1464–1480.

Grigorenko, E. L. (2000). Doing data analyses and writing up their results: Selected tricks and artifices. In R. J. Sternberg (Ed.), *Guide to publishing in psychology journals* (pp. 98–120). New York: Cambridge University Press.

Grosofsky, A., Adkins, S. M., Bustholm, R., Meyer, L., Krueger, L., Meyer, J., et al. (2003). Tooth color: Effects on judgments of attractiveness and age. *Perceptual and Motor Skills, 96,* 43–48.

Guthrie, J. S. (Ed.). (2003). *Encyclopedia of education.* New York: Macmillan Reference USA.

Heilman, M. E., Wallen, A. S., Fuchs, D., & Tamkins, M. M. (2004). Penalties for success: Reactions to women who succeed at male gender-typed tasks. *Journal of Applied Psychology, 89,* 416–427.

Heinberg, L. J., Thompson, J. K., & Stormer, S. (1995). Development and validation of the Sociocultural Attitudes toward Appearance Questionnaire. *International Journal of Eating Disorders, 17,* 81–89.

Holmes, D. S. (1976a). Debriefing after psychological experiments: I. Effectiveness of postdeception dehoaxing. *American Psychologist, 31,* 858–867.

Holmes, D. S. (1976b). Debriefing after psychological experiments: II. Effectiveness of postexperimental desensitizing. *American Psychologist, 31,* 868–875.

Hough, R. L., Tarke, H., Renker, V., Shields, P., & Glatstein, J. (1996). Recruitment and retention of homeless mentally ill participants in research. *Journal of Consulting and Clinical Psychology, 64,* 881–891.

Howell, D. C. (1992). *Statistical methods for psychology* (3rd ed.). Boston: PWS-Kent Publishing Co.

Humphreys, L. (1970). *Tearoom trade: Impersonal sex in public places.* Chicago: Aldine.

Hyde, J. S. (1990). Meta-analysis and the psychology of gender differences. *Signs, 16,* 55–73.

Iaffaldano, M. T., & Muchinsky, P. M. (1985). Job satisfaction and performance: A meta-analysis. *Psychological Bulletin, 97,* 251–273.

Ittelson, W. H. (1962). Perception and transactional psychology. In S. Koch (Ed.), *Psychology: A study of a science,* vol. 4 (pp. 660–704). New York: McGraw-Hill.

Jacobson, J. W., Mulick, J. A., & Schwartz, A. A. (1995). A history of facilitated communication: Science, pseudoscience, and antiscience. *American Psychologist, 50,* 750–765.

Jensen, P. S., Fisher, C. B., & Hoagwood, K. (1999). Special issues in mental health/illness research with children and adolescents. In H. A. Pincus, J. A. Lieberman, & S. Ferris (Eds.), *Ethics in psychiatric research: A resource manual for human subjects protection* (pp. 159–175). Washington, DC: American Psychiatric Association.

John, O. P., Donahue, E., & Kentle, R. L. (1991). *The big five inventory—Versions 41 and 54.* Berkeley, CA: University of California, Berkeley, Institute of Personality and Social Research.

Jonassen, D. H. (1996). *Handbook for research for educational communications and technology.* New York: Macmillan Library Reference.

Jones, J. (1981). *Bad blood.* New York: The Free Press.

Kahneman, D., & Tversky, A. (1973). On the psychology of prediction. *Psychological Review, 80,* 237–251.

Kallgren, C. A., & Tauber, R. T. (1996). Undergraduate research and the institutional review board: A mismatch or happy marriage? *Teaching of Psychology, 23,* 20–25.

Kanner, A. D., Coyne, J. C., Schaefer, C., & Lazarus, R. C. (1981). Comparison of two modes of stress measurement: Daily hassles and uplifts versus major life events. *Journal of Behavioral Medicine, 4,* 1–39.

Kaplan, R. (1973). Some psychological benefits of gardening. *Environment and Behavior, 5,* 145–162.

Kaplan, R. (1977). Patterns of environmental preference. *Environment and Behavior, 9,* 195–216.

Kaplan, R., & Kaplan, S. (1989). *The experience of nature: A psychological perspective.* New York: Cambridge University Press.

Kaplan, S., Kaplan, R., & Wendt, J. S. (1972). Rated preference and complexity for natural and urban visual material. *Perception and Psychophysics, 12,* 354–356.

Kapp, M. B. (2002). Regulating research for the decisionally impaired: Implications for mental health professionals. *Journal of Clinical Geropsychology, 8,* 35–51.

Kass, N. E., & Sugarman, J. (1996). Are research subjects adequately protected? A review and discussion of studies conducted by the Advisory Committee on Human Radiation Experiments. *Kennedy Institute of Ethics Journal, 6,* 271–282.

Kather, R., Chestnut, E., Ellyson, S. L., & Yarab, P. (2000, March). Is professional wrestling becoming more violent? Perception versus reality. [Abstract]. *Proceedings and Abstracts of the Annual Meeting of the Eastern Psychological Association, 71,* p. 61.

Kazdin, A. E. (Ed.). (2000). *Encyclopedia of psychology* (Vols. 1–8). Washington, DC: American Psychological Association and New York: Oxford University Press.

Kendall, P. C., Silk, J. S., & Chu, B. C. (2000). Introducing your research report: Writing the introduction. In R. J. Sternberg (Ed.), *Guide to publishing in psychology journals* (pp. 41–57). New York: Cambridge University Press.

Keyser, D. J., & Sweetland, R. C. (Eds.). (1987). *Test critiques compendium*. Kansas City, MO: Test Corporation of America.

Kirkpatrick, L. A., & Feeney, B. C. (2005). *A simple guide to SPSS® for Windows® for version 12.0*. Belmont, CA: Thomson Wadsworth.

Knowles, A. K. (2002). *Past time, past place: GIS for history*. Redlands, CA: ESRI Press.

Kopka, D. L. (1997). *School violence: A reference handbook*. Santa Barbara, CA: ABC-CLIO, Inc.

Krapp, K., & Longe, J. L. (Eds.). (2001). *The Gale encyclopedia of alternative medicine* (Vols. 1–4). Farmington, MI: Gale Group.

Kurtz, L. (Ed.). (1999). *Encyclopedia of violence, peace, and conflict* (Vols. 1–3). San Diego, CA: Academic Press.

Landrum, R. E. (1999). Introduction. In G. Chastain & R. E. Landrum (Eds.), *Protecting human subjects: Departmental subject pools and institutional review boards* (pp. 3–19). Washington, DC: American Psychological Association.

Landrum, R. E., & Chastain, G. (1999). Subject pool policies in undergraduate-only departments: Results from a nationwide survey. In G. Chastain & R. E. Landrum (Eds.), *Protecting human subjects: Departmental subject pools and institutional review boards* (pp. 26–42). Washington, DC: American Psychological Association.

Lazarus, R. S., & Folkman, S. (1989). *Manual for the hassles and uplifts scale*. Palo Alto, CA: Consulting Psychologists Press.

Lenert, L., & Skoczen, S. (2002). The Internet as a research tool: Worth the price of admission? *Annals of Behavioral Medicine, 24,* 251–256.

Leong, T. L., & Austin, J. T. (Eds.). (1996). *The psychology research handbook: A guide for graduate students and research assistants*. Thousand Oaks, CA: Sage Publications.

Lesieur, H. R., & Blume, S. B. (1987). The South Oaks Gambling Screen (SOGS): A new instrument for the identification of pathological gamblers. *American Journal of Psychiatry, 144,* 1184–1188.

Liddle, B. J., & Brazelton, E. W. (1996). Psychology faculty satisfaction and compliance with IRB procedures. *IRB: A Review of Human Subjects Research, 18*(6), 4–6.

Lynch, K. (1960). *The image of the city*. Cambridge, MA: The MIT Press.

Macklin, R. (1989). The paradoxical case of payment as benefit to research subjects. *IRB: A Review of Human Subjects Research, 11,* 1–3.

Maloney, D. M. (1984). *Protection of human research subjects: A practical guide to federal laws and regulations.* New York: Plenum Press.

Martin, D. (1985). *Doing psychology experiments* (2nd ed.). Monterey, CA: Brooks/Cole Publishing Co.

Mason, M. J. (1999). A review of procedural and statistical methods for handling attrition and missing data in clinical research. *Measurement and Evaluation in Counseling and Development, 32,* 111–118.

Mathes, S. A., & Battista, R. (1985). College men's and women's motives for participation in physical activity. *Perceptual and Motor Skills, 61,* 719–726.

McConahay, J. B. (1986). Modern racism, ambivalence, and the modern racism scale. In J. F. Dovidio & S. L. Gaertner (Eds.), *Prejudice, discrimination, and racism* (pp. 91–126). Orlando, FL: Academic Press.

McEvoy, J. P., & Keefe, R. S. E. (1999). Informing subjects of risks and benefits. In H. A. Pincus, J. A. Lieberman, & S. Ferris (Eds.), *Ethics in psychiatric research: A resource manual for human subjects protection* (pp. 129–157). Washington, DC: American Psychiatric Association.

McHale, S. M., Crouter, A. C., & Tucker, C. J. (2001). Free-time activities in middle childhood: Links with adjustment in early adolescence. *Child Development, 72,* 1764–1778.

McNair, D. M., Lorr, M., & Droppleman, L. F. (1992). *EdITS manual for the profile of mood states.* San Diego, CA: EdITS/Educational and Industrial Testing Service.

Menard, S. (2002). *Longitudinal research* (2nd ed.). Thousand Oaks, CA: Sage Publications.

Mendelson, B. K., & White, D. R. (1982). Relation between body-esteem and self-esteem of obese and normal children. *Perceptual and Motor Skills, 54,* 899–905.

Mikulinsky, R. (2002). *Vocational indecision in adolescents enrolled in college and secondary school.* Unpublished honors thesis. New London, CT: Connecticut College.

Milgram, S. (1974). *Obedience to authority: An experimental view.* New York: Harper & Row.

Miller, G. A. (1956). The magical number seven, plus or minus two: Some limits on our capacity for processing information. *Psychological Review, 63,* 81–97.

Miller, R. B., & Wright, D. W. (1995). Detecting and correcting attrition bias in longitudinal family research. *Journal of Marriage and the Family, 57,* 921–929.

Mind Garden. (2001). *Mind Garden catalog.* Redwood City, CA: Author.

Moffitt, K. H., & Singer, J. A. (1994). Continuity in the life story: Self-defining memories, affect, and approach/avoidance personal strivings. *Journal of Personality, 62,* 21–43.

Moos, R. (1968). The development of a Menstrual Distress Questionnaire. *Psychosomatic Medicine, 30,* 853–860.

Moos, R. (1988). *University Residence Environment Scale* (2nd ed.). Palo Alto, CA: Consulting Psychologists Press.

Moos, R., & Moos, B. S. (1994*). Family environment scale manual: Development, applications, and research* (3rd ed.). Palo Alto, CA: Consulting Psychologists Press.

Moreland, R. L. (1999). Evaluating students' research experiences via credit slips. In G. Chastain & R. E. Landrum (Eds.), *Protecting human subjects: Departmental subject pools and institutional review boards* (pp. 87–108). Washington, DC: American Psychological Association.

Mostert, M. P. (2001). Facilitated communication since 1995: A review. *Journal of Autism and Developmental Disorders, 31,* 287–313.

Mostert, M. P. (2003). Response: Now you see it, now you don't: A response to Bebko, Perry, and Bryson. *Journal of Autism and Developmental Disorders, 33,* 221–222.

Muchinsky, P. M. (2003). *Psychology applied to work: An introduction to industrial and organizational psychology* (7th ed.). Belmont, CA: Thomson Wadsworth.

Mulick, J. A., Jacobson, J. W., & Kobe, F. (1993). Anguished silence and helping hands: Autism and facilitated communication. *Skeptical Inquirer, 17,* 270–280.

Murstein, B. I., Chalpin, M. J., Heard, K. V., & Vyse, S. A. (1989). Sexual behavior, drugs, and relationship patterns on a college campus over thirteen years. *Adolescence, 24,* 125–139.

Murstein, B. I., & Holden, C. C. (1979). Sexual behavior and correlates among college students. *Adolescence, 14,* 625–639.

Murstein, B. I., & Mercy, T. (1994). Sex, drugs, relationships, contraception, and fears of disease on a college campus over 17 years. *Adolescence, 29,* 303–322.

Nadel, L. (Ed.). (2003). *Encyclopedia of cognitive science* (Vols. 1–4). New York: Nature Publishing Group.

Najjar, L., & Devlin, A. S. (2000, March). Intercultural marriage: Satisfaction levels and gender roles. [Abstract]. *Proceedings and Abstracts of the Annual Meeting of the Eastern Psychological Association, 71,* p. 33.

Neisser, U. (1976). *Cognition and reality: Principles and implications of cognitive psychology.* New York: W. H. Freeman and Company.

Neisser, U., & Harsch, N. (1992). Phantom flashbulbs: False recollections of hearing the news about Challenger. In E. Winograd & U. Neisser (Eds.), *Affect and accuracy in recall: Studies of "flashbulb" memories* (pp. 9–31). New York: Cambridge University Press.

Neisser, U., & Hyman, I. E., Jr. (2000). *Memory observed: Remembering in natural contexts* (2nd ed.). New York: Worth.

Neisser, U., Winograd, E., Bergman, E. T., Schreiber, C. A., Palmer, S. E, & Weldon, M. S. (1996). Remembering the earthquake: Direct experience vs. hearing the news. *Memory, 4,* 337–357.

Nelson, R. M. (2002). Research involving children. In R. J. Amdur & E. A. Bankert (Eds.), *Institutional review board management and function* (pp. 383–388). Mississauga, Ontario: Jones and Bartlett Publishers.

Nezu, A. M., Ronan, G. F., Meadows, E. A., & McClure, K. S. (Eds.). (2000). *Practitioner's guide to empirically-based measures of depression.* New York: Kluwer Academic/Plenum.

Nosek, B. A., Banaji, M. R., & Greenwald, A. G. (2002). E-research: Ethics, security, design, and control in psychological research on the Internet. *Journal of Social Issues, 58*(1), 161–176.

Oakes, J. M. (2002). Risks and wrongs in social science research: An evaluator's guide to the IRB. *Evaluation Review, 26,* 443–479.

Office for Protection from Research Risks. (1993). *Protecting human research subjects: Institutional review board guidebook.* Washington, DC: Office for Protection from Research Risks.

Opie, I., & Tatem, M. (1989). *A dictionary of superstitions.* New York: Oxford University Press.

Orne, M. T. (1962). On the social psychology of the psychological experiment: With particular reference to demand characteristics and their implications. *American Psychologist, 17,* 776–783.

Pattullo, E. L. (1984). Institutional review boards and social research: A disruptive, subjective perspective, retrospective and prospective. In J. E. Sieber (Ed.), *NIH readings on the protection of human subjects in behavioral and social science research* (pp. 10–17). Frederick, MD: University Publications of America.

Paulhus, D. L. (1991). Measurement and control of response bias. In J. P. Robinson, P. R. Shaver, & L. S. Wrightsman (Eds.), *Measures of personality and social psychological attitudes* (pp. 17–59). San Diego, CA: Academic Press.

Porter, J. P. (1986). What are the ideal characteristics of unaffiliated/ nonscientist IRB members? *IRB: A Review of Human Subjects Research, 8*(3), 1–6.

Porter, J. P. (1987). How unaffiliated/nonscientist members of institutional review boards see their roles. *IRB: A Review of Human Subjects Research, 9*(6), 1–6.

Presley, C. A., Meilman, P. W., & Lyerla, R. (1993). *Alcohol and drugs on American college campuses: Use, consequences, and perceptions of the campus environment.* Vol. 1: 1989–91. Carbondale, IL: The Core Institute.

Pritchard, I. A. (2001). Searching for "research involving human subjects": What is examined? What is exempt? What is exasperating? *IRB: Ethics & Human Research, 23*(3), 5–12.

Propst, R. L., & Propst, C. G. (1973). *The University of Massachusetts dormitory experiment: An examination of the influence of the direct living environment on the attitudes and behavior of residents in high rise dormitories. A report on the introduction of innovative changes and their implications to the satisfaction of residents and to management feasibility.* Ann Arbor, MI: The Herman Miller Research Corporation.

Publications and databases. (2004, July–August). *American Psychologist, 59*, 301–302.

Ramachandran, V. S. (Ed.). (1994). *Encyclopedia of human behavior* (Vols. 1–4). San Diego, CA: Academic Press.

Reis, H. T. (2000). Writing effectively about design. In R. J. Sternberg (Ed.), *Guide to publishing in psychology journals* (pp. 81–97). New York: Cambridge University Press.

Reiser, S. J., & Knudson, P. (1993). Protecting research subjects after consent: The case for the "research intermediary." *IRB: A Review of Human Subjects Research, 15*(2), 10–12.

Robertson, G. J. (1992). Psychological tests: Development, publication, and distribution. In M. Zeidner & R. Most (Eds.), *Psychological testing: An inside view* (pp. 159–214). Palo Alto, CA: Consulting Psychologists Press.

Robles, N., Flaherty, D. G., & Day, N. L. (1994). Retention of resistant subjects in longitudinal studies: Description and procedures. *American Journal of Drug and Alcohol Abuse, 20*, 87–100.

Rosenberg, M. (1965). *Society and the adolescent self-image.* Princeton, NJ: Princeton University Press.

Rosenberg, M. (1979). *Conceiving the self.* New York: Basic Books.

Rosnow, R. L., Rotheram-Borus, M. J., Ceci, S. J., Blanck, P. D., & Koocher, G. P. (1993). The institutional review board as a mirror of scientific and ethical standards. *American Psychologist, 48*, 821–826.

Rudy, E. B., Estok, P. J., Kerr, M. E., & Menzel, L. (1994). Research incentives: Money versus gifts. *Nursing Research, 43*, 253–255.

Russell, M. L., Moralejo, D. G., & Burgess, E. D. (2000). Paying research subjects: Participants' perspectives. *Journal of Medical Ethics, 26*, 126–130.

Salovey, P. (2000). Results that get results: Telling a good story. In R. J. Sternberg (Ed.), *Guide to publishing in psychology journals* (pp. 121–132). New York: Cambridge University Press.

Sandberg, J. (2003, September 10). Why U.S. workers are losing the tug of war over toilet paper. *The Wall Street Journal*, p. B1.

Schachtel, E. G. (1959). *Metamorphosis: On the development of affect, perception, attention, and memory.* New York: Basic Books.

Schon, C. (2003). *Sexual behaviors relating to attitudes, contraception, drug use, religion, relationships, gender, attractiveness, and fear of STDs and pregnancy at Connecticut College over three decades.* Unpublished honors thesis. New London, CT: Connecticut College.

Schwarz, N. (1999). Self-reports: How the questions shape the answers. *American Psychologist, 54,* 93–105.

Shaw, G., Brown, R., & Bromiley, P. (1998, May–June). Strategic stories: How 3M is rewriting business planning. *Harvard Business Review,* 41–50.

Sherer, M., Maddox, J. E., Mercandante, B., Prentice-Dunn, S., Jacobs, B., & Rogers, R. W. (1982). The self-efficacy scale: Construction and validation. *Psychological Reports, 51,* 663–671.

Sieber, J. E. (1992). *Planning ethically responsible research: A guide for students and internal review boards.* Newbury Park, CA: Sage Publications.

Sieber, J. E. (1996). Typically unexamined communication processes in research. In B. H. Stanley, J. E. Sieber, & G. B. Melton (Eds.), *Research ethics: A psychological approach* (pp. 73–104). Lincoln, NE: University of Nebraska Press.

Sieber, J. E. (1999). What makes a subject pool (un)ethical? In G. Chastain & R. E. Landrum (Eds.), *Protecting human subjects: Departmental subject pools and institutional review boards* (pp. 43–64). Washington, DC: American Psychological Association.

Sieber, J. E., & Baluyot, R. M. (1992). A survey of IRB concerns about social and behavioral research. *IRB: A Review of Human Subjects Research , 14*(2), 9–10.

Simsek, Z., & Veiga, J. F. (2001). A primer on Internet organizational surveys. *Organizational Research Methods, 4,* 218–235.

Singer, J. A., & Blagov, P. (2000, June). *Classification system and scoring manual for self-defining and autobiographical memories.* Paper presented at the Meeting of the Society for Applied Research on Memory and Cognition, Miami, FL.

Singer, J. A., & Moffitt, K. H. (1991–1992). An experimental investigation of specificity and generality in memory narratives. *Imagination, Cognition, and Personality, 11,* 233–257.

Singer, J. A., & Salovey, P. (1993). *The remembered self: Emotion and memory in personality.* New York: The Free Press.

Smail, M. M., DeYoung, A. J., & Moos, R. H. (1974). The University Residence Environment Scale: A method for describing university student living groups. *Journal of College Student Personnel, 15,* 357–365.

Smelser, N. J., & Baltes, P. B. (2001*). International encyclopedia of social and behavioral sciences* (Vols. 1–24*).* New York: Elsevier.

Smith, J. A. (2003). Introduction. In J. A. Smith (Ed.), *Qualitative psychology: A practical guide to research methods* (pp. 1–3). Thousand Oaks, CA: Sage Publications.

Smith, J. A., & Osborn, M. (2003). Interpretative phenomenological analysis. In J. A. Smith (Ed.), *Qualitative psychology: A practical guide to research methods* (pp. 51–80). Thousand Oaks, CA: Sage Publications.

Smith, R. A. (2000). Documenting your scholarship: Citations and references. In R. J. Sternberg (Ed.), *Guide to publishing in psychology journals* (pp. 146–157). New York: Cambridge University Press.

Smith, S. S., & Richardson, D. (1983). Amelioration of deception and harm in psychological research. *Journal of Personality and Social Psychology, 44,* 1075–1082.

Sokolov, R. (2003, August 22). Lobster chronicles. To test conventional wisdom we eat a plus-size crustacean. *The Wall Street Journal,* W1, W5.

Spence, J. T., Helmreich, R., & Stapp, J. (1973). A short version of the Attitudes toward Women Scale (AWS). *Bulletin of the Psychonomic Society, 2,* 219–220.

Spielberger, C. D., Gorsuch, R. L., & Lushene, R. E. (1970). *Manual for the State-Trait Anxiety Inventory.* Palo Alto, CA: Consulting Psychologists Press.

Srebro, K., Hodges, J., Authier, C., & Chambliss, C. (2000, March). Campus stereotypes of student smokers. [Abstract]. *Proceedings and Abstracts of the Annual Meeting of the Eastern Psychological Association, 71,* p. 61.

Stein, G. (Ed.) (1996). *The encyclopedia of the paranormal.* Amherst, NY: Prometheus Books.

Sternberg, R. J. (2000a). Article writing 101: A crib sheet of 50 tips for the final exam. In R. J. Sternberg (Ed.), *Guide to publishing in psychology journals* (pp. 199–206). New York: Cambridge University Press.

Sternberg, R. J. (2000b). Titles and abstracts: They only sound unimportant. In R. J. Sternberg (Ed.), *Guide to publishing in psychology journals* (pp. 37–40). New York: Cambridge University Press.

St. Pierre, M., & Wong, A. (2003). Accuracy of memory recall for eyewitness events. *Connecticut College Psychology Journal, 15,* 44–49.

Sullivan, C. M., Rumptz, M. H., Campbell, R., Eby, K. K., & Davidson, W. S., II (1996). Retaining participants in longitudinal community research: A comprehensive protocol. *Journal of Applied Behavioral Science, 32,* 262–276.

Sullivan, H. S. (1954/1970). *The psychiatric interview.* New York: W. W. Norton & Company.

Suzuki, L. A., Meller, P. J., & Ponterotto, J. G. (Eds.). (1996). *Handbook of multicultural assessment: Clinical, psychological, and educational applications.* San Francisco, CA: Jossey-Bass Publishers.

Taylor, J. E. (1953). A personality scale of manifest anxiety. *Journal of Abnormal and Social Psychology, 48,* 285–290.

Tickle, J. J., & Heatherton, T. F. (2002). Research involving college students. In R. J. Amdur & E. A. Bankert (Eds.), *Institutional review board management and function* (pp. 399–400). Mississauga, Ontario: Jones and Bartlett Publishers.

Torrance, P. E. (1977). *Torrance tests of creative thinking: Thinking creatively with pictures.* Bensenville, IL: Scholastic Testing Service, Inc.

Tracy, D. M. (1987). Toys, spatial ability, and science and mathematics achievement: Are they related? *Sex Roles, 17,* 115–138.

Tropp, R. A. (1982). A regulatory perspective on social science research. In T. L. Beauchamp, R. R. Faden, R. J. Wallace, Jr., & L. Walters (Eds.), *Ethical issues in social science research* (pp. 391–415). Baltimore: The Johns Hopkins University Press.

Tver, D. F., & Hunt, H. F. (1986). *Encyclopedic dictionary of sports medicine.* New York: Chapman and Hall.

Tversky, A., & Kahneman, D. (1974). Judgments under uncertainty: Heuristics and biases. *Science, 185,* 1124–1131.

Ulrich, R. S. (1981). Natural versus urban scenes: Some psychophysiological effects. *Environment and Behavior, 13,* 523–556.

Ulrich, R. S. (1984). View through a window may influence recovery from surgery. *Science, 224,* 420–421.

Ulrich, R. S., Simons, R. F., Losito, B. D., Fiorito, E., Miles, M. A., & Zelson, M. (1991). Stress recovery during exposure to natural and urban environments. *Journal of Environmental Psychology, 11,* 201–230.

Vandenberg, S., & Kuse, A. (1978). Mental rotation: A group test of three-dimensional spatial visualization. *Perceptual and Motor Skills, 47,* 599–604.

Van Volkom, M. (2000, March). The relationship between tomboys, their siblings, and androgyny in adulthood. [Abstract]. *Proceedings and Abstracts of the Annual Meeting of the Eastern Psychological Association, 71,* p. 60.

Verderber, S. (1986). Dimensions of person–window transactions in the hospital environment. *Environment and Behavior, 18,* 450–466.

Wadman, M. (1998, April 23). Row erupts over child aggression study. *Nature, 392,* 747.

Waggoner, W. C., & Mayo, D. M. (1995). Who understands? A survey of 25 words or phrases commonly used in proposed clinical research consent forms. *IRB: A Review of Human Subjects Research, 17* (1), 6–9.

Walker, A., Jr. (Ed.). (1997). *Thesaurus of psychological index terms* (8th ed.). Washington, DC: American Psychological Association.

Wallston, K. A., Wallston, B. S., & DeVellis, R. (1978). Development of the Multidimensional Health Locus of Control (MHLC) Scales. *Health Education Monographs, 6,* 160–170.

Wampold, B. E. (1996). Designing a research study. In F. T. L. Leong & J. T. Austin (Eds.), *The psychology research handbook: A guide for graduate students and research assistants* (pp. 59–72). Thousand Oaks, CA: Sage Publications.

Waterman, A. S. (1993). Two conceptions of happiness: Contrasts of personal expressiveness (eudaemonia) and hedonic enjoyment. *Journal of Personality and Social Psychology, 64,* 678–691.

Watson, D., & Friend, R. (1969). Measurement of social-evaluation anxiety. *Journal of Consulting and Clinical Psychology, 33,* 448–457.

Weger, D. M., Fuller, V. A., & Sparrow, B. (2003). Clever hands: Uncontrolled intelligence in facilitated communication. *Journal of Personality and Social Psychology, 85,* 5–19.

Wiederman, M. W. (1999). Sexuality research, institutional review boards, and subject pools. In G. Chastain & R. E. Landrum (Eds.), *Protecting human subjects: Departmental subject pools and institutional review boards* (pp. 201–219). Washington, DC: American Psychological Association.

Williams, J. G. L., & Ouren, L. H. (1976). Experimenting on humans. *Bulletin of the British Psychological Society, 29,* 334–338.

Wohlwill, J. F. (1968). Amount of stimulus exploration and preference as differential functions of stimulus complexity. *Perception and Psychophysics, 4,* 307–312.

Wohlwill, J. F. (1970). The emerging discipline of environmental psychology. *American Psychologist, 25,* 303–312.

Wolf, J. W., & Singer, J. A. (2000, March). Substance abuse and ADHD in homeless men. [Abstract]. *Proceedings and Abstracts of the Annual Meeting of the Eastern Psychological Association, 71,* p. 38.

Wolman, B. B. (Ed.). (1983). *International encyclopedia of psychiatry, psychology, psychoanalysis, and neurology* (Vols. 1–12). New York: Aesculapius Publishers, Inc.

Year Book Medical Publishers. (2002). *The year book of sports medicine.* Chicago: Author.

Zeisel, J. (1981). *Inquiry by design: Tools for environment-behavior research.* Monterey, CA: Brooks/Cole.

Zuckerman, M., Kolin, E. A., Price, L., & Zoob, I. (1964). Development of a Sensation-Seeking Scale. *Journal of Consulting Psychology, 28,* 477–482.

Zuckerman, M., & Link, K. (1968). Construct validity for the Sensation-Seeking Scale. *Journal of Consulting and Clinical Psychology, 32,* 420–426.

Zuckerman, M., & Lubin, B. (1965). *Manual for the Multiple Affect Adjective Check List.* San Diego, CA: EdITS/Educational and Industrial Testing Service.

INDEX

Abstract, 30, 207–208
Academic Search Premier, 23
Ackerman, T. F., 129, 130, 251
Active consent, 165, 245 (*see
also* Human Subjects
Institutional Review
Board)
Actual criterion, 91, 245
Adair, J. G., 76, 79,
84, 251
Adams, P. L., 19, 251
Alkin, M. C., 18, 251
American Anthropologist, 20
American Antiquity, 20
American Educational
Research Association,
110, 251
*American Educational Research
Journal*, 20
American Ethnologist, 20
American Journal of Sociology, 20
American Psychiatric
Association, 19, 251
American Psychological
Association,
annual conference, 230
debriefing, 169
deception, principles
related to, 167–168
ethical principles of and
code of conduct, 120,
139, 167, 170, 251

membership directory
of, 99
publication manual, see
Publication Manual
American Sociological
Association,
15, 251
American Sociological Review,
20, 93
Analyze function (*see* SPSS)
Analyzing results,
see Results, analyzing
Anchoring, 127, 245
Anchors,
on scales, 107–108
Anderson, J. C., 94, 251
Animal measures, 116
Angoff, N. R., 162, 251
Anonymity,
part of informed consent,
162, 245
Antony, M. M., 112, 251
APA, *see* American
Psychological
Association
Apparatus,
section of Method,
33, 212
Appendixes,
format of, 219
Applied research,
vs. basic, 30

TO THE OWNER OF THIS BOOK:

I hope that you have found *Research Methods: Planning, Conducting and Presenting Research* useful. So that this book can be improved in a future edition, would you take the time to complete this sheet and return it? Thank you.

School and address: _____

_____

Department: _____

Instructor's name: _____

1. What I like most about this book is: _____

_____

_____

2. What I like least about this book is: _____

_____

_____

3. My general reaction to this book is: _____

_____

_____

4. The name of the course in which I used this book is: _____

_____

5. Were all of the chapters of the book assigned for you to read? _____

    If not, which ones weren't? _____

6. In the space below, or on a separate sheet of paper, please write specific suggestions for improving this book and anything else you'd care to share about your experience in using this book.

_____

_____

DO NOT STAPLE.   TAPE HERE   TAPE HERE   DO NOT STAPLE.

FOLD HERE

THOMSON ™
WADSWORTH

NO POSTAGE
NECESSARY
IF MAILED
IN THE
UNITED STATES

BUSINESS REPLY MAIL
FIRST-CLASS MAIL   PERMIT NO. 102   MONTEREY CA

POSTAGE WILL BE PAID BY ADDRESSEE

Attn: Vicki Knight / Psychology Publisher

Wadsworth/Thomson Learning
60 Garden Ct Ste 205
Monterey CA 93940-9967

FOLD HERE

OPTIONAL:

Your name:_____ Date: _____

May we quote you, either in promotion for *Research Methods: Planning, Conducting and Presenting Research* or in future publishing ventures?

Yes: _____ No: _____

Sincerely yours,

Ann Sloan Devlin